'Black Butterfly' by Cezanne (2009)

Dear Samantha,
Follow your HEART
(not your mind)
love,
Cezanne ♡ 18.11.17

Even when crawling through life
The caterpillar still has the HEART of a butterfly,
and still aspires to fly;
No matter where you are in life right now,
Stay focused on your heart's desires
You can only rise as high as your aspirations
The sky is no limit – aim higher!

~ Cezanne Poetess

Introduction

"Who am I?"
"Why am I here?"

If you have never asked your Self these questions, you have not yet begun your journey of Self discovery!

Have you been wandering through life aimlessly? Are you unsure of your purpose? Do you get the feeling there's 'more to life' than what you've been led to believe? This is how I felt eight years ago; I was a practicing Christian but I lacked Self-identity, had low self-esteem, and lacked purpose in life. I had a victim mentality and suffered from severe bouts of depression. I constantly sabotaged my own success in relationships, business, and finances. I had been programmed for failure, and unless something drastic changed, I was destined for a life of misery, with a faint hope of making it into heaven when I die.

What changed? Fortunately for me, despite my human failures I was able to develop a relationship with my Creator through prayer, fasting, reading my bible, and spending time in 'the Silence' waiting to hear back from 'Him' (at the time, I only thought of God as my spiritual Father because that's what I'd been taught to believe). Yet I had reached a point where I could no longer continue walking in blind faith; I had so many unanswered questions. Because I had a close relationship with this Source of Love, I gained the confidence to ask all the questions the church couldn't answer in a fearless letter, which I ended by asking for 'the Truth!'

Your ***quest*** *for 'the Truth' begins when you ask the right* ***quest****ions!*

I was given a huge task to complete:
I was to go through the whole bible and select all the scriptures that;
1) Made me **feel good** 2) **Empowered me** *especially as a woman*, and 3) **Set me free**. As I was doing this huge task, John 8:32 played on repeat in my mind:

'You will know the Truth and the Truth will set you FREE!'

When I had finished compiling these scriptures, I was then led to speak them over my life daily, and thus began my first use of Positive Affirmations!

"An affirmation is a strong, POSITIVE statement that something is ALREADY so." ~ Shakti Gawain

An example would be;
"I am like a tree planted by the rivers of water, that brings forth its fruit in due season; my leaf does not wither, and whatever I put my hands to PROSPERS!" (Psalm 1).

I wanted to share everything I've discovered since asking God for 'the Truth!' in 2007, and chose to do it in story form.

The aim of this book is not to negate religion, but to use it to build greater spiritual awareness upon. I am grateful for my Christian upbringing, which built a firm foundation for where I stand now. Whether you are in 'the faith' or not, and whether you are a sister or a brother, you will be able to relate to this story. It is 'our' story.

Although this book is part-autobiographical, I also used it to practice Creative Imagination; when I discovered that I could be, do and have whatever I could *imagine*, and that my thoughts were powerfully creating my future, I decided to use this story to stretch my imagination to its limit – and then I discovered it didn't have any!

You will notice that sometimes I capitalize the word 'Self'. This is when I'm referring to our Higher Self. If you are a believer, you probably call this inner guidance the Holy Spirit. We all have an inner teacher, but for some reason we were never taught how to be guided by our 'in-tuition' at school. Yet that still, small voice is the part of us that is directly connected to our Source. This is what I'm referring to when I capitalize 'Self'.

I designed the front cover in Photoshop using three different images; my interpretation is that the woman is coming out of a dark place and stepping into 'enlightenment'. The face looking down from

above represents guidance from her Higher Self, which could also be the personification of *Wisdom*, who according to Proverbs 8, is a woman. She could also represent Mother Nature.

The image is not making the statement 'God is a woman' (which would be no better than saying 'God is a man'), I am simply bringing *balance*, and acknowledging the Feminine Aspect of God.

My aim in writing this book is to plant *Seeds of Love*, in the hope that you will ask your Self *"Could this be true?"* – then go and do your own research. We live in the age of Information and Technology, make use of it while you can!

While I was writing this story I realized some of my paintings and poems could be used to illustrate it; if you haven't got this book's complimentary poetry collection *'Seeds of Love'*, you can order it from the **Poetry** page at **www.journeyofasister.com** along with its Book of Lyrics (all 13 poems feature in the story).

Start the journey!

Cezanne

Cezanne Taharqa aka Cezanne Poetess

Year One: The 'Truth!'

"Who am I?" I ask my Self as I lay here, eyes closed, in deep contemplation.

"Why am I here?"

I have always been a deep thinker. I always seek to get to the bottom of things, instead of looking at them from a surface level.

Born in England of Jamaican parentage, I was raised in the Christian faith. Ever since I was told there was a God who had created me and loved me, my deepest desire has always been to get to know Him, and to find out why He created me – to discover my 'destiny'. So as an adult, I continue to attend church, read my bible, pray, and deny myself of life's pleasures, to the best of my abilities.

However, I could be described as a 'non-conformist free spirit', which makes it somewhat difficult for me to abide by all the rules and regulations. My biggest weakness is 'fornication' – sex before marriage. I sincerely desire to serve God in spirit and in truth, but my *natural* desires do, every now and then, prevent me from keeping my vow of remaining celibate – my *spirit* is willing, but my *flesh* is weak.

I did have the opportunity to marry, but I wasn't ready. Besides, the principle of 'marriage before children' was never instilled into me by my mother, despite my Christian upbringing. She never married.

Still, the bible makes it very clear that sex before marriage is wrong. It's like a taboo topic in my church; everyone appears to be so *spiritual*.

I remember the turmoil I went through when I found out I was pregnant with my first son nine years ago; what should I do? What would church members *think* of me? Now everyone would know I'd had sex! Distraught, I confided in a church sister who advised me to have an abortion: "Loads of girls do it," she had said. But that seemed even worse than having the baby! According to the bible *'(all) children are a heritage from the Lord'*. My 'friend' informed me that many church sisters were sexually active but if they accidentally conceived, they would terminate the pregnancy so they stood a better chance of getting married. Thank God I didn't listen to her.

Instead, I went to God in prayer;

"What kind of a life will this child have?" I asked in distress; "I'm not married, I'll have to give up my job, the father has done a runner, I've got nothing to offer a baby!"

That day God spoke to me so clearly, I remember his reply like it was yesterday:

"The same way you were born in sin and I have a plan for your life, is the same way I have a plan for your ***son****'s life."*

I can't begin to describe the peace that swept over me; every negative emotion I was feeling was erased as I felt God's presence surrounding me, as if comforting me. From that moment on, I remained at peace with myself and with the world. I had heard from God directly, and he had even informed me I was having a *boy*, which was confirmed at my first scan! I continued to attend church until I began to show at around 6 months – returning to a new, local church after my son's birth.

When I fell pregnant with my second son two years later, I really thought I'd blown it this time! Again distraught, I went into God's presence, and this time he gave me a promise concerning both my sons, based on Isaiah 44:3-5;

"...I will pour out my Spirit upon your offspring, and my blessings on your descendants; one will say 'I belong to the LORD, and the other will write on his hand 'the LORD's'

Micah and Elijah are now aged six and eight. My relationship with their father broke down when they were only three and five; it took over two years for me to heal emotionally from the break-up. To be honest, we were never really a proper couple; when I told him I was pregnant with our first son, he'd done a disappearing act for months, only re-emerging when I was due to have the baby. Suddenly, he wanted to play the proud father, but after a few short months the novelty of the new baby wore off, and he was off again. I didn't rely on him for anything, buying everything I needed for the baby myself. Then just as I was getting my life back on track he came back, wanting to start over. At the time I had a part-time job in the admin department of the Museums & Galleries Commission, and our year-old son went to private nursery. Before I knew it, I was pregnant again. On this occasion he tried to stay, but it wasn't long before he started straying away. This time, it was over for good.

So here I am aged 28, a single mum with two young sons on a low income. I have no man, no job and no savings.

What I *do* have though, is a dream.

The Bible and Sex

It was a warm spring evening in 2001. The boys were with their father for the weekend.

Suzanne was feeling more sensual than usual.

As she lay on the sofa with her eyes closed contemplating life, she slid her hand up her skirt, down into her panties, and began pleasuring herself. She wondered why God had created the clitoris; 'is it there for me to please myself, or for my *husband* to give me pleasure?' According to her pastor, it was even a sin to masturbate, since the mind is likely to start conjuring up images of a sexual nature. If you so much as *think* about having sex, it's just as bad as *doing* the act. But how many men actually know how to stimulate the clitoris well enough to bring a woman to orgasm?

With all these thoughts running through her mind, Suzanne couldn't help re-creating the outline of her imaginary lover, who visited her whenever she needed a release. As she pictured him riding her silently back and forth, she increased the pressure and speed of her finger while simulating sex on the sofa. With every withdrawal, she let out a sigh, and with every penetration, a deep moan. Before long, she came to climax…and he had slipped away before she even opened her eyes.

Suzanne felt like she was *always* sinning, which left her in a perpetual state of 'unworthiness'. She just couldn't seem to stay on the straight and narrow path! Her *spirit* was willing, but her *flesh* was weak. Suzanne couldn't understand why God would give her sexual urges then command her to ignore them until she got married; but what if she didn't *want* to get married? Or what if she ended up being one of the sisters in the church who didn't *get* married, since there weren't enough men to go around?

It was only through having children of her own that Suzanne really began to understand God's Unconditional Love for her. There seemed to be nothing she could do to make God stop loving her. No matter what she did, he always did something to prove that he still loved her, much like a spiritual Father. As such, he would give her instructions on how to live her life, but if she chose to do her own thing and 'fell', he would just pick her up, dust her off, and stand her back on her feet again. And that's how she developed her relationship with God; his strength really *was* made perfect through her weakness.

As their relationship developed, Suzanne was inspired to write 'messages from God' based on his word, which she thought were personal to her, but when she placed them on the walls around her home as a constant reminder, her visiting friends were so touched by them that they asked for copies. Soon, she was printing them unto fancy paper and framing them for her friends as gifts.

However, the more Suzanne studied the bible, the more questions arose for her, and lately she had found her Self questioning a lot of what she had been taught to believe. She especially questioned the 'no sex before marriage' rule:

"Who created the institution of marriage, God or man?"

She couldn't find any stories in the bible of a couple going to a church to get married, or signing a register. In most instances, the man simply approached the father of the woman he wanted to marry, and if the father agreed to the union, he would pay him a dowry, or work for the father to pay the price of his bride. A feast of ceremony would be held for family and friends to join in the celebration, and then the father would take him into the room (or tent) to get to 'know' his wife. Sometimes it would be months between the time the marriage was agreed, to when he would actually get to consummate the marriage. And there was no honeymoon.

Suzanne began with the first couple mentioned in the bible; how did Adam and Eve get married? It simply stated that Adam 'knew' his wife, so what did the word '*knew*' mean? Suzanne dug deeper and discovered that the Hebrew word for 'knew' was '*Yada*' which had several meanings, but in the context of 'Adam *knew* his wife and she conceived...' this seemed to indicate a very intimate type of knowledge – they had sex! Was there a church or priest to marry them first? Did churches or registry offices even exist in those days?

Suzanne wondered if, in God's eyes, the very act of having sex with someone means you are married to them? This didn't appear to be the case, since having a strictly sexual relationship with someone didn't mean you were experiencing 'Yada'. This type of Yada meant *'total dedication to a person in order to engage them with love and affection'.*

Suzanne found other instances in the bible where the word 'Yada' was used as a euphemism for sexual intercourse; in Genesis 4:17 Cain 'knew' his wife and she conceived and bore Enoch. Genesis 24:16 described a virgin who had not 'known' a man, and in the genocide of Numbers 31:17-18, all women who had 'known' a man were murdered, while the young virgins were captured and turned into sex slaves. In Genesis 19: 5-8, even sodomy (anal sex) translated from Hebrew into the word 'know'. It was rumoured that King James, (who commissioned the King James Version of the bible) had gay lovers outside of his marriage, who he openly expressed 'yada' for.

King Solomon, a man renowned for his great wisdom and insight which led him to great riches, fell for the charms of the beautiful, dark-skinned Queen of Sheba and impregnated her before she returned to her native land. *They* never married, but he also had 700 wives and 'other women'.

The Old Testament had plenty of stories relating to sex outside of marriage. Multiple wives, concubines and one-off sexual encounters, including sex with prostitutes appeared to be the norm, and wasn't considered 'immoral'.

Still, Suzanne accepted the teaching that fornication is a sin, so she decided to find out what the root meaning of the word 'fornication' was.

Since the New Testament was originally written in Greek, her research led her to the Greek language. She was surprised to learn that the Greek word for *fornication* was '*porneia*' which meant 'to prostitute'.

Suzanne suspected that this might also be where the term 'porn' originated from, since they both related to the sex industry. 'Porneia' was the activity of *porné*, or prostitutes, and literally meant 'whoredom'. Anyone who sold their body for money (or goods) was called a whore, or harlot. But what did all this have to do with 'sex before marriage'?

Suzanne reminded herself what she was meant to be discovering; the root meaning of the word *'fornication'*.

She visited her local library to study Greek bible concordances in her search for 'the Truth'.

She discovered that Greek-speaking Jews and the apostle Paul (who used the term 'sexual immorality' extensively) used *porneia* as a universal term for all sexual sin prohibited by the Law of God, as set out in Leviticus 18. Incest was big on God's list, as was adultery, sleeping with a woman while on her monthly cycle, idol worship (Molech was a fire god whose worship included child sacrifices, astrology and temple prostitution), blaspheming the name of God, homosexuality, and bestiality (sex with animals).

No mention of sex before marriage.

'Sexual immorality' in the New Testament also referred to cult prostitution in idolatry; in those days there were 'sacred prostitutes' who had devoted their life and body to a 'god'. Some people believed that by having sex with a temple prostitute they could join with her god, which made sex with the prostitute a religious experience. This pagan worship is what Paul was warning against. This, he said, is the only sin that a believer can commit against his own body; no sin is as harmful as this, because sexual union with a temple prostitute invited demonic entrance which then had the potential to drive out the indwelling Holy Spirit; the person would then become possessed by an unclean spirit.

Suzanne concluded her research with the knowledge that *'fornication'* did not mean *'sex before marriage'*.

'Does this mean sex before marriage is okay?' she wondered; 'In an ideal world we *should* marry young and spend the rest of our lives together, but the world hasn't been ideal since Genesis chapter 3!'

Suzanne also learned that the word *'woman'* translated into *'wife'* in both Hebrew and Greek. So when Jesus had said 'any man who looks at a *woman* with lustful intent has already committed adultery with her in his heart', he was talking about *married* women. This made sense to her, since adultery *is* unfaithfulness in marriage.

Suzanne was shocked to discover that in some Old Testament customs, a woman's virginity didn't belong to her, it belonged to her father. It was then transferred to her betrothed husband once he had paid the dowry. She had no rights where her sexuality was concerned. If it was discovered that she wasn't a virgin on her wedding night, she risked being stoned to death. At the same time, men were permitted to have multiple wives (preferably virgins), sex outside of their marriage, and could write the woman a 'certificate of divorce' and send her out of the house, whereas she couldn't divorce him.

Did Jesus come to liberate women?

He didn't judge the Samaritan woman at the well who had five previous husbands, and the man she was now with wasn't her husband. He also forgave Mary Magdalene of her sins, who then went on to become his closest 'disciple', and one of a group of women who supported his ministry financially.

It was the apostle Paul, who in his quest to do away with sexual immorality, succeeded in *repressing* church folk's sexual energy. Sex before marriage now became 'immoral' in The Gospel According to Paul. Suzanne believed that this repression of sexual energy had become the root cause of much sexual deviancy, including rape.

Suzanne wasn't ready for marriage, so what was she supposed to do with her sexual energy? Get married just so she could have sex?

The bible depicting Jesus as a celibate man who never married is supposed to show Christians that it can be done. Yet wasn't it God's will for man and woman to unite, to be fruitful and multiply the earth? Ancient manuscripts even suggested Jesus and Mary Magdalene had married. It was common knowledge that Jesus loved Mary more than any of his other disciples, which explains why she was the first person he showed himself to upon his resurrection.

Suzanne concluded her research on marriage with the decision that the 'white wedding' was a contract with the government, not a covenant with God. Walking down the aisle with a 'veil over your eyes', exchanging rings, signing a register, the wedding reception and honeymoon were all creations of man, not 'of God'.

She wondered how many couples in church were currently going through 'hell' in their marriage. There were many married couples who weren't experiencing 'yada' in their relationship, but who stayed together out of religious obligation. She didn't want to be one of them.

She decided to find out what was *God's* idea of marriage.

Potential

Despite becoming another statistic, Suzanne knew she had the potential to better her life.

When her boys had reached the ages of two and four, she had completed a part-time college course in Multi-Media. She wanted to devote her time to raising her sons rather than an employer, so looked for things she could do that would fit around them. Working from home was the best option, she thought. But doing what? The only thing she was really good at was writing poetry, but her friends and family were always telling her "writing poetry won't pay the bills", and that she should just think of it as a hobby. But somewhere deep inside, Suzanne believed she *could* make a living doing what she loved – *how* she was going to achieve this goal though, she didn't know.

She felt like a caterpillar, yet;

'Even when crawling through life,
The caterpillar still has the HEART of a butterfly,
and still aspires to fly…'

...But they were right – writing poetry *wasn't* paying the bills. So Suzanne went back to work part-time, only to discover that she had joined the rat race of working to pay the bills. She still couldn't afford to buy a car, take the boys on holiday, or even save.

But she continued to write whenever she felt inspired, and was compiling her first collection.

The Rebellion

After a day at work and collecting the boys from school, Suzanne returned home and instructed the boys to change out of their uniform while she started dinner. She took the chicken she had seasoned the night before out of the fridge, stuck it in the oven, and put the rice on to cook slowly. Returning to the living room, she reclined in the sofa and switched on the T.V. As usual, all the news reported were the bad things going on in the world. As she watched images of starving children in Africa, listened to the latest report of another 'black on black' murder and the plummeting economy, fear and anxiety began to set in. Feelings of helplessness overwhelmed her; what could *she* do to help heal the world? Suzanne often wondered what life was really all about; was it to live a meaningless existence, get saved, then spend the rest of her life waiting to go to heaven?

"There's got to be more to life than this!" was the mantra that played over and over again in her mind.

Was there 'more to life'?

On a conscious level, Suzanne believed that as a 'child of the King' she was entitled to the best of everything; *'The earth is the Lord's and the fullness thereof'*, the bible said. So if the earth is abundant (which it is) what was stopping her from claiming her piece of the pie?

The *devil.* That's what the bible said; the 'devil comes to kill, steal and destroy' anything good that she was entitled to. The only way to stop him from stealing her stuff was to fight him every day; *'Put on the whole armor of God, so that you can withstand the fiery darts of the devil'.* That's what she had been taught to do. But she was tired of fighting. She was tired of always having to be on guard against what the devil was going to do to her next. Why wasn't God, her 'spiritual Father' protecting her from the devil anyway? And with all her bible study, going to church every week, paying her tithes, praying in Jesus' name and even fasting sometimes, she still wasn't any better off than a non-Christian! The only believers *she* knew living the 'abundant life' she wanted were Pastors of the big churches.

What was the point in being a Christian if she wasn't going to live a better life here *on earth* than a non-Christian? Why did she have to wait until she got to heaven? How could she even be sure she was going to get *into* heaven? What if she ended up being one of those who got to the pearly gates, only to be told *"Depart from me, I never knew you"*?

That evening, feeling melancholic, Suzanne decided to confront her Heavenly Father with all the questions the church didn't seem to be able to answer. She believed that if it wasn't for the devil, she would be living in 'heaven on earth'. So sitting up in bed with a heavy heart, she reached for her journal on the bedside table and wrote what some might call 'an angry letter to God'. She started off by informing Him that she was going to be open and honest, since He could see what was in her heart and thoughts anyway. She was going to 'tell it as it is' regardless of the consequences. Besides, she was sure many of her brothers and sisters in Christ wanted to ask these same questions, but were too scared for fear of His wrath, so she took it upon herself to stand in proxy for them.

She started off with the 'The Fall of Lucifer' story, which she believed was the *root cause* of all the world's problems. She re-told the bible story back to God as *she* understood it; that Lucifer, His 'Lead Worshipper' the most beautiful angel of them all, got a bit egotistical and decided that *he* was worthy of some of this praise too; *"He obviously didn't understand why You Alone should be worshipped, and why everyone else has to bow to You! This is where all the trouble started..."*

She continued telling how Lucifer managed to get a third of the angels to join him in rebelling against God, resulting in Him kicking them out of heaven. She asked why He hadn't been banished them to one of the far distant planets in the galaxy, and put some kind of force-field around it. Instead, they were allowed come to earth to corrupt His creation, as if He had no control over what Lucifer and his posse did!

She questioned whether God really *could* kill Satan because if He could, surely He would have done it by now? *"...after all, you were quick to punish humans when WE rebelled!"*

She then proceeded to examine 'The Fall of Adam and Eve' story, again trying to get to the *root cause* of all of the world's (and her) problems. She reminded God that he made Adam and Eve in his *very own image* and created a beautiful garden for them to inhabit. He gave them free access to all the fruit of the garden – except the fruit from the tree right in the *middle* of the garden; the 'Tree of Knowledge of Good and Evil'. She pointed out that Lucifer also had free access to the Garden of Eden, and even though Eve should have been under the protection of God and her husband, Lucifer was successful in tempting her to eat the forbidden fruit. Instead of God and Adam taking responsibility, Eve was blamed for the fall of humankind. God then *cursed* his creation, *evicted* them from their home, and sent them out into the Big Wide World only to be tempted and corrupted by the devil even more!

Only *after* they were evicted did God place a Guardian Angel with a fiery sword at the entrance of the garden, to stop Adam and Eve from going back in to eat from the *Tree of Life,* which was situated *right beside* the Tree of the Knowledge of Good and Evil.

None of this made any sense to Suzanne; was the Tree of Life more important to God than the human race?

She then asked God why He had placed the Tree of Knowledge of Good and Evil right in the *centre* of the garden, if Adam and Eve weren't supposed to eat of it. Had they been deliberately set up to fail?

Suzanne believed that even if Adam and Eve hadn't been tempted by the serpent, *curiosity* would have got the better of them sooner or later anyway;

'...As a mother, I know that if I placed a handful of sweets in the middle of a table, in the middle of the sitting room and then told my children "Don't eat those sweets!" and just left them there for weeks and weeks, I guarantee that it would only be a matter of time before those sweets started disappearing down their throats!' Suzanne knew *her* children would eventually take the risk of whatever punishment they would have to suffer later, just for that moment of pleasure. She continued; '*...Now what if I then said to my children "Right, because you ate those sweets I'm not going to give you any dinner for a week!" wouldn't you think I was being a bit – harsh?'*

Suzanne stood in Adam and Eve's defense saying that the punishment God served on *His* 'children' far outweighed their actions.

They were naïve, inexperienced, gullible. They didn't stand a chance against the guile of His enemy.

Instead of making Adam and Eve feel as if it was *their* fault that Satan came to tempt them, Suzanne suggested that God should have *apologized* to them for putting them in such jeopardy in the first place! *"But instead, You cursed the whole of the human race, and now generations later, we are still suffering because 'Adam and Eve ate of the forbidden fruit'."*

The intensity of her Scorpio energy flowed unto the pages as she continued her critical examination of what she had learned from years of studying the bible. She pointed out that the world has been in a state of anarchy literally since the beginning of time; *"The bible has barely begun, when already there's disobedience, damnation, murder, incest, war, famine and woe! But who's really to blame; man, the devil, or dare I say it – YOU?"*

At this point she cringed as if waiting to be struck by a bolt of lightning............when it didn't happen, she carried on more boldly;

Referring to another scripture, Suzanne asked God *why* He had instructed her not to react to people who acted wickedly towards her; instead, she was to see 'past' the flesh and deal with it in the spiritual realm, since they were just 'pawns in the devil's game'. She told God she had a problem with that, because from what she had read in the bible, He had consistently reacted to flesh and blood people, destroying them when He could no longer stand their wicked ways! She reminded Him of Sodom and Gomorrah and The Flood, two occasions where God, in His anger, had wiped out whole populations:

'...But you didn't kill SATAN, the ORIGINATOR of the corruption, so when the earth became re-populated, the whole cycle just started all over again!'

Pausing to think about this, she wrote;

'In fact, I doubt these stories, as I don't think you would be so naïve as to believe that by wiping out the whole of humankind without destroying the ROOT CAUSE, you would ERADICATE the problem? You are far too wise a God to not see that...'

For a moment she appeared to come back to her senses as she watched the sun setting through her window, turning the sky a hazy blue-red. But returning to her journal, her questions instantly re-surfaced; she asked God why He had allowed Himself to be portrayed as a Jekyll and Hyde character (loving us in one instance, then cursing us the next). She especially wanted to know *why* God had allowed His adversary the devil to come to earth and corrupt His creation;

'What did you expect Satan to do? Leave us alone, knowing we were made in the image of the person he hated the most – You?'

Suzanne needed to understand God's thinking *behind* His decisions, so she implored '*...I know Your ways are not my ways but please, help me to understand...'*

After reminding God that the battle was in fact between *Him* and the *devil* and didn't really have anything to do with *us*, His creation, she pointed out that the war was getting *worse* and *worse:*

'People are being murdered, raped, tortured, beaten; children are starving, going missing, being abused, corrupted, killed! The earth is dying from pollution, there's famine, earthquakes, and polluted water and air everywhere, and there's a big hole in the ozone layer! This isn't the world that You created for me to live in, I was meant to live in peace, and harmony, joy and happiness with You and my fellowmen...the fact that there's some devil making my life a living hell isn't my fault, I didn't create him, You did! So why don't You take responsibility and protect me when you see him coming for me, like the Loving Father you're meant to be?'

Suzanne paused for a moment to reflect on what she had just written. She cringed at the thought of what would happen to her if she allowed *her* children to be abused by some crazy tyrant. Wouldn't she be held accountable? So why not God, the ultimate Heavenly Father?

And why wasn't He supplying all her needs like He'd promised in His Word?

Returning to her journal she continued to write; *'We're expected to 'wait on You' and we have no way of knowing when You're going to come up with the goods! So many times I've waited on You, believing and praying for my miracle, and when it doesn't happen, we're expected to resort to the conclusion that it was just 'not God's timing'. You seem to play with us like we're a chess game, only moving when it suits You!'*

She again implored; *'I want to know and understand You more; I want to understand Your ways.'*

She recalled the times she walked closely with God, thinking they were the most beautiful; *'...I mean, there's nothing like waking up in the morning and feeling Your presence all around me, or being inspired to write a piece of poetry... But I want more: I want a big house! I want nice clothes! I want to be able to go on holiday yearly with my family, buy myself a decent car, have plastic surgery to correct all those things You got wrong with me...'*

She acknowledged that it was probably due to her lack of the 'fear of the Lord' why she was *not* walking in His blessings. Still, she wanted to know *why* she was expected to do God's will without questioning His word;

'...What good is a 'free will' when you command me to do things YOUR way? What kind of a free will is that, anyway?'

She demanded the answers to her questions through her sheer *will power*.

In all honesty, Suzanne loved the Lord and really wanted to serve Him 'in spirit and in truth', but the truth was, she was finding it hard to put her trust in Him totally and follow His ways:

'...I know Your Word; I've read it, spoken it, meditated upon it, memorized it, and I still have ***so many needs****! Is it because I didn't BELIEVE enough, or perhaps I didn't PRAY enough, or maybe I just didn't have enough FAITH? ...All I want to do is live the life of my dreams, is that asking too much?*

Why can't I just live in heaven – on EARTH?'

Because she had experienced God's pure, unconditional Love, Suzanne was finding it difficult to equate the character in the bible with the God she had built a relationship with. When she thought everything through, she came to the conclusion that even though Lucifer had taken a third of the angels with him, there were still *two thirds* left in heaven with God! She told God she believed He was mightier than the devil, and since He also had twice as many angels, where was the battle, really? So writing her last lines she ended; *'...You know, the more I think about all of this, the more these stories just don't sound true, nor do they reflect the character of You, so now what I really want is…the TRUTH!'*

Feeling pleased with her Self, she entitled her letter to God *'The Rebellion'*. Writing it had felt cathartic. She had put it 'out there', and now she would wait for His response.

God's Reply

The following morning as soon as Suzanne woke up, she felt inspired to write. So picking up her journal and pen still lying on the bed beside her, she turned over to a fresh page and wrote:

Think on My Love,
Think on My goodness,
Think on My grace,
And all the things I've done for you.

When you think on these things,
Your problems will become small
Your mountains will become molehills
And everything you aspire to WILL become reachable.

Don't look at your situation,
Look to Me.
You can do all things, through Me.
I Am the Way that makes crooked paths straight
I Am the Key that unlocks the doors
I AM the Great I AM.

Do not fear when trials come your way
Do not bend when temptation is at your door
Always remember that in trials there are testimonies
And no ***test****imony without a TEST.*
So don't be discouraged,
Don't feel downhearted,
Be of good cheer

And always remember that in Me
There is victory.
(Track 1 on the '*Seeds of Love*' CD)

God responded to her promptly, and in a language that she could relate to – poetry! As she was writing, she could feel God's presence surrounding her, as if comforting her. Tears rolled down her cheeks as she wrote a letter of apology back, for allowing her Self to lose focus.

Synchronicity

Later that morning as Suzanne was running water into the sink to wash the dishes, she had an inspired idea to design some backdrops for her poems. She was proficient in Photoshop, so she had a go at creating layers of photographs, and adding her text on top. She was pleasantly surprised with the results. 'I can sell these!' she thought.

Quite by chance (or should we call it *synchronicity*?) the next day she attended a community event where she met a local Councilor. She told him about her new poster designs, and he informed her of an International Caribbean Trade Expo which would be taking place the following weekend. He gave her a number to call to find out if there were any stands left, and said to mention his name.

When she called, she was offered a stand at a reduced rate. She called her sister Janice and asked if she wanted to share the stand; Janice travelled to places like Egypt, West Africa and the Caribbean to buy things of black interest to sell.

The Caribbean Expo

The Expo was a much bigger occasion than Suzanne had anticipated; thousands of people flocked to the venue in the Docklands for the three day event. She made over three times as much money as she had invested in the stand and printing her posters. But it was the third day that was to change her life forever...she spotted him in the distance; he seemed to stand out like a neon light, appearing head and shoulders above everyone else. As he approached her stand, Suzanne began to get all excited, with butterflies in her stomach; did she know this man?

Now only a few feet away; she could see that she *didn't* know him, and standing over six feet tall he really *was* head and shoulders above everyone else! She also realized he wasn't heading towards *her* stand, but the stand opposite! She just *had* to get his attention;

"EXCUSE ME!" she called out to him on impulse.

He turned, saw her waving at him, and began walking towards her. She suddenly felt nervous; what was she doing? She wasn't in the habit of pursuing men, plus, she was meant to be working! But as their eyes met, she flashed him a huge, inviting smile. He accepted her invitation.

She knew he thought she was attractive, and she thought he was attractive too.

As he reached her stand she flicked her hair and said cheerfully "Hi! I thought you might be interested in my posters."

"Hmmm....they're nice, did you design them?" He asked, perusing them.

"Yes, I wrote the poetry too."

He stood silently, reading one.

"I can tell, you're deep," he commented when he had finished.

Suzanne laughed.

"Would you like one?" she asked.

"How much are they?" he enquired.

"Well you can buy one for £4.50, two for £8.00 or three for £10"

He chose three different designs, saying "My mum will appreciate these," and paid her the £10.

"What made you come here today?" Suzanne asked, trying to prolong his stay as she rolled the posters up slowly before putting an elastic band around them. Neat, heavy eyebrows adorned his sparkling dark brown eyes. He was dressed casually but neatly in a pair of jeans, a shirt and polished shoes. As she handed him the posters he smiled with full, luscious lips revealing perfect teeth. But it wasn't his *looks* that had attracted her to him in the first place. In fact, she couldn't quite put her finger on *what* it was.

"My friend invited me," he answered, pointing to another brother at the stand opposite.

"Oh sorry, I didn't realize you were with someone!"

"It's okay. So how long have you been doing this?" he asked, indicating towards her posters with his tube.

"I've only just started actually – this is my first time selling them!" she smiled proudly.

"What were you doing before this?"

"I used to work in Admin, but I left my job two weeks ago so I could focus on starting my own business."

"Wow, sounds pretty much like me..."

He proceeded to tell her how he had just left the job he had been working in for 7 years, as well as ending his long term relationship. It sounded as if they were both at a turning-point in their lives. In a weird kind of way, during the time they were talking, everything around them became like a blurred whirlwind, as if they were in some kind of time warp; time literally stood still. Suzanne forgot she was meant to be selling. In that moment, nothing else existed in the room but the two of them. For the two minutes or so that they conversed, they both shared personal information about themselves, as if they had known each other already.

"…I have to go – do you have a card?" he asked.

Suzanne picked up one of her home-made business cards and handed it to him. He read it and smiled at her slogan; *'Promoting LOVE through Creativity!'*

"I'll call you," he said with promise in his eyes.

"I'll look forward to it," she smiled encouragingly.

"My name's Charles, by the way," he added, extending his hand. His smile was as warm as a summer's day, making her feel all hot and flustered.

As their hands made contact, what felt like an electrical current passed through Suzanne's whole body; she wondered if he had felt it too. They shook hands quite formally, but there was a lingering in the time they should have let go.

"Suzanne."

As Charles walked away, Janice asked "Who was *THAT*?"

He Calls

Two days later, true to his word, Charles called. A number came up that wasn't stored in Suzanne's phone, and she instinctively knew it was him. The boys hadn't come up in their conversation at the Expo, and they were playing in the living room, making quite a lot of noise.

"BE QUIET!" she called out to them as she answered her mobile phone.

"Hello, Suzanne speaking" (in her business-voice).

"Hi Suzanne, its Charles – remember we met at the Expo on Sunday?"

"Oh *hi* Charles, of course I remember – lovely to hear from you!"

Charles sensed the genuine appreciation in her voice and responded to it;

"Well, I couldn't wait to call, but I thought I should give you a day or two to rest after the weekend...how did it go?" he asked.

"It was great! I was really surprised at the amount of people who turned up; I sold loads of posters and made lots of new contacts too – including you!" She answered excitedly.

"How many other 'contacts' did you make?" Charles asked, as if defending his territory.

Suzanne laughed. "Not like that, I mean *business* contacts!"

"Oh, well that's alright then – so I don't have any competition?" Charles pushed for confirmation.

Suzanne could see where this was heading so asked "Could you do me a favour and call back after eight please? I've got to put the boys to bed; once they're asleep I'll be free to talk. Is that okay?"

"Oh! I didn't know you had children – how old are they?" he asked in a surprised tone. Judging by her sylph-like figure, he'd figured she was childless.

"Six and eight" she responded tentatively.

"Okay no problem, I'll call back after eight then."

As Suzanne replaced her mobile on the armrest, she wondered whether he *would* call back. He obviously hadn't banked on her having children.

After dinner, spending 'Quality Time' with the boys and tucking them into bed, she sat down to relax. It was 8.30pm. Just as she was about to think 'I knew he wouldn't call back' her mobile phone started to ring. It was him!

"Hi Charles! Thanks for calling back – and sorry about earlier."

"Nothing to be sorry about, I understand. Are you okay to talk now?"

"Sure, what would you like to talk about?"

"Well I'm not one to beat around the bush – are you single?"

She could hardly believe he was still interested even though she had two young ones!

"Yes I'm *single* but I'm not *available*, if that's what you mean," she said though.

"Why not?" he asked inquisitively.

"Well, I'm just starting my business, and I have to focus on getting it off the ground."

"That's all well and good, but…couldn't you do with some help?" he asked again.

"Maybe, but I just feel this is something I have to do on my own."

Out loud he said "Fair comment," but in his head, he was thinking 'Another Independent Black Woman!'

He decided to change the topic by asking "So what do you do for fun?"

"Oh, I *love* writing poetry, and occasionally, I go out and perform as well."

"Hmmm....sounds interesting, maybe I'll join you next time you go."

Suzanne panicked at the thought – she wasn't *that* good! She was still building her confidence performing in front of a crowd.

"Okay...that would be nice!" she lied.

"What about you? What do *you* like to do?" she changed the subject.

Charles told her that he was an Accountant by profession, but he also liked to study Numerology in his spare time. There was a lot more to numbers than meets the eye, he informed her. Suzanne told him about her fascination with the way people's date and time of birth seemed to affect their personality. They already had something in common.

She asked him if he had any children.

"No, not yet."

She thought this was unusual for a Black man of his age group.

"How old are you?" she asked.

"36, why, how old are you?"

"28"

The age gap didn't seem to bother either of them. They spent the next two hours getting to know each other over the phone that evening. Suzanne told him she was a church-going Christian, and how much she loved the Lord. Charles told her he loved God too, but didn't go to church anymore, saying he'd outgrown it. She was tempted to press the issue further, but decided to wait. She told him she liked going for early morning walks in the park to 'breathe in the trees' which helped clear her head. He told her he went to the gym most mornings for a work-out which helped set him up for the day. She said the only thing *she* liked to go to the gym for was a sauna and steam. He asked about the boys, and she told him all about them. He told her that he had joined the 100 Black Men of London to mentor young black boys, and that she should consider bringing them to the Saturday morning sessions, which she thought was a great idea. Before ending the conversation Charles said, "It's been really nice talking to you Suzanne; I'd like to carry on this conversation over dinner, if that's alright with you – what are you doing on Saturday evening?"

It was Suzanne's weekend to have the boys.

"I'm taking the boys to their cousins, but I'm free *next* Saturday," she replied.

"Okay it's a date!" Charles responded confidently. "But don't think I won't be calling you every day up until then," he added.

Suzanne laughed.

"Yes, it's been lovely talking with you too, I'll look forward to it!"

"Goodnight then."

"Goodnight Charles."

Self-Esteem Demon

Over the next two weeks, Suzanne and Charles spent every evening talking on the phone. They learnt of each other's likes and dislikes, hopes and dreams, past, and future plans. Despite not having children of his own, Charles always asked about the boys, which she appreciated. They discussed any issues the boys were facing at school, and he offered whatever advice he could give. Charles was single, owned his own home, had a good job, was polite and well-mannered, and to put the icing on the cake, was tall, dark and handsome. Did I mention that he was *Black*?

But Suzanne wondered what he saw in *her?* Instead of looking at the things she could bring to the table, she focused on the things she didn't have.

During one of their conversations, Suzanne's low Self-esteem demon reared its ugly head;

"What do you see in *me*?" she asked him.

"What do you mean, what do I see in you?"

"Well, I'm hardly on your level, am I?"

"I'm...not sure what you mean?"

"Well, look at you; you own your home, you drive, you've got a good job, you have no children..."

"Suzanne, do you really think having a house, car and job make me happy? Those are just *things*, Suzanne. *Things* don't make you happy; having someone to *share* those things with can, though."

"I see what you mean, but I still wouldn't feel right joining myself to someone else in my current situation, especially someone like you."

"Why not?"

"I wouldn't feel good enough."

"Well how will you know when you're good enough for say, someone like me?"

"When I've achieved something."

"Like what; what is your goal?"

"Well...I'd like to run a successful business doing what I love."

"Which is?"

"Writing and performing my poetry."

"Okay….so what steps are you taking towards your goal?" Charles asked in an interested tone.

"Well, I'm working on my first poetry collection, and I also plan to record my poems to go with the book."

"Good!" Charles commended her; "So how will you know when you've reached your goal?"

Suzanne closed her eyes and imagined holding her first book of poetry with its complimentary CD. She thought about all the people that would benefit from listening to them, and the feedback she would receive, confirming that her poetry had an important message. She thought about how in turn, it would help her achieve financial independence.

"I'll be financially free," she answered.

"Okay...what does 'financial freedom' mean to you; what will it enable you to *do*?" Charles probed.

"I'll be able to buy my own house, take my boys on holidays, buy a decent car, buy the clothes I like..."

"Alright stop there...how will achieving your goal make you *feel*?"

"I'd feel fulfilled, like I've achieved what I said I was going to do…I'd feel like I'm actually making a difference in this world doing something that I love."

"That's great Suzanne, really great. So do you know anyone who's already achieved your goal?"

"I do actually – I know someone who's recorded *three* poetry collections and he travels all over the world performing his poetry!"

"Wow…so what resources do they have that you could possibly use?"

Up to that point, Suzanne hadn't even considered asking that brother if she could use his recording equipment to record *her* CD, or for help guiding her through the process! She thanked Charles for helping her 'see the light'.

"So are you ready for me now?" he asked.

"What do you mean?" She asked in a puzzled tone.

"Well, you just made the necessary changes internally to help you attract the things you desire, so it's only a matter of time before they show up. Are you ready for *me* now?"

"You deserve the best, Charles."

"Don't you believe you *are* the best Suzanne? Don't put yourself down; I mean, where's all this *coming* from?"

His question jolted Suzanne's memory back to her childhood; visions flashed through her mind of her mother beating her mercilessly while telling her she was worthless and good for nothing. She was labelled 'the ugly duckling of the family' because she was the darkest of the girls. Her mother showed her no affection, but made her feel as if she didn't even *like* her, let alone *love* her. Nothing she did was ever 'good enough'. Worse than the beatings were the negative *words* spoken to her, which had gone straight into her subconscious, and had festered there for years. With Charles prompting her to uncover where her low self esteem issues were coming from, those memories were only now resurfacing. When she explained this to him, he responded;

"I'm so sorry to hear that Suzanne; it sounds as if your mother was *herself* a victim of the slave mentality. I'm sure growing up in church didn't help either. Most people I know who grew up in church have serious low self esteem issues. Unfortunately, you had a double-whammy."

"What do you mean?"

"Well, both at home and at church you were made to feel inferior. You had that going on at home, then you went to church where you were taught that you were a poor, wretched sinner, unworthy – it's no wonder you grew up with low self esteem!"

"I see what you mean…what can I do to change the way I feel about myself?"

"That's a very good question Suzanne, because until you change the way you *feel*, you'll continue to attract things on the vibration of how you feel about yourself."

"Well I attracted *you*, didn't I?" Suzanne answered cheekily.

"Yes, and you feel you don't deserve me, so you're trying to push me away. See what I mean?"

"But surely I must be doing *something* right…I mean if I can attract someone like you, surely there must be something good going on internally."

"Yes, what would you say that was?"

"Well, I really do believe I deserve the best God has for me. I just feel something's blocking it."

"And you really *love* God, right?"

"Yes, with all my heart!"

"Then that's your answer; you attracted me because you love God wholeheartedly. The thing that's blocking it is *you* Suzanne. To really begin living the life you desire, you have to change the way you feel about *yourself*. It's time to face your demons."

"You're right Charles, I never thought of low self esteem as a demon before, but when I think about all the opportunities I've missed because of it, it's stolen from me time and time again."

"Well thank God you didn't let it to stop you from calling out to me!"

They both laughed.

Charles concluded the conversation;

"You ask me what I see in you so let me tell you; I see an attractive young woman with great ideas who lacks the knowledge to take things further at this time. Still, you have the courage, strength and determination to pursue your dreams and care for your boys with limited resources."

The other things didn't matter to him, what mattered was the way he was beginning to feel about *her*.

First Date

The day of their date finally arrived. Charles had said he would pick her up at 6.30pm, and sure enough, his black BMW pulled up at almost six-thirty on the dot. Suzanne looked excitedly in the mirror one last time to make sure her wig was in exactly the right place and that her make-up was perfect. It was a warm summer evening; she was wearing a red sleeveless dress that hugged her figure, dropping in folds just below her knees. 5-inch heeled red sandals, lipstick and nail varnish finished off the look, coupled with diamente drop earrings. She carried a light jacket in case it got cold later. Her clothes weren't expensive, but she looked and felt like a million dollars.

As she stepped outside and pulled her front door shut, Charles was already standing by her side of the car with the door open. She kissed him lightly on the cheek before getting into the car. After making sure her dress wouldn't get caught, he shut the door firmly.

'A real gentleman!' she thought.

All the way to the restaurant, they laughed and joked as they listened to music. It was as if they had known each other for ages. When they discovered they had the same taste in music, they agreed to do a compilation CD for each other.

Charles pulled up outside a Thai restaurant in Muswell Hill. He had pre-booked a table, so they didn't have to wait to be seated; they followed a waitress to their table and sat down. Charles excused himself to use the men's. Suzanne looked around; the restaurant was nice; not overly posh, but pleasant surroundings with a warm atmosphere and soft piano music playing in the background.

When Charles returned, the waitress brought their menus. As Suzanne looked through hers, Charles made his recommendations;

"Do you want to try the mixed platter? I always have it when I come here, I like the variety."

"Alright then, I'll try it!" Suzanne agreed. She liked a man who knew how to take control in a situation without dominating, if you know what I mean.

"What would you like to drink?" he asked.

"Water for now."

"Me too."

Charles called the waitress over and ordered the meal and a bottle of spring water.

While they were waiting for their food to arrive, Suzanne took the opportunity to pose the question she had been waiting to ask him face to face:

"So tell me Charles, why don't you go to church?"

"Well..." Charles paused to think carefully before responding;

"God lives inside me, that's why I don't feel I need to go to church to find him. Plus, I don't see anywhere in the bible that says you should go to church every Sunday."

"True, but it *does* say not to forsake the gathering of the brethren."

"Yes, well I'm more interested in *relationship* than religion."

"But how can you have a relationship with God if you refuse to mix with his people?"

"I don't; his people are *everywhere*, not just in church – I serve God every day by serving my fellow human beings. I see God in *every* body…I see God in *you.*"

Suzanne blushed, but he didn't notice.

"Really?"

"Of course…I used to go to church, but I grew out of it. I hope that answers your question."

"It does…to a point, but what about when you die? Aren't you afraid of going to hell?"

Charles chuckled.

"See that's the problem with religion, it's fear-based. Would you still be a Christian if you weren't afraid of going to hell?"

Suzanne paused to think before replying;

"Yes of course I would! I'm a Christian because God loved me so much that he sent his only son to die for me. I *love* God, that's why I choose to serve him, not because I'm afraid of anything."

Charles put his hand over hers on the table and looking her straight in the eyes smiled and replied "Well I love God too, so we both have something in common."

Just then, the waitress returned with their food. As she served the various dishes, they smiled at each other from across the table.

Suzanne complimented the look of the food as they tucked in. After a few mouthfuls, she continued probing:

"You didn't answer my question…how do you know your life is right with God?"

Charles took a deep breath before continuing; "Well first of all I need to say, I don't really feel comfortable with all this 'God' business, it just sounds so…*impersonal.* I much prefer to call Him by His name, *Jehovah.* Do you mind?"

"Not at all…are you a Jehovah's Witness then?"

"No I'm not, so to answer your question, the reason I don't go to church anymore is because I haven't found one that aligns with my new way of thinking. For instance, most churches today meet on a

Sunday, when the bible clearly says *Saturday*, the Sabbath, as His holy day."

"Yes but we're no longer under the old law, we're under a *new* covenant," Suzanne defended the move.

"That's *your* belief, Suzanne, based upon what they told you in church – but is it *scriptural?* The day was changed by Roman Catholics in direct defiance of the Laws set in place by Jehovah. I think we should all learn to follow our own inner guidance, then we wouldn't need religions and governments to impose their *man*-made laws on us."

"But surely if there were no governments or religions the world would be in a state of anarchy?" Suzanne responded incredulously.

"Not necessarily; we all have an internal guidance system that lets us know right from wrong. But when you take away people's moral right to follow their own inner guidance, they either rebel, or turn into sheeple."

"Sheeple?"

"Yeah, that's what I call people who just go along with anything they've been told without asking any questions. I mean, what do you know about the history of Christianity?"

"Well, 2000 years ago, a man named Jesus…."

Charles watched in amusement as Suzanne re-told the story of the virgin birth, Jesus' ministry, and his death upon the cross.

"What if I told you that most of the main characters in the bible were Black – that *Jesus* was Black – would you believe me?"

"What difference does it make if he was Black or white? Surely what matters is that you accept him as your Lord and Saviour?"

"It makes a *big* difference actually Suzanne – if it didn't matter, why did they *change* his image from Black to white? It's things like this that bother me; nobody asks any questions. Considering most of the people who go to church look like you and me, don't you think there's something wrong with them worshipping to a *white* saviour?"

"I don't see it like that."

"Ok, let's conduct a little experiment; close your eyes."

(Suzanne does as he says.)

"Now think of Jesus…what image do you see?"

Suzanne opened her eyes and stared at him blankly.

"Well?"

Suzanne's mind ran back to her childhood; the main picture that had dominated the family's living room was of a white Jesus hung on the cross. And in her children's bible, all the images were white too.

"You're right, he's white. But what's most important to me is that I accept him as Lord and Saviour of my life, not what colour he is."

Charles sighed; "It's psychological warfare against my people, that's how I see it…It's okay, you follow your religion, and I'll follow Universal Laws – doesn't mean we can't get along."

"What are 'Universal Laws'?"

"There were certain Laws put in place during the process of Creation. I reckon if everybody was living by these Laws instead of man-made laws, we would all be living in peace and harmony."

"That's interesting; can you name some of these Laws?" Suzanne's thirst for knowledge grew.

"*'You Reap What You Sow'* is one of them," he explained; "Scientifically they call it *'Cause and Effect'*, some people even call it *Karma*, meaning for every *action* you take, there has to be a re*action*. Everything you do produces a knock-on effect, or a *harvest*. So if you do good deeds – or sow good seeds – you'll reap a good harvest. If you sow bad seeds, you'll reap the results of your actions."

Suzanne processed the information before responding;

"Oh, no wonder Jesus said to *'love your neighbour as yourself'* – if everybody treated others the way they wanted to be treated, this world *would* be a better place!"

She could now see why Charles always seemed to be calculating his movements.

"…But that still doesn't answer the question about where your soul will end up when you die. You can't get to heaven by good works, you know."

"I'll worry about that when the time comes, okay?" Charles responded, taking another bite of food.

Suzanne sat silently looking down at the table, making it clear to Charles she was unhappy with his response. Not wanting to get on her bad side, he added;

"Look, if I *was* to go back to church, it would have to be based upon what I *know*, not on what I *believe*."

"What do you mean?"

"Well I'd want to go to a church that acknowledged the Divine Mother as well as the Father, which meets on God's holy day, *Saturday*, not Sunday. They would call God by his name, *Jehovah*, and acknowledge that Jesus, or *Yeshuah*, looked more like me, not a white man. And instead of making everyone give 10% of what they earn – which is unscriptural – some of the money collected would be shared with those members in need."

"That sounds like a good church! I don't think it exists though."

"And that's why I don't go! Now can we enjoy our meal without all this church business please?"

"Ok…but can you tell me more about Universal Laws?"

"I can lend you some books on the subject, you're welcome to come over to my place sometime and pick a few if you like."

"I might just take you up on that!"

Charles went on to explain that his father, a Ghanaian, had been the spiritual head of their home, and made sure he was connected to his African roots. He taught him all about the black leaders who had died in the process of trying to save their people from white supremacy and oppression. His mother on the other hand, who was Barbadian, was brought up in a Christian home, and had passed that down to her children. She had often taken him and his two sisters to church with her, but religion had not played a key role in their household. Despite their opposing beliefs, his parents had focused on raising their children well. His father had never tried to stop his mother from taking them to church with her, but instead made sure they also knew their history. This, he believed, would help them make an informed decision when they came of age. Charles shared an African proverb his father used to say:

"THEY had the bible and WE had the land,
Now WE have the bible and THEY have the land!"

He re-told the story his father had told him as child, of how missionaries had arrived in Africa with thousands of bibles, under the guise of converting Africans to Christianity, but with a secret plot to steal the wealth-creating resources of their land. They convinced the natives that they needed a white saviour to save them from their sins, and that Jesus was to be their new Lord and Master. This, Charles said, psychologically set Africans up to think of the white man as being more superior to them, and that they couldn't do anything without him. This new form of Christianity taught them to be meek, humble servants, not to covet earthly riches, but instead, to wait until they got to heaven to receive 'riches untold'. By tricking Africans into this new belief system, it pacified them enough to make them willingly hand over the wealth-creating resources of their land. Europeans were then able to help themselves to their gold, diamonds, oil, and other natural resources, which they used to build up their own countries economies.

Suzanne smiled at him apologetically.

"You seem to know more about my religion that I do…maybe I should do some research of my own."

"You should."

Even though they were talking about church and God, they were both aware of the underlying current; they were inches away from each other across the table and the heat they both seemed to be generating was beginning to set sparks flying.

Charles was wise and knowledgeable, and had *standards*, Suzanne thought. He was a one-in-a-million kinda guy; good-looking, well-mannered, well-spoken, loving, spiritual, respectful, intelligent, financially astute, and...Black! What more could she ask for?

"HE MUST BE BORN AGAIN!"

She could already hear the voice of her Pastor booming from the pulpit.

If the brother hasn't accepted Jesus Christ as Lord and Savior of his life, she would be 'unequally yoked to an unbeliever'. But Charles was *perfect*, she argued within herself; she was sure they had met by some kind of Divine Order – he was everything she had hoped and prayed for, God's best promise; Faith, Hope and Love all rolled into one. There was only one problem...he wasn't a born again Christian. Did it matter? Her conscience wouldn't allow her to say 'no'. 'If we're going to carry on this relationship' she thought, 'he has to get *saved*, and we're going to have to get *married.*'

After their meal, Charles took her for a drive; they ended up on the Embankment where he showed her a huge Sphinx carving, which had apparently been given to the British by the Head of State of Egypt in the 1800's. He informed her that the original name for Egypt was '*Ancient Kemet*' which meant 'Land of the Blacks'. Suzanne was intrigued, and asked Charles if he knew what the significance of the animal body and human head was? Charles explained that it symbolized the ability to rise above the lower animal nature. They took photos of each other with the silhouetted Sphinx in the background.

As they crossed the bridge, Charles put a protective arm around her shoulder and asked "Will you go out with me?"

"We *are* out!" Suzanne joked with him.

"You know what I mean."

"We'll see..."

Suzanne would have loved to have said "Yes!" but she was still thinking about being 'unequally yoked to an unbeliever'.

The evening went even better than they had both anticipated; they felt comfortable in each other's company, and conversation flowed easily. Because they had spent the past two weeks talking over the phone, they already felt like they knew each other intimately. They both had a good feeling about this.

It was getting late, and cold. Charles offered to drop her home, although neither of them wanted the evening to end. They had waited nearly two weeks to see each other again, and weren't in a hurry to part company so easily.

Although Suzanne was a practicing Christian, her weakness was strong Black men. It had been two years since she'd had sex, but she knew she didn't want to sleep with Charles, especially on the first date.

As they pulled up outside her house, she invited him in for a cup of tea.

They spent the next few hours talking, drinking herbal tea and listening to music in the living room. As they sat on the sofa, Suzanne was still trying to think of a way to get him to agree to go to church with her.

"Don't you think going to church and having a belief in something is good?" she couldn't help asking him.

"Let me put it like this; religion in its purest form *was* good – it was created by *us*; the ancient manuscripts that the bible and other holy books were created from *did* show us how to get the best out of life. But somewhere along the line religion was hijacked, and now, it's just a form of control to mentally enslave the masses. I still read my bible, there's still a lot of Truth in it, but I see my *body* as God's temple. That's where I go to find God; *within*."

With that, he pulled her close to him in a warm embrace, changing the subject. He didn't want to fall out with her over her beliefs. They continued to talk as they sat huddled on the sofa.

By 1.30am it became apparent than he didn't want to leave, and she didn't want him to go either. She was determined not to fall into temptation though. Still, he managed to convince her that they could just lie on the bed together and cuddle; they didn't have to take their clothes off, they could just lie on *top* of the bed – after all, they both had will-power, didn't they? So they moved to her bedroom, and talked and talked into the early hours of the morning, until finally falling asleep in each other's arms, fully clothed.

The Following Morning...

The following day was Sunday. No work for Charles, and the boys would be at their dad's until the evening, so Charles and Suzanne had the day to themselves. Suzanne had adopted the habit of getting up early from when the boys were babies, and it had stuck with her ever since. No matter what time she went to bed, she was normally up by 6am. She liked to get up early to pray, read her bible, exercise and get washed and dressed before the boys got up at 7.30am. Sometimes she would just be inspired to write. Charles was an early riser too. He habitually went to the gym before going to work and on weekends, so even though it was Sunday and they'd had a late night, they were both awake by 7am. Suzanne woke up first, headed for the bathroom, stripped, and did some stretches before taking a shower. While she was showering, Charles had woken up, and needing to use the toilet urgently, knocked on the bathroom door.

"Can I come in?" he asked.

"Yes…it's open."

Suzanne smiled at the sound of Charles emptying his bladder.

"Did you sleep alright?" she asked.

"Like a baby."

"Me too."

She could hear Charles washing his hands at the sink.

"Do you need to freshen up?" she asked.

"I was thinking I'd do that when I got home."

"Are you leaving already?"

Charles sensed her disappointment at the thought.

"Don't you want me to?"

"Well, not if you don't need to…"

"Can I take a shower then?"

"Okay…I'm nearly finished."

"Do you want me to scrub your back for you?" Charles asked hopefully.

"Er…okay. You might as well get in then."

Just what he wanted to hear!

Charles stripped quickly, hanging his clothes on the hooks behind the door.

As he peeled back the shower curtain, Suzanne had her back turned to him, but greeted him with a smile over her shoulder. She passed him the bottle of liquid soap and her body scrub as he got in.

"Don't get any ideas, this is just a shower, okay?"

"Okay."

Charles stood behind her and began soaping her back gently, admiring the way the soap bubbles glistened against her skin, and her pert backside. He was getting aroused. He stood back so she couldn't notice.

"Put some elbow grease into it!" Suzanne encouraged him.

Charles scrubbed harder, covering her whole back and the nape of her neck, just below her shower cap.

"Do you want me to do anywhere else?" he asked optimistically.

"No, I'm done. Do you want me to do yours before I get out?"

"That would be great!"

Charles turned around quickly as she took the scrubber from him. He held his manhood down with both hands as she began soaping his back quickly and purposefully.

She stopped suddenly.

"What's wrong?" he asked, turning to look at her.

"Nothing…"

Suzanne had suddenly become aware of Charles' body; she was now admiring his smooth dark chocolate skin, the shape of his back, from his broad shoulders which narrowed down to his waist, his firm backside, and his strong, muscular arms and legs.

'I've struck black gold!' she thought.

Now, her movements were slower and more deliberate.

"I don't have any clean boxers to put on, I'll have to go home commando!" Charles joked.

But Suzanne was making plans of her own.

When she had finished scrubbing his back, she left him to complete his shower alone and headed back to her room. After oiling her skin, she got into bed, naked.

It wasn't long before Charles entered, with the towel she had left for him wrapped around his waist. Suzanne couldn't help eyeing him up from top to bottom – especially the bulge in the middle!

As he made his way towards the bed he said "So what's the plan for today?"

Suzanne held up the covers and invited him to join her.

"I thought we could just chill and relax for an hour or so – it's still early – then I'll make breakfast, how does that sound?"

Charles wasted no time joining her.

"Sounds good to me…so what do you want to do?" he remembered her earlier caution, but was hopeful.

Suzanne didn't say another word, instead, as he lay on his back, she moved on top of him, pressing her naked body against his, and proceeded to give him his first kiss.

Charles put his arms around her waist, pulling her into him, as they kissed passionately. They were both aroused; neither of them had had sex in months; Charles' manhood was as hard as a rock, catching Suzanne's attention.

She kissed her way down to greet it. Kneeling before him, Suzanne took his throbbing manhood in her hand, and examined it closely. It was a piece of art; her fingers could hardly meet around its girth, and as it stood erect, all nine-and-a-half inches of it leaned to one side. A large vein ran down its underside, and with the skin pulled back, its head stood out loud and proud. This was her smooth dark chocolate-colored dream!

"Does it have a name?" she asked, knowing men like to do this.

"Pride."

"Pride?"

She thought this was a bit of an odd name for a dick, until Charles explained;

"You read the bible, don't you? Doesn't it say 'Pride *comes* before a fall'?"

It took a few seconds for Suzanne to get it, but when she did, she burst out laughing.

"No it doesn't, actually!" Still, she thought it was funny.

"It also *stands* for 'Black Pride'" Charles added, raising his hand in a fist.

"Hello Pride!" Suzanne introduced herself, then looking up at Charles, she slowly took Pride into her mouth. Charles let out a deep-throated groan. Suzanne lubricated his shaft with her tongue, as she slowly and rhythmically moved her mouth up and down over his organ, using her hand to massage the bottom end that wouldn't fit. "Oh...*damn*!" Charles gasped, as she continued licking, paying particular attention to his bare helmet. Charles groaned and grabbed her head to push her down unto him further, but moving her head away, she gave him a look that let him know the only place out of bounds to him was her hair.

After Suzanne had finished introducing herself to Pride, Charles pulled her up by the hand and invited her to lie next to him. They pressed against each other hungrily, exploring each other's bodies; kissing, touching, discovering, learning, bonding. Charles straddled her body on all fours like an animal that had just caught its prey, and branded his mark all over her face, neck, shoulders and chest with every hot kiss. Cupping her breasts in each of his hands, he pushed them close together and sucked on one erect nipple, then the other, paying each one individual attention. Suzanne's nipples were super-sensitive; she moaned and writhed underneath him as he continued to lick, suck and tease them gently with his teeth. When he had finished, he continued his journey of exploration around the map of her body, kissing every place he encountered. He left a burning trail on her arms, fingers, abdomen, thighs, calves, ankles and feet. Then he traced a wet line with his tongue gently back up from her foot to her inner thigh, until he reached her garden.

Her flesh tingled in anticipation of what she knew was coming. Parting her labia, he revealed the juicy pink flesh underneath. He thought it resembled a flower. As the tip of his tongue made contact with her sweet spot, what felt like an electrical current ran through her, causing her whole body to shudder; she let out a soft gasp. Tasting her sweet nectar, he began moving his tongue slowly backwards and forwards, then in circular motions, as her back arched involuntarily with each cycle. He increased the speed; soon his tongue was darting up and down, back and forth, making her clitoris go as hard as a man's erection. He ate her like it was his favorite meal. Suzanne moaned with pleasure, and holding his head between her hands, guided him to make sure he was hitting exactly the right spot. She raised her head from the pillow to catch a glimpse of his face, to see if he was enjoying this as much as she was; his focus was totally on the job in hand (or should I say 'tongue'?)

"Oh Charles, that feels *sooooo gooooood*!" she whispered to him. He raised his head briefly to say "I aim to please" before burying his head between her legs again. He loved the way she smelled; her fragrance reminded him of a garden in full bloom; it left him feeling all heady. As he continued working his magic, she could feel the waves of orgasm approaching;

"Oh my god, I'm coming!" she gasped as her eyes rolled to the back of her head. The thought of her coming in his mouth excited him; he pulled the whole of her mound deep into his mouth and concentrated his effort on her clitoris, licking with increased pressure.

"Charles, I'm coming!" she cried out as the waves hit. Her body convulsed with one spasm after another, sending an electrical current travelling from her clitoris, up her torso, down her arms and legs to every other nerve in her body, ending in the tips of her fingers, toes, and the top of her head.

He drunk every last drop of her sweet juices.

After Suzanne had climaxed, Charles was ready to mount her. Looking deep into her eyes, he entered her slowly inch by inch. She sighed deeply as he delved deeper and deeper into her hot tunnel. He was a perfect fit; it was as if they were made for each other, like Adam and Eve.

"I love the way you said my name when you climaxed," He murmured in her ear.

"And I love the way you made me come," she whispered back to him.

As they kissed passionately, he increased the intensity and speed of his thrusts while Suzanne moaned softly.

"Oh my god, that feels so good!" she whispered to him.

Without warning, Charles drove deep into her. She cried out, as pleasure and pain mingled together in a bitter-sweet combination. He watched her breasts rise and fall beneath him as she breathed deeply, holding on to his shoulders for support. He did it again; one hard, then one soft. Each time he drove in hard, she cried out, turning him on even more.

"""Give it to me baby!" he called out to her.

"I'm giving it to you!" she cried back.

He took hold of her ankles and placed them on his shoulders. Crossing her feet behind his head, her back naturally rose off the bed. At this angle, he was able to penetrate even deeper; entering her again, he continued kissing her feet and legs as he drove Pride in and out of her wet vagina, which made a soft slurping noise with each thrust as if saying 'thank you, thank you, thank you, thank you, thank you'.

"Tell me what it feels like, inside of me," Suzanne moaned to him.

"Oh man, it feels like...it feels like... " he could hardly get the words out, he was so intoxicated;

"...It feels like I'm entering the centre of your yoni-verse; the deeper I go, the hotter it gets!" he finally managed to get out, quite eloquently.

This was sheer, unadulterated bliss;

'How could something so wrong feel so right?' Suzanne questioned in her mind. Her religious beliefs were trying to creep in and spoil her fun; she'd save the guilty conscience for later.

Pulling her up off the bed while still inside her, Charles carried her across the room, trying to suck her nipples at the same time. *Now* she understood why he worked out so much! As he propped her up against the wall, she wrapped her legs around his back while he took her weight in his hands and lifted her up and down on his manhood. She felt as if she was stealing something from her wedding night; this is just how she would have liked it to be! Returning to the bed, he placed Suzanne on her back, while she squeezed her vaginal muscles around his great obelisk.

"Oh…shit, that feels great, do it again!" Charles groaned in his deep, sexy voice.

She squeezed again, harder this time, muscle-massaging him as he slid slowly back and forth.

"Oh, F**K!" he cried out. She had never heard him swear before.

As he directed her into the doggy position, she placed her hands on the bed for support, with both feet on the floor. The versatility of her body drove him crazy. As he entered her front passage from behind, he let one hand dangle at his side as he admired the view of her small waist and curvy backside. She buried her face in a pillow to muffle her cries of passion; she could feel the bend in his banana-like organ massaging her g-spot, sending small electrical currents rippling through her body with each thrust. Reaching round, Charles played with her breasts, squeezing her nipples in between his thumb and forefingers. He then reached down and stimulated her clitoris while still pounding her from behind. With all her erogenous zones being catered for, she could feel herself coming again.

Grabbing hold of her hips and riding her like a black stallion, Charles headed for the finish line...

When the ultimate moment 'came', they both froze for a moment within their own ecstasy before collapsing in a heap of skin and sweat. With Charles still inside her, Suzanne lay face-down, bearing the weight of his body. She could feel his heart beating rapidly against her back, as their frantic breathing slowed down in unison with every passing second. With his arms wrapped around her waist from behind, she felt like a captured prey.

She had no desire to be freed.

She could feel him still throbbing inside her, and if it wasn't for the condom he was wearing, their body fluids would have mingled together. In that moment it was as if time stood still as they drifted off slowly into sleep together...........

...............I feel like a Butterfly as I flutter amongst the flowers – then I realize I have the power to go higher, so upwards I fly until I see the treetops way below me. Still higher I flutter until I become like one of the stars illuminating the night sky. It feels so free, to be able to rise limitlessly; the night air brushes against my face as I am drawn to the light above me.....Suddenly I'm aware that I am not alone and looking down, I see a man with Wings of an Eagle flying just below me; his arms are outstretched as if waiting to catch me. The look on his face resembles that of an angel and I know, I just know I would be safe in his embrace, but it is not my intention to fall from this place, so I beckon him to come up and join me.......yet even though the space between us is only that of a ladder, he struggles to reach me, as if some invisible force is holding him back. I wait patiently for him, fluttering my red wings to help him focus, eager to experience the warmth of his embrace...

Finally he's just below me; and as I place my arms across my chest he catches me, kissing me gently on my neck, the warmth of his breath............

........Suzanne is awakened from her dream by Charles planting warm, gentle kisses on her neck as she lay cradled under his arm.

"Oh wow....what time is it?" she asked him, still in a daze.

"It's nearly five o'clock," he murmured into her ear.

"Oh my god, the boys will be back at six!" she jumped up in a panic.

"That's okay, I have to go anyway; I've got to prepare for work tomorrow."

It was at this point that Suzanne fully woke up to the realization of what had just happened; she had lost it all – track of time, her dignity...and her favorite wig!

She suddenly felt bare and exposed; as Charles turned his back to start getting dressed, she searched around the bed, hoping he hadn't noticed. Finding it down the side of the bed, she picked her robe off the floor, slipped it on, and tucking the wig inside, excused herself quickly to use the bathroom. She hoped the closed curtains would have limited his ability to see what she was doing.

Five minutes later a calm Suzanne re-entered, wig now intact. Charles was tying his shoelaces. He *had* noticed, and couldn't help commenting;

"You have a beautiful face Suzanne, why do you hide it underneath that wig?"

Embarrassed, she replied "It's just easier for me to manage, that's all – my hair is so *thick*!"

"Oh...well I think you'd look good even if you were bald." Charles meant it, but the thought of walking around with a bald head did *not* appeal to Suzanne! She was sure men preferred long, straight flowing hair. Walking him to the front door she caught a glimpse of herself in the hallway mirror. 'Was he being serious about me looking better without the wig? Nah, he was just saying that to make me feel better!' she thought.

As Charles left, he kissed her *long* and *slow.* As they engaged in one final embrace, she could feel her knees giving way beneath her.

"I'll call you later," he whispered into her ear as he left.

Closing the door behind him she leant back against it and slowly slid down to the floor, smiling to herself as she replayed the whole night and day in her head.

"He is definitely 'The One!'" she thought.

As frantic as the sex was, there had been something deeply spiritual about their lovemaking. But it didn't take long for feelings of guilt and condemnation to start creeping in.

"Oh no, I've sinned *again*!" she thought in despair.

With her head in her hands she realized she was going to have to repent again. Yet the experience had felt so natural, so beautiful, so *right* – how could it have been wrong? As Suzanne knelt to ask for forgiveness, she questioned God;

"Why do you have so many expectations of me, when you have made me so *weak*?"

Lucid Dream # 1

Suzanne had been on the phone with Charles until nearly 1am. It was now 7.00am, and the boys would be up in half an hour. No matter what day of the week it was, they were always up by 7.30am. Suzanne never used an alarm clock either, preferring to let her body clock wake her up naturally. So she woke up late, emerging from a lucid dream. In it, Charles was walking towards her in a cream suit and tan-colored shoes. The suit had a red rose in its lapel...they were getting married! She recalled the way his broad shoulders shifted from side to side as he walked, and the big smile on his face as he sauntered towards her. It didn't last long, but she remembered it vividly when she awoke. She called Charles and relayed the dream back to him.

"*Me* in a cream suit and brown shoes?" he laughed. Charles always wore dark colors; grey, black or blue.

'Well at least he wasn't laughing at the idea of us getting *married*', she thought happily.

She wrote the dream, and Charles' response into her journal, before praying to God that if this was indeed her husband, let him get saved.

Love vs. Fear

They were on the phone again.

It was as if they couldn't get enough of each other, but due to their individual circumstances (Suzanne's boys and Charles's work schedule) they only really got to spend quality time with each other every other weekend. However, sometimes Charles would visit Suzanne during the week after the boys had gone to bed, and leave before they got up in the morning.

This particular evening they were discussing how much power the devil has. Charles was trying to get Suzanne to focus on the greatness of God, rather than anything the devil could do. He told her he didn't believe the devil had the power to do anything to him.

"How can you *not* believe the devil has power?" Suzanne asked in disbelief; "Look at the state of the world! If it wasn't for the devil, we'd all be living in peace and harmony!"

Charles responded calmly; "You've got to take responsibility for your life Suzanne, you can't keep blaming the devil for everything. Your life is the way it is because of how you *think* about it."

"God is in control of my life," she said with conviction.

"Sweetheart, think about it – if God is in control, why *don't* you have everything you say you need? Do you honestly believe the Lord would withhold anything good from you?"

She didn't know what to say in reply to that;

"Hun, when you realize that you're creating your life with your *thoughts, words* and *actions* then you will have taken responsibility for it. Until then, you're powerless to change it for the better. You said you want to learn more about Spiritual Laws, so here's another one: *'What you focus on expands'*. If you keep thinking about the devil and being *fearful*, all you're going to do is attract more things to be fearful about!"

"So are you saying you don't believe in the devil?" she asked, still feeling perplexed.

"No…I'm saying I choose not to *focus* on that energy. I prefer to think of God and the devil as two opposite forces; both are needed to make up the universe, it's a Spiritual Law. Without one, you wouldn't be able to experience the other. I mean, if there was no evil, how would you know what good is? So my dear, if you were to think of God as a Positive, Creative Force, and the devil as a Negative, Destructive Force, which would you choose?"

"God of course!"

"Exactly! So stay centred in that...there *are* people who choose to worship the dark side, but if you're a believer, you should stay focused on Love – God. Our Source is Pure Love and Light, and just remember, *light always overcomes darkness*, like a candle lit in a dark room, so you really have nothing to fear. That's why whenever an angel appeared in the bible, the first thing it would say is FEAR NOT. *Love* is a much stronger force than fear."

"But isn't *hate* the opposite of love, not fear?"

"Hate is a *product* of fear. People hate what they fear, it's that simple."

Changing the subject, Charles asked what she would like to do on their next weekend together.

They agreed to spend it at his place for a change.

Conversation with God

They pulled into the driveway of Charles's end-of-terrace house.

It was a typical bachelor's pad; the living room was spacious with large brown soft leather sofas, a plasma T.V. screen on the wall, and a neat piles of books and newspapers on the coffee table.

She liked his taste in decor, it was similar to hers; wooden floors, plain walls, and minimal furniture. She looked over at one wall lined with shelves of books from top to bottom. The saying...

'If you want to hide something from a Black man,
put it in a book!'

...certainly didn't apply to him! Remembering Charles' offer to lend her some books to learn more about the Universal Laws, she walked over to his library and scanned the rows of Self-development,

African History books and novels on his shelves. One particular book *'Conversations with God Book One'* stood out. She selected it and opened it at a random passage:

'...Words are merely utterances: noises that stand for feelings, thoughts, and experience. They are symbols. Signs. Insignias. They are not Truth. They are not the real thing.

Words may help you to understand something. Experience allows you to KNOW. Yet there are some things you cannot experience. So I have given you other tools of knowing. And these are called FEELINGS...Now the supreme irony here is that you have all placed so much importance on the Word of God, and so little on experience. In fact, you place so little value on experience that when what you experience of God differs from what you've heard of God, you automatically discard the experience and own the words, when it should be the other way around...Many words have been uttered by others, in My name. Many thoughts and many feelings have been[49] *sponsored by causes not of My direct creation. Many experiences result from these. The challenge is one of discernment. The difficulty is knowing the difference between messages from God and data from other sources. Discrimination is a simple matter with the application of a basic rule: Mine is always your Highest Thought, your Clearest Word, your Grandest Feeling. Anything less is from another source.'*

Tears welled up in Suzanne's eyes. It was as if God was standing there talking to her himself. She recognized his words immediately.

"Can I borrow this book?" she turned and asked Charles.

He walked over to see which one she had chosen.

"Good choice...why that one in particular?"

"It reminds me of a letter I wrote to God – it's as if he's replying in this book!"

"Oh okay...well feel free to choose another one."

"No, this will do for now, besides I can always come back and exchange it when I've finished, can't I?"

"Of course you can."

Right Time to Meet

Suzanne had been dating Charles for three months now, and felt it was a good time to introduce him to the boys. So during Quality Time one evening, she told Micah and Elijah that she had met a really nice man, and asked if they would like to meet him. They had both said yes, so Suzanne had invited Charles over for Sunday Dinner.

Suzanne believed it was important for the boys to have some spiritual grounding, so apart from taking them to church, she prayed and read the bible with them every night before they went to bed. She also used this time to find out how their day at school had been, and to discuss anything else they wanted to talk about. This is what they called 'Quality Time.'

Sunday arrived, and Suzanne took the boys to church; they had missed last week because they had been at their dad's (and she had been at Charles' house).

Charles had passed on her invitation to accompany them, offering to pick them up outside and take them back home instead.

Praise and Worship was Suzanne's favorite part of the service. As Suzanne and the whole congregation joined the choir in giving glory to God, His presence filled the room; tears streamed down her face.

Afterwards, the Pastor began his sermon:

"I have a message this morning for certain members of the church (pronounced 'choch')" he informed his congregation.

"As I relay this message that the Lord has given me I am sure that those for whom this message is intended will recognize themselves. Are you listening to me somebody? Is it okay if I pass on the message that the Lord has given me today?" he asked in his strong West African accent.

"It's okay!" The congregation responded in anticipation.

"Do you promise not to shoot the messenger?" he asked.

"We promise!"

"Oh, you say you will not shoot the messenger, but Jesus had a message of Love from the Father – and they crucified him! Ladies, do you promise not to crucify your Pastor this morning?"

"Yes Pastor!"

"The message the Lord wants me to tell you is this: *HE SEES YOU!* Somebody turn to your neighbor and say 'Your Father sees you'!"

The congregation obey.

Pastor Mensah then added "Somebody turn to your *other* neighbor and say 'My Father, He sees you'!"

There is murmuring and laughter in the congregation as they do as he commanded.

Pastor Mensah takes it a step further;

"Tap the person in front of you and say 'My Father, He sees you!"

(The congregation obliges).

Still not satisfied, he added "Turn to the person behind you and say 'My Father, He sees you!"

And to make sure no-one had been left out he insisted; "Turn to the late-comers hiding right at the back of the choch, point to them and tell them 'My Father, He sees you'!"

When he was sure everyone had got the message, he continued;

"Now, I want you to open your bibles to Hebrews 4:13. Sister Sonia, will you read what the Lord has to say?"

Sister Sonia, a young, attractive woman in her early twenties stood up and read in a steady, confident voice;

"Nothing in all creation is hidden from God. Everything is naked and exposed before His eyes, and He is the One to whom we are accountable."

Pastor Mensah echoed the last line;

"To whom we are *accountable*? To whom we are *what*?"

The congregation responded as one:

"Accountable!"

"Now will you turn your bible to Psalm 33:13."

He picked out another young attractive woman in the church; "Sister Letishia, will you read what King David had to say to the Lord – beloved children of God, are you listening? The Lord is waiting for you to heed His word so you might be saved – sister Letishia, read!"

Sister Letishia stood up:

"The LORD looks down from heaven and sees all the sons of men."

"And sister Suzanne, will you be so kind as to read for us Proverbs 15 verse 3?"

Suzanne found the scripture quickly and stood up to read;

"The eyes of the LORD are in every place, beholding the evil and the good."

"Ah-*HA*! Please read that again sister Suzanne, because some people weren't paying attention!"

Suzanne read the scripture again, this time slower, steadier and louder.

"So you see my dear people, this essential quality of our God as an *all-seeing God* is found throughout Holy Scripture! Do you know what this means, ladies? This means that the LORD is not merely telling you He has *good* vision, He does not need reading glasses like your Pastor (peering over the ones perched at the end of his nose) He has *more* than 20-20 vision – the Lord our Father is telling you that He has *X-ray vision*! ARE YOU LISTENING TO ME SOMEBODY?"

Suzanne wondered where Pastor Mensah was going with this.

He elaborated;

"This means that there are NO SECRETS! This means you cannot hide from Him...but the LORD has revealed to me that some of His children are attempting to keep secrets from Him! Some of you are not married, yet you are sitting in His holy house in unholy undergarments... *Vic-toria's Secrets*!

(The congregation gasped at his revelation, including Suzanne).

"Yes! You are not satisfied with Marks & Spencer's anymore...now you are going to *Ann Summers*! Now you are going to *Victoria's Secrets*, but there are no secrets from the Lord! Now I ask you ladies, do you think it is *appropriate* to wear this kind of clothing to choch?"

Suzanne started to feel agitated. 'Here we go again!' she thought as he continued admonishing the young women about wearing underwear that accentuated their sexuality. She had come here to be edified, not bombarded with misquoted scripture.

Pastor Mensah read from 1 Timothy 2:9 himself; *"Likewise also that women should adorn themselves in modest apparel with shamefacedness and Self-control'.* In other words sistars, you are sending your brothars to HELL because it is written in Matthew 5 verse 28 '*that whoever looks on a woman with lustful intent has ALREADY committed adultery with her in his heart'*. Is this your intention sistars? Do you want to send your brothars to HELL?"

Suzanne began to lose interest; she couldn't even *afford* Victoria's Secret lingerie! Her mind wandered to the chicken she had left on a slow cook in the oven. The peas were already cooked, and when she got back in, she would add the rice and boil it down, and make the macaroni cheese. She didn't want to spend too long in the kitchen, as Charles would be meeting the boys for the first time today.

When Pastor Mensah quoted Lauren Hill's *'that was the sin that did Jezebel in'* Suzanne began to imagine herself wearing expensive sexy lingerie for Charles.

After the service, she and the boys left the church to find Charles double-parked outside waiting to pick them up.

Micah and Elijah took to Charles immediately. They supported the same football team, so that got them off to a good start.

All the way back to Suzanne's, the four of them laughed and joked. Looking at them, anybody would have thought they were a regular happy family.

The boys weren't sure *when* their mum had started seeing Charles, because by the time she introduced him to them, it was obvious they had known each other for quite a while already.

As they got to know Charles, they looked up to him with respect because they could see that he loved their mum and treated *her* with respect.

As long as she was happy, they were happy.

Year Two: Who Am I?

Undoing the Indoctrination

Suzanne learned from *'Conversations with God Book One'* that in order to undo the indoctrination she had received around sex, she had to *reverse* the thought-word-deed process. That is, she had to *do* the deed (have sex!) then have a new *thought* about it. So while she was making love with Charles, she thought about how wonderful the experience was, and that it was the best gift God gave. Instead of thinking that she was doing something 'wrong', she now thought about how 'right' it felt, and how much she loved having sex.

"I LOVE sex!" she spontaneously exclaimed once during their love-making.

"You don't have to tell *me* that!" Charles remarked.

In time, she began to feel better about having sex with the man she loved, and the feelings of guilt and condemnation passed away.

She did the same thing around money. Whereas she had been brought up to believe that *'it is easier for a camel to pass through the eye of a needle, than for a rich man to enter the kingdom of heaven',* she now began to go by her *own* experience of having money; the more she had, the better she felt. When she didn't have much money, she felt anxious, wanting and needy. So she developed new thoughts around money, and changed her mind to believe that money was neither good nor bad, it was just a *tool* to be able to buy the things she needed. Having plenty of money was not *bad*, it would just enable her to do *more*.

She opened a savings account and started saving 10% of her income. She still put money in the offering, but no longer felt obliged to give 10%, she would give as she felt led. She also took every opportunity to give money to people who were in need. Now that she understood the Natural Law of Sowing and Reaping, she knew that if she wished to *have* more money, she had to plant *money seeds*. Saving was a good way to watch her money grow. She started off with £5 a week, and was surprised to see how quickly her money began to grow. She soon noticed that she was able to save £10 a week easily, and decided to save towards a holiday with the boys, who had not yet been out of the country.

She began treating her boys to more of the things they wanted so they wouldn't develop a poverty mentality. She opened savings accounts for each of them, and saved part of their Child Benefit towards their future. She encouraged them to save out of their pocket money so they could watch their money grow too.

Even though the love of money was supposedly the root of all evil, from her experience it was the *lack* of money that was the root of all evil...

Visualize to Materialize

Suzanne lived in the heart of Camden, which had an amalgamation of both rich and poor living side by side. She occupied the top half of a run-down council house, on the same road as privately-owned houses which sold for millions. Not that long ago, a house four doors down had sold for over £1,000,000. She went to view it out of curiosity. She was amazed that a house of that standard could be just four doors away. It was decorated just as she liked, with real wooden floors and plain walls, and a naturally matured garden. It had a newly fitted kitchen with white lacquered cupboards and new appliances. Each bedroom had its own en-suite shower and toilet. It was perfect for her and her boys, she thought. She tried to believe God for the money to buy it in cash, and began playing the lottery religiously, hoping to win the jackpot. But nothing happened. Maybe she didn't really believe it was possible – or maybe God had a bigger and better plan for her?

At the top of her road, there was a pub. In the middle of the night she would often be awakened by people returning home 'in the spirit', talking to each other loudly, singing, whooping and laughing at the top of their voices, fuelled by the alcohol they had been drinking. In stark contrast, she would wake up early to the sound of birds singing.

Despite her current situation, Suzanne's ultimate goal was to buy her own home outright. *How* she was going to achieve this though, she didn't know. She just believed she could somehow. To support her desire, the universe would send her little gifts; every month, a free

Fabric magazine would drop through her door. It advertised expensive houses of the highest standard, with swimming pools, landscaped gardens, in-house cinemas, gyms, Jacuzzis, everything a heart could desire. Suzanne would cut out pictures from these magazines and put them on her 'vision board', where she stuck images of the things she wanted to attract into her life. At times when she was relaxing, she would imagine herself actually *living* in her dream house; watching films with the boys in their home cinema, relaxing in the steam room and Jacuzzi with her partner, writing poetry in their beautiful garden; she saw it all in detail.

Suzanne's dream was far from her current reality, but her current situation was not her destination; she stayed focused on her goal despite her circumstances. Her plan was to build a business that she could hand down to her sons – she didn't want them to have to rely on the government like her; she wanted them to be able to earn enough money to support a family comfortably, without feeling like the responsibility was too much, and bailing out like their father had done. Although her sons were doing well in school and were headed for university, even a degree didn't guarantee that they would get well-paying jobs, so she was thinking ahead.

Invitation

The house phone rang. It was Charles. Suzanne hadn't heard from him in a couple of days.

"Hi babes, how are you today?" He asked cheerfully.

"I'm fine, how are *you*?" She replied, trying her best to sound as chirpy as him.

"I'm good! I was just wondering, what are you doing tomorrow evening?"

"Tomorrow? Oh….I'm going to a networking event with a friend," she remembered. Every so often she would attend these business meetings where she could meet other professionals and hand out her business cards.

His ego couldn't help asking; "Is that a *male* or *female* friend?"

"Female...why?" she half-laughed, but in her mind she was thinking; "Do you expect me to be sitting around waiting for *you* to call?"

Masking his embarrassment for asking, he replied "Oh, I just thought you might be free that's all – what about Thursday?"

"Let me check my diary..." she paused, pretending to be checking the date, knowing full well she had nothing planned.

"Well it looks like I'm free on Thursday. What did you have in mind?"

"I thought I might come over to yours and just chill and relax, you know?"

Suzanne did enjoy his company, but he seemed to be getting into a comfortable routine – with still no commitment from him. She wasn't even 100% sure if she was the only woman he was seeing.

Still, she invited him over. She had the whole evening planned; dinner, a Tyler Perry DVD and then sex! Suzanne had a whole collection of Black films, and even though they didn't all portray her people in positive light, she still preferred watching characters of her own colour.

The Preparation

After she had showered and oiled her skin, Suzanne traced a line of her favorite inspired aroma *'Lovers Attraction'* in dots from behind her ear down to her groin area, hoping he would join them up.

Charles arrived carrying a bunch of orchids; he had taken note that she always liked to have freshly-cut flowers in her living room. He looked drained, yet she could see he had still made an effort.

As he handed them to her he sniffed the air and said "Something smells good!"

"Thank you! How was your day?" she replied in gratitude as she helped him remove his coat.

"Oh, don't ask – terrible. I really don't want to bore you with it all, either. I'd rather just forget about it for a while..." he moved in for an embrace. As he hugged her tightly, she could feel that despite being stressed and tired from his day at work, he was still turned on.

Breaking away from him, she hung up his coat and placed the flowers on the table before heading for the kitchen asking "Are you hungry?"

"Starving!"

"I ate earlier with the boys, so I'll just share yours." (Suzanne rarely ate after 8pm, unless she was out on a date).

"What did you cook?" he called out, rubbing his hands together. Charles had worked late preparing Tax Returns, so had built up quite an appetite since lunchtime.

"I made a pot of soup with yam, sweet potato, pumpkin, dumplings, green banana, plantain, carrots, kale..."

"Sounds good to me!"

While she was warming his serving in a small pot, she had the idea to treat him to an aromatherapy bath. Leaving him at the table to eat alone, she went in the bathroom and ran a hot bath, adding some Epsom salts, and the essential oils of Lavender and Chamomile; the mixture would help relax his muscles and ease his tension. As she was preparing his bath, the sound of the running water got her inspiration flowing; she felt a poem coming on, so ran for her notebook and pen and wrote a poem-song;

'As you walk in, I can feel your passion...rising
But you're not ready for me
See, you're still carrying the negative energy
you picked up along the way during your day,
So let me run you a bath
and help you wash all your troubles away
Leave behind all the pressures of life,
The worries and strife
And enter, if you will, into my Queendom...

(Track 2 on the *'Seeds of Love'* CD)

The words flowed as easily unto the page as the water into the bath. By the time it was filled, Suzanne had finished. She titled it '*The Preparation*'. She then lit some candles and placed them around the bath, which created a warm, ambient glow; this would also help to relax his mind and body. Finally, she started the CD she had compiled earlier, and with the soft music playing and the bath ready, she called out to Charles. He had finished his soup and fallen asleep on the sofa. She smiled as she watched him sleeping, and allowed him to nap for 15 minutes before waking him gently. Taking him by the hand, she led him into the bathroom.

He smiled in appreciation at the scene she had created.

"Get naked," she ordered in a soft-spoken voice. He only needed to be told once; before you could say "Jack Robinson" he was starkers. She watched as he eased himself slowly into the bath, then turned to leave so he could relax undisturbed.

"Aren't you going to join me?" he asked.

"No, I showered earlier – this is for you."

Charles closed his eyes and allowed the aromatherapy to do its work. Twenty minutes later, Suzanne returned with just a sarong wrapped around her body. She pulled the plug, and as the water was draining, proceeded to scrub him down. She then showered him down to get rid of any residual negative energy, dirt and soap, before rubbing his body down with a soft, clean towel. Letting his manhood lead the way like a divining rod, he followed her into her Queendom.

Suzanne took another clean towel and placing it on the bed, instructed Charles to lie face down on top of it. Resting his head to one side with arms straight down and eyes closed, he waited in eager anticipation. Suzanne straddled his body, and kneeling on either side of him, poured some of Aziza's *Aphrodisiac Love Potion Massage Oil* into her hand, rubbing them both together. Starting with his shoulders, she used her thumbs to get into the deep tissue muscle between his shoulder blades to get rid of all the knots. Charles encouraged her to go deeper. He could feel the tension easing as she applied pressure, as if she was kneading dough to make bread.

To bring his energies into balance she gave him a Spinal Flush; first she loosened up his back by massaging down both sides of his spine, applying her body weight to get pressure. Then using her thumbs, she massaged between the notches of his vertebrae from the base of his neck all the way down to his sacrum. Staying on each point for a few seconds, she massaged his skin in a circular motion, pressing each point with firm pressure. When she reached the bottom of his spine she went back to the top and repeated the process to ensure she had released all the congestion stored in his spine, which was blocking the flow of his vital energies. To complete the final flush, Suzanne brushed her open palms down the length of his back in a sweeping motion, admiring the way his mahogany skin glistened from the oil she was administering.

"Mmmm....you really know how to make a man feel like a king," he murmured.

"Well, you're *my* king," she leaned down to kiss him on the cheek.

She told him to roll over, while helping him onto his back.

Opening his eyes, he saw that she was still wearing her sarong. He removed it saying he didn't want her to get oil on it. She straddled his torso, and while she massaged his chest, he played with her breasts, squeezing her nipples between his thumbs and forefingers. This got Suzanne aroused, but she was determined to finish her job.

"Your turn," he offered.

"I haven't finished yet!" she was enjoying giving the massage just as much as he was receiving it.

Rubbing some more oil into the palms of her hands, she gently massaged his temples, face, top of his bald head, and neck. She then proceeded down to his shoulders, arms, and hands, giving each finger a gentle pull to release any tension in them. Continuing down his torso, she admired his six-pack and the defined lines in his groin as she proceeded down his legs, giving his toned muscles a good knead. She finished off by massaging his calves and feet, making sure to apply pressure to the points in his soles.

"You've missed something."

She knew what he meant, but pretended she didn't.

"What?" she asked naïvely.

He took Pride in his hand and wiggled it at her.

"He's feeling left out."

She laughed, and talking to it cooed "Oh, are you feeling neglected? Let me see what I can do about that then..."

She began to massage Pride with some more of the oil. She could feel it pulsating as her fingers slipped up and down, while she used a twisting action. Charles let out a grateful moan. He had long since taught her how to handle his family jewels; she gripped and pulled his balls back gently with one hand, stretching the skin which he'd told her created even greater sensitivity. She then continued to massage his tightened shaft using slow, then fast wrist-action, with the other hand.

"Oh my goddess, that feels so…*good!*" he groaned.

She quickened her pace, alternating between squeezing and stroking.

His breathing became erratic.

"Sh....IT!" he cried out.

By now, he was writhing as if in agony, unable to control himself. Suzanne could tell he was about to come, so she pressed a finger on the large vein on the underside of Pride near the scrotum, and squeezed the shaft at its base.

When Charles had regained control, she mounted him.

"Oh, yeaaah!" Charles sighed in appreciation as she began riding him. When his entire length was inside her completely, she paused. Charles looked up to see why she had stopped. Leaning forward with her hands on the bed at either side of his head, she looked into his eyes and asked "Are you enjoying this?"

The look of satisfaction on his face told her she didn't need to ask.

"You bet I am!"

"Good, because I aim to please," she resumed riding him.

Charles grabbed hold of her hips, begging her to go faster with his hands. He watched as her 34c breasts bounced up and down before his eyes like two gazelles as she rode him, slipping up and down with ease. He cupped each breast in his hands, offering them support. The look on her face as she let herself go said it all; she was in complete ecstasy. Suddenly Charles took control; in one quick movement he flipped her over and proceeded to give it to her hot and cool, fast and slow, wicked and wild; one moment pushing and grinding urgently, the next more soft, slow, tender and deep; between her soft sighs and his heavy breathing, their love-making matched the slow R 'n B tracks still filling the room. As she surrendered her body to him fully, the intoxicating elixir she radiated filled his nostrils, completely consuming him.

"F***ING HELL!" he cried out as he climaxed.

"I'd rather f*** in heaven," Suzanne replied with a giggle.

He felt totally rejuvenated.

Another Level?

They awoke in a warm, sticky embrace.

"Good morning, my queen," Charles whispered in her ear as she stretched, opening her eyes.

She snuggled under his arm and replied "Good morning....my king!"

He'd never called her 'his queen' before.

'Does this mean we've moved to the 'next level'?' she wondered.

"Man, last night was phenomenal!" Charles exclaimed, "You blew my mind!"

Suzanne laughed. "Well it takes two, you know!"

They had been dating for just over a year now, but Suzanne still wasn't sure where she stood in the relationship.

"Where do we go from here?" she asked, trying to get some kind of commitment out of him.

"What do you mean?"

"Where do you see this relationship going?" she made herself clear.

"Let's just go with the flow and see where it takes us, shall we?" he responded calmly.

But Suzanne was beginning to feel impatient. When was he going to be ready to *commit*?

He kissed her gently on the forehead and gave her a tight squeeze before getting up to use the bathroom. She watched as he rose from the bed and made his way across the room. His body reminded her of carved mahogany, dark and shiny, his muscles flexing with every move he made.

A random line *'Natural muscle definition under your skin, with rich tones of melanin!'* came to mind. Scribbling it down, she thought 'I must put that in one of my poems!'

He had no idea how much he inspired her. Suzanne always had a notebook to hand, for when those moments of inspiration struck, like lightening. If she didn't write it down straight away, she couldn't guarantee she would remember it later. Sometimes they would come in the middle of the night. She had learned by now that if she didn't yield to the spirit and capture it there and then, it could be forgotten and lost by the morning. So she kept a Dictaphone in her bedside table drawer, and carried a notebook wherever she went.

'I wonder if he'll have time for a quickie before he leaves?' she wondered. She could hear him in the shower singing away to himself. In a swift movement, she impulsively jumped from the bed and quick-stepped towards the bathroom.

"Can I join you?" she asked, pulling back the shower curtain.

Squinting through the soap around his eyes, he smiled broadly and replied "Be my guest!"

Suzanne pulled a plastic cap over her weave and stepped into the bath, joining him under the water. He welcomed her in by wrapping his arms around her from behind. With her back against his front, he began soaping her body to match his. Using both hands, he started with his favorite part, her breasts, and worked his way down her torso to her stomach, round to her firm backside, up her back, down her arms, up her thighs, until reaching her yoni. Then moving in front of her, he unhooked the shower head and knelt on one knee.

As if about to perform an operation, he carefully parted her labia with his left hand and directed the flow of water at her clitoris with his right. Moving it backwards and forwards, he watched as it hardened. In between watering her garden, he used his tongue.

Suzanne moaned and writhed, struggling to hold on to the bathroom tiles to prevent herself from slipping. Nevertheless, she could feel her knees giving way beneath her. Just as she was about to collapse, Charles stood up and held her around the waist. She wrapped one leg around him as he put the shower head back in its holder. Lifting her unto his erection, he directed Pride into her wet opening. As Suzanne began gyrating up and down and around, he held onto her bum cheeks and bending his knees, supported her weight with his muscular legs. It wasn't long before he gave a deep-throated groan of gratitude as he came, while she gave a kind of sigh of relief.

Surprise

That evening, Charles returned to spend the night. They enjoyed just lying entwined around each other's bodies, talking until they fell asleep. Suzanne got up early the following morning and started doing her stretches, while Charles hit the floor and started doing press-ups. After 20 minutes of exercising together Suzanne declared "I'm hungry. What would you like for breakfast?"

"A bowl of thrusties would be nice!" Charles joked, with a cheeky smirk on his face.

"Ha ha very funny – Do you want to go back to bed?"

"We can either do that, or we can get ready and go out," he announced.

"Out where?" she asked in anticipation.

"Shopping!"

"Shopping? To buy what?"

"Well, what do you need?"

Suzanne wasn't sure if he was being serious. No man she'd ever dated had taken her shopping before, so she thought she'd play along.

"That depends on what my budget is!"

"Would £250 be enough for you?"

"£250! Are you serious?" She still thought he was joking.

"Listen honey, today is all about you," he said. "Whatever you need, we'll go get it – as long as you stick within the budget!"

Suzanne finally realized he *was* being serious, and gave him a big hug and a kiss.

"I really appreciate that Charles – let's go shopping then!"

"And pack a bag," he added "We're going out tonight, you might as well stay over at my place."

Suzanne looked up at Charles, and gazing deep into his eyes, said "I love you, you know."

"Yeah, I love you too...now let's get moving!" he replied, slapping her playfully on the bum.

They arrived at Charles' house laden with bags of shopping. Charles had bought Suzanne a new outfit to wear that night (which he had chosen) and he had even bought her some new underwear – Victoria's Secret! Suzanne knew how to buy clothes cheap, not buy cheap clothes, so she had money left in her budget to buy something each for the boys as well.

"So where are we going tonight?" Suzanne asked.

"I've booked a table at this nice Caribbean restaurant I know you'll like, and then *you* can decide what we do after that."

"Sounds lovely! What time did you book the table for?"

"7 o'clock."

"Well we'd better get a move on, it's nearly 5 o'clock already!"

They enjoyed getting ready together; Suzanne had her shower first, then while Charles was having his, she applied her make-up and brushed her weave. Charles came out of the bathroom still wet, with just a small white towel wrapped around his waist. Admiring his physique, a line came to Suzanne's mind; *'Look at you, standing tall and strong, brilliantly black, sun-kissed skin, with beautiful eyes for looking in...'* She ran for her bag to get her notebook so she could write it down before she forgot.

"What are you writing?" he asked.

"Oh, nothing, just an idea for a poem," she responded shadily as she scribbled into her notepad.

He looked at her suspiciously; "What are you up to?"

"Nothing!"

"Then let me see…." He tried to get a peek.

"No!" (She didn't like showing people her work until it was finished).

He made a dash at her notebook, trying to catch a glimpse of what she'd written.

"Get off!" she cried out playfully, as he tried to tackle it out of her hands.

"I know it's about me, I want to see it!"

"Okay okay, I'll show you!" she gave in; she didn't want her hair and make-up getting messed up.

He read the line of poetry and smiled.

She felt embarrassed.

"I wish I hadn't shown it to you now," she mumbled.

"Why? It's a great line; it shows how deep you think."

His answer put her at ease.

"Do you think I should use it in a poem?" she asked.

"It's not what *I* think that matters, it's what *you* think – follow your spirit," he replied.

"I'm just glad I could inspire you," he added, smiling at her broadly as he creamed his skin.

She loved the things he came out with sometimes. He had a way of helping her to believe in her Self and her abilities.

Awakening His Inner Child

Charles was an accountant, but secretly he wished he'd followed his dream of becoming an artist. He had been very good at drawing and painting at school, but his father had advised him to study for a 'proper job' if he wanted to be able to support a family in the future. Since he was also good at Maths, he'd decided Accounting was a safe bet, and would provide a good, steady income.

Charles was excellent at his job and this was reflected in his pay-packet, but still, he felt unfulfilled. His inner child was crying out to be heard; he wanted to draw and paint, but he just couldn't find the time. Or was it that he didn't *make* the time? He admired Suzanne for not giving up on her dreams, and not giving in to 'the system'. She refused to go down the 9-5 route, and even though money was tight, she certainly seemed happier than him. She believed there was 'more to life' and was following her bliss at whatever cost. Something had to give, and Suzanne had decided to make whatever sacrifices necessary to achieve her goal of making a living from doing what she loved – writing and performing her poetry. Charles could see that despite her limited resources, she was striving towards her goals. He was willing to do whatever he could to help, but she always refused, telling him this was something she felt she had to do by herself.

"I just need a reason to get up and go to work in the morning," he would tell her, to no avail. Suzanne couldn't see that her prayers had been answered; Charles was willing to provide the financial support she needed to pursue her dreams, but she was unwilling to unwrap the gift.

Still, she inspired him in more ways than one…

Lace Seduction

As they lay huddled on the sofa together listening to soft music playing in the background, Charles admired Suzanne's strong African-Caribbean features in the dim light.

"Can I paint you?" He asked, seemingly randomly.

Suzanne was taken aback, since he had never shared his secret passion for art with her before.

"*Paint* me?" she asked curiously.

"Well, I could start by drawing you – just for fun," he replied.

She looked at him in surprise; "I didn't know you could draw!"

"Well I haven't done anything in years, but I'm thinking about getting back into it again, and what better way than to start by drawing my favourite lady!"

She paused, smiled, shrugged her shoulders and said "Okay, when?"

"No time like the present!" he stated, reaching over for his briefcase.

"Alright then! What are you going to draw on?"

Charles pulled out a drawing pad, pencil and rubber.

"Oh, so you had this all planned!" Suzanne remarked.

"Well I was hoping you'd say yes, and I just thought I'd better be prepared."

"Well then let me change into something a bit more... *interesting,*" she said, heading towards her Queendom.

"Er, before you go..." Charles called out "...Can you...lose the wig? I'd prefer to draw you in all your *natural* beauty."

"...Sure," she replied hesitantly, not feeling sure at all. She couldn't believe that Charles wanted to draw her with her 'nappy' hair, whereas *he* couldn't understand why *she* insisted on wearing the wigs and weaves when she had a perfectly good head of natural hair underneath.

Ten minutes later Suzanne re-appeared wearing the red and black Victoria's Secret lingerie set that he had bought her, with her own natural hair out. Because it had been in plaits under the wig, it was a mass of wild curls. Charles eyed her up from top to bottom; her 'fro was striking in all its natural, untamed glory. The lace and satin bodice she was wearing pushed up her breasts enhancing her cleavage, while the matching thong barely covered her yoni. Suzanne had also adorned herself in black suspenders and stockings, and the whole look was completed with a pair of high-heeled black patent shoes. The whole ensemble drove him crazy – he could feel Pride rising, but now was not the right time, he thought – down boy!

"Damn!" Charles reacted, "How am I supposed to concentrate with you in *that*?"

"Come on, be professional about this," Suzanne teased, strutting sexily over to the couch.

"How do you want me?" She continued to seduce him as she perched herself provocatively on the edge of the sofa, crossing her legs.

"This woman!" Charles thought, smiling to himself.

"Okay..." He really wanted to catch her striking profile, the contours of her eyes, full lips, broad nose and high forehead, and her slender figure. For a mother of two, she had a great body, he thought.

"...Why don't you kind of lie back, rest on your elbows, and drop your head back a bit?" he responded to her question.

She got into the position requested, bending one knee.

"How long do I have to stay like this?" she inquired.

"I'm not sure; do you think you can hold that position?" He asked back.

"I don't think so, not for long, anyway."

"Okay, you get yourself into a comfortable position, and I'll be happy with that."

Suzanne rolled unto her right side, propped her head up with her right hand, and looking at him seductively, rested her left knee in front on the couch.

"Perfect!" Charles called out, as if directing a film.

A sudden surge of panic hit him; he hadn't drawn in over 20 years; what if he made a mess of it? What if she didn't like it, and thought he was insulting her looks? What if.....he had to stop these thoughts from crippling his creativity before he even got started;

"I can do this. I'm a *good* artist. I know she will like it," he told him Self. With pencil in hand ready to begin, he thought he had better protect his interests for later that night;

"Babe, can I just say before I start that you are a beautiful work of art yourself, and no matter how this turns out, I couldn't improve on what God has already done naturally."

"Oh, that's so sweet!"

Suzanne left her position on the sofa and started making her way towards him. He dropped his artist's pad and pencil on the floor ready to receive her. Straddling his lap, she French-kissed him full on the lips, wrapping her arms around his neck and her tongue around his tongue. He grabbed each of her bum cheeks, pressing her against his hard-on.

Suddenly she broke away saying "Okay, let's get back to business! You've got a drawing to do, remember?"

As she slowly meandered her way back to the sofa, she took a fresh red rose from the bouquet in the vase on the table, and getting back into the pose, positioned the rose strategically under her nose.

"Mmmm...nice touch!" Charles commented. But secretly he was beginning to wish he'd never asked to draw her. 'Look at her! All ready for a good sex session and now I have to spend God knows how long *drawing* her instead! Mind you, she wouldn't *be* dressed up like this if I hadn't asked to draw her in the first place...' All these thoughts were going through his head as he sat there staring at her, pencil in hand, ready to begin. Then his imagination began to go wild as he pictured himself taking her from behind, watching her ass jiggle as he drove Pride in and out of her wet vagina with the thong still on, pulling it to one side...

"Have you started yet?" Suzanne burst his bubble.

"Uh? Oh...Yes, I'm just starting now..."

Charles put pencil to paper.

'Where do I begin, with her eyes? The outline of her face? Her hair?' Before feelings of doubt could set in, his inner child took over and began to play by putting bold strokes onto the paper. He allowed his inner child the freedom to create – this was fun! Charles began to feel something inside coming alive as he set him Self free. He did his best to capture not only her outer beauty, but her *inner* beauty and femininity as well. He emphasized the fullness of her lips, the sensual curve of her hips, and the ancient seductive look in her eyes. He enjoyed drawing her cleavage, accentuated by the tight bodice. He then took time to draw the lace detail on the top of her stockings, and the shine in the shoes she was wearing. He'd never seen them before – in fact, they looked new. He hoped she would wear them next time they went out together.

'Why has she given me all this extra work to do with the rose?' he wondered as he copied each petal carefully. 'It *does* add to the composition, though'.

As he was drawing the thorns on the stem, he thought about how much a rose is like a woman; beautiful to look at, but hurtful if not handled correctly.

Suzanne observed Charles as he focused entirely upon his work. It was as if he no longer saw her as his woman, but an object to be studied. She saw him go into his 'zone' and respected it, as she had often been there when engaged in her writing. He stared intently as he studied different parts of her body; drawing, rubbing out, and drawing again. She thought she may as well use this time to think about the business empire she was planning on building...

Some forty-five minutes later, Charles announced that he had finished. Suzanne couldn't wait to see it; jumping up from the sofa, she quickly wiggled over to where he was sitting. As he handed her the picture, she sat on his lap. As soon as she saw it she gasped "Oh Charles, it's... it's... *beautiful*! I had no idea you were *this* good at drawing!"

"I'm glad you like it," Charles breathed a sigh of relief.

"Can I keep it?" She asked.

He had poured his heart and soul into that drawing, and now she wanted to *keep* it!

"I...suppose so," he consented reluctantly.

Suzanne noticed that he had titled the drawing *'Lace Seduction'.*

"Mmmm...nice title!" she smiled at him.

"You have real talent here Charles, you should take it more seriously." Noticing he hadn't signed it yet, she asked for his paw print. He signed and dated it, and gave it back to her half-heartedly.

Placing the drawing on the floor, Suzanne wrapped her arms around his neck again, and kissing him passionately, gave him what he had been dreaming about all along...

'Trust'

Suzanne loved spending time in Charles' company. Their relationship was intense and passionate – and their arguments equally so. Sometimes they would have a disagreement and then wouldn't speak for weeks. Despite this, it was as if the Forces of Nature kept pulling them back together. But was it Love, obsession, or just a natural reaction to each other's chemistry?

On this occasion, they had just spent a lovely weekend together, and now Suzanne hadn't heard from him in *two days*. She called his mobile. No answer. Should she call his landline? No answer. She wondered what he was doing when they weren't together. Was he dating other women? Or was he just so busy with work that he didn't have time to call? Her low self-esteem demon usually reared its ugly head at times like this, and while she tried to get visions of him with other women out of her head, evil thoughts would tell her she wasn't good enough, pretty enough, or successful enough for him. The only way to combat them was by constantly telling her Self that she *was* good enough for him. She wanted to call his mobile again, but her inner voice was advising her to relax. She didn't want her negative Scorpio trait of jealousy and possessiveness to rule, so she tried to focus on something else. To get rid of the tension she was feeling, she had a go at writing a song:

When we come together
We're like a river flowing effortlessly,
Safe in your arms
Your embrace is the only protection I need.

But we both need time to grow, baby
To develop ourselves individually
So I'm giving you the space that you need
With no expectations from me

(And I want you to know)

I trust you baby,
I know you've got your things to do
And I've got mine too...

(Track 3 on the *'Seeds of Love'* CD)

She felt much better after she had finished. Her inner voice was always telling her to have no expectations of Charles, that *'expectations inhibit the flow of love'* and that *'the least expectations you have of someone, the more likely they are to surpass them'*. But having no expectations of him was proving to be difficult. How could she *not* expect more from the relationship, when everything was going so good? Why *shouldn't* she expect him to want to take it to the 'next level'? Commitment! That's what she wanted. Was that asking too much?

'Stuff that – next time he calls, I'm gonna give him a piece of my mind!' she thought, going against her inner guidance.

Later that evening, Charles called.

"Hi babes, how are you?" he asked cheerfully.

"Could be better," she replied, off-key.

"Why, what's wrong?" he asked in a concerned tone.

"I don't think you appreciate me!" she started.

"What makes you say that?" he asked, surprised.

"Well look, we spent a lovely weekend together, then you don't even call for *two days*!"

"Babe, I've been busy, you know my work schedule."

"What, too busy to even pick up the phone?"

Silence.

Charles was tired. He didn't need this headache right now. He'd only called to hear her voice, and now she was *attacking* him with it!

"Charles? Are you still there?"

Silence.

"I know you're listening! Don't ignore me when I'm talking to you!"

"What do you want me to say?" he asked wearily, coming across one of her bouts of Angry Black Woman Syndrome for the first time.

"Well you could at least have the decency to answer me when I'm talking to you!"

Silence. He didn't wish to add any fuel to the fire.

If Suzanne had taken the time to listen to what her inner voice was saying, she would have known to stop right there. Maybe if it hadn't been her time of the month, she might have handled the situation differently, but no, she kept on going;

"How do I even know you're not sleeping with other women? For all I know you could have a dozen other women out there besides me!"

He felt offended.

"Babe, you know I'm a one-woman man."

"So where are you when you're not with me then?" she demanded to know.

He wanted to remind her that apart from working full time, he was also developing him Self; he studied Numerology in his spare time, and was also learning how to apply Spiritual Laws. He had set Suzanne on *her* Path of Truth, but he still had his *own* journey to make as well. So when he got home from work in the evenings, after having a shower and making something to eat, he would study for an hour or two, before retiring to bed. If he called Suzanne, he knew they would be on the phone for ages. Texting didn't work either – after receiving a text from him, she would then try to hold a whole conversation by text! So he rather waited until he had the time to talk with her properly. But he didn't tell her that.

"Suzanne, I really have to go, I have another busy day ahead of me tomorrow."

"Charles, if you hang up on me, we're through!"

"We'll talk properly at the weekend, okay?"

"I'm serious Charles, if you hang up on me, it's over!"

Charles hung up.

In a fit of rage, Suzanne deleted his number from her phone.

But out of the chaos and confusion something beautiful was growing, like a rose growing out of the crack in a concrete pavement.

Her Story (not His-story)

'It is not taboo to go back and fetch what you have forgotten'

Suzanne joined an African History course and absorbed herself learning about her origins.

She had to start from scratch, because her mother had never talked about coming from Africa. She and *her* mother appeared to be suffering from amnesia; they had no stories to tell of their ancestors who were kidnapped from the Motherland and brought to Jamaica to work on the plantations. She had never identified herself as being of African origin; in fact, to even imply it seemed offensive to her.

The descendents of enslaved Africans who were taken to America had at least identified themselves as 'African-American'. There was no such term as 'African-British', and those who remained in the

Caribbean didn't even call themselves 'African-Caribbean'. They seemed to want to have nothing to do with their African origins.

Suzanne needed to get to the bottom of what exactly had taken place during her ancestors 400 years of enslavement, which had caused their descendants to become so totally disconnected from their roots.

It all started in Africa.

Long before Europeans arrived, Africans were in conflict with each other, and were enslaving each other's tribes. They had forgotten the First Law: *Treat Others How You Would Like to Be Treated.* When Europeans arrived and saw their lack of unity, they used it to their advantage; they offered to buy each tribe's captives in exchange for guns, alcohol, tobacco, cloth, and worthless trinkets. The problem was, none of the things African leaders were trading their fellow human beings for was able to grow their economy. Whereas the manpower the Europeans purchased enabled them to run plantations to produce sugar, cotton, coffee, cocoa, to mine gold and silver, to construct buildings, to cut timber for ships (to transport the enslaved), and to have unpaid domestic servants – not to mention, sex slaves.

Before long, Europeans stopped trading with the tribe leaders and began kidnapping and enslaving Africans themselves. The Dutch, Portugese, French, British and Spanish took slavery to another level.

Over 12 million Africans were forcefully removed from the Continent and transported to the Americas, Brazil, France, and the Caribbean to work on plantations. Each 'slave' was branded with a hot iron to show they had been bought and now belonged to the slave trader. Their African names were stripped from them and replaced with their slave master's name. They were torn from their families, physically, sexually and psychologically abused, made to work long hours with no pay, and were not permitted to speak their own language or to practice any of their cultural traditions, such as playing the 'talking drums'. Neither were they allowed to practice their own spirituality or to honour their ancestors as was their custom. Instead, they were given a new religion with a white male god to pray to. Any slave that refused to worship this new god was whipped until he submitted, or died.

There were many uprisings and revolts, and many committed suicide rather than live in the horrific conditions.

Suzanne read *The Willie Lynch Letter*. It explained how the slave traders had devised a system to 'break in' their captives so they would stop rebelling:

They would take the strongest male who appeared to be the leader, tar him up, whip him in front of the whole community, tie his legs to two horses, then whip the horses so they would bolt, ripping the man in two. This sent the Black Woman into an emotional state of shock – the image of the Black Man who she had looked up to was completely destroyed. She now had to fend for herself. The women were repeatedly raped by their enslavers in front of the men, who were powerless to do anything to stop it, as they were likely to lose their own lives, or a limb, or be whipped until the skin on their backs was raw. Some of the men were kept solely as 'studs' to 'breed' the women to provide more 'stock', like animals. They were not allowed to marry young or live as families, and because they never knew when their children were going to be taken away and sold, they were encouraged not to form any emotional bonds with them. They beat their children mercilessly as *they* were beaten, to teach them how to behave – if *they* didn't do it, the slave master would. The Mulatto children, products of the frequent rapings, were treated better than the Black children because they had 'better quality blood'. Enslaved Africans were taught that 'the lighter or *whiter* you are, the better and prettier you are'. The women were trained to rely on their slave master as their provider, and to raise their boys to be *physically strong*, but *mentally weak,* while raising their daughters to be strong and independent of the Black man. The male captives were stripped of their power and influence, and reduced to nothing more than slave labour and baby-making machines. Their warrior-spirit was broken. Within this system, enslaved Africans whole way of life, culture, spiritual practices, names, language and inheritance was stripped from them – but some of them still managed to practice in secret, and carry them across the waters.

The Slave System was run with brutal force, yet religion played a major part of it. While enslaved Africans weren't permitted to learn to read or write, enslavers taught them from the bible to 'turn the other cheek', think of themselves as poor and wretched sinners, to be humble servants, and to forgive those who persecuted them.

Growing up in church, Suzanne had received the same indoctrination.

"If you show me your religion,
I will show you your conqueror"
~ Molefi Kete Asante

Suzanne recognized some of her behaviors to be directly linked to her past, as if it was in her bloodline. Her inability to rely on her Black brother for anything had been passed down to her genetically. Fiercely independent, she now got *why* she found it difficult to look up to him; he had failed to protect her and her children when she needed him the most. Still, she couldn't see herself with anyone *but* her Black man. It now made sense *why* her son's father had done a disappearing act each time she got pregnant; he was most likely the descendant of a 'stud', whose only responsibility was to impregnate the woman; he had no say in how the child was raised.

Up to this point, Suzanne had never considered that the skin lightening cream she used to 'even her skin tone' was from social conditioning that lighter, or whiter, was better. Her low self esteem was a result of negative programming reinforced both at home and at church. On top of that, the media was now brainwashing her to believe that unless she looked, talked and dressed European, she wasn't beautiful or cultured. White was the standard of beauty and status.

And it wasn't just her; she could see how the after-effects of slavery were still affecting her community today; many of her sisters were bleaching their skin, wearing long straight hair, raising their children alone, and allowing themselves to be abused sexually.

Many of her brothers were still socially disempowered, unable to get well-paying jobs unless they were oppressing their own people, idolized white woman over their own, and still acted like 'studs', neglecting their fatherly duties.

There was a general lack of trust with each other, while relying on the white man for a job, approval in family matters, money matters, and social standing. If you didn't look or act European, you weren't 'cultured' or 'civilized'. Broken families, dysfunctional relationships, low self esteem and a poverty mentality were all remnants of the slave trade.

Suzanne was soon able to spot the descendants of enslaved Africans (those who still had the slave mentality) and the descendents of enslavers (those who still had the slave *trader* mentality).

A friend gave her the film 'Sankofa' to watch. Seeing what her ancestors had endured traumatized her, yet inspired her to write a poem-song called *'We Belong Together'*, a message to the brothers from the sisters, reminding them that they needed to stick together and work together to heal themselves. (Track 13 on the *'Seeds of Love'* CD)

Suzanne wondered how she could help her community to heal; it seemed like such a large job.

She remembered a part in the *Willie Lynch Letter* which explained how to *reverse* the programming; his blueprint guaranteed plantation owners that they wouldn't need to keep breaking in new slaves being born, because the females would automatically 'train' their children. He said the only way to *reverse* the programming resided in the female slaves, because they were the ones raising the children. If she didn't change her way of thinking, she would automatically pass the 'slave mentality' down to her children, and it would continue to be passed down from one generation to the next without the slave owners having to do anything more. It suddenly occurred to Suzanne that many descendants of enslaved Africans were still running on the programming! She realized it was the *mothers* who had to break the chain.

She recognized the slave mentality in herself and committed to the process of Self-healing. In order to make sure she didn't pass the slave mentality down to her own children and future generations, Suzanne was going to have to 'change her mind', starting with her Self-love and Self-worth issues.

Africa Divided

On her African History course, Suzanne learned that economically, the Transatlantic Slave Trade and Colonialism were Europe's greatest triumphs. Europeans had devised a long-term strategy of how they could make as much money as possible out of Africa's rich natural resources. At the point slavery was abolished, they had amassed great fortunes from gold, silver, diamonds, copper, sugar, rice, cotton, and coffee, not forgetting all the money they saved from years of free labour forced upon millions of enslaved Africans.

So much, that they are still living off the profits today.

Suzanne discovered that most of the white men in Politics today are descendants of enslavers, and still have the slave trader mentality.

After slavery was abolished in 1807, the displaced and mistreated Africans weren't compensated for helping to build the economies of these countries with their free labour, nor were they given any means to return to their homeland. Many were forced to continue working for their former enslavers for a minimum wage, because they had no money and nowhere else to go. To add insult to injury, enslavers were paid millions of pounds by the British government in compensation for the loss of their 'stock'.

When slavery was abolished, the plan to Colonize Africa began. The 'Scramble for Africa' took place between 1885-1910; in just 25 years the Continent had been divided up by the British, French, Belgians, Germans, Dutch, and Portugese, who claimed parts of Africa and its rich natural resources for themselves. Any African leader who resisted Colonization was killed or exiled.

An example of this was when they exiled Kwame Nkrumah from Ghana. When the British visited Ghana and saw the magnificence of the Ashanti king's palace, they plotted to bring down his empire. From their own account, the palace was described as *'...an immense building of a variety of oblong courts and regular squares with exuberantly adorned bold fan and trellis work of* ***Egyptian*** *character. They have a suit of rooms over them, with small windows of wooden lattice, of intricate but regular carved work, and some have frames cased with thin gold. The squares have a large apartment on each side, open in front, with two supporting pillars...They are lofty and regular, and the cornices of a very bold cane-work in alto relievo. A drop-curtain of curiously plaited cane is suspended in front, and in each we observed* *chairs and stools embossed with gold, and beds of silk, with scattered regalia.'*

The original palace of the Ashanti king before it was burnt down and ransacked by the British in 1875.

One of their strategies for Colonizing Africa was to send in missionaries to spread the 'gospel' in order to pacify the people. This made it easy for them to extract the wealth of Africa with little resistance.

Other strategies used were *'Assimilation'*, the process of 'civilizing' Africans to become more like Europeans, and *'Divide and Conquer'* – setting the men and women against each other, light-skinned against dark-skinned, young against old etc. Both strategies had worked really well during the Transatlantic Slave Trade.

Suzanne saw the devastating effect slavery and Colonialism had had on both Africans who had remained on the Continent, and the descendents of enslaved Africans who had been displaced (including herself). Their inheritance had been stolen from them, and the religion forced upon them only promised an inheritance after *death*, while Europeans benefitted financially from the natural God-given earthly riches of their land.

So here she was in England, far away from her Motherland, cut off from her spiritual roots, disinherited, brought up in a dysfunctional family who were suffering from 'Post Traumatic Slave Syndrome', and disempowered by the religion she had been indoctrinated into.

The History of Christianity

In Suzanne's quest for the Truth, she discovered that Christianity had originated in Africa, and in its purest form, was beneficial to her people. But the same religion that Africans had created was stolen, re-packaged, and handed back to them in the form of mental slavery.

The people of ancient Kemet (meaning 'Land of the Blacks') ruled the 11 dynasties *before* it was invaded by Arabs and Europeans and renamed 'Egypt'. The ancient Egyptians were wise in their knowledge of spiritual matters, including how to use the full power of the mind, the roles of Masculine and Feminine energies, the proper use of sexual energy, and how to prepare for the afterlife. They taught meditation as a way of connecting with the Source, and that everything is energy, and connected to each other. They lived by the principles of Ma'at: Truth, Balance, Order, Harmony, Law, Morality and Justice.

42 Ideals of Ma'at

1. I honor virtue
2. I benefit with gratitude
3. I am peaceful
4. I respect the property of others
5. I affirm that all life is sacred
6. I give offerings that are genuine
7. I live in truth
8. I regard all altars with respect
9. I speak with sincerity
10. I consume only my fair share
11. I offer words of good intent
12. I relate in peace
13. I honor animals with reverence
14. I can be trusted
15. I care for the earth
16. I keep my own council
17. I speak positively of others
18. I remain in balance with my emotions
19. I am trustful in my relationships
20. I hold purity in high esteem
21. I spread joy
22. I do the best I can
23. I communicate with compassion
24. I listen to opposing opinions
25. I create harmony
26. I invoke laughter
27. I am open to love in various forms
28. I am forgiving
29. I am kind
30. I act respectfully of others
31. I am accepting
32. I follow my inner guidance
33. I converse with awareness
34. I do good
35. I give blessings
36. I keep the waters pure
37. I speak with good intent
38. I praise the Goddess and the God
39. I am humble
40. I achieve with integrity
41. I advance through my own abilities
42. I embrace the All

They had no need for police, armies or a criminal justice system, because everyone abided by Spiritual Laws.

Living this way allowed them to live a life of abundance.

People travelled from all over the world to be taught in their Mystery Schools, including noble kings and queens. The Ancient Egyptians happily taught Europeans their ancient wisdom including philosophy, sacred geometry, physics, music and the arts, writing, astrology, astronomy, the science of numbers (numerology), and the true nature of humanity and its relationship with its Source.

But after learning everything he could from them, Alexander the Greek plotted to conquer Ancient Kemet; in 332 BC his army burned down their universities and stole all their ancient manuscripts, taking them back to Greece, where he set up his own library, naming it the Library of Alexandria. It was from these ancient manuscripts that the New Testament of the bible was devised. Suzanne learned that the Old Testament had been translated into English from *Hebrew*, and the New Testament from *Greek*.

Ancient Kemet, the Land of the Blacks, was easy to invade because they had no armies, unlike the Europeans who were notorious for using them to go around the world killing, stealing, raping, plundering any new place they set foot upon, then claiming it as their own.

This reminded her of the scripture John 10:10.

'What is *wrong* with them?' she thought. 'Why do they feel the need to steal everything they come across? Why don't they care about their fellow human beings? Why don't they believe in sharing equally?'

The once-great dynasty that had tried to teach Europeans how to be civilized was usurped, and the knowledge was now in their deadly hands.

It was from these ancient manuscripts that they conspired to devise *new* religions which would still contain a lot of Truth, but would leave out important information that would empower the masses. For example, instead of informing believers of the creative power of their thoughts, they planned how they could use *other people's thoughts* to create what *they* wanted instead.

The aim of their new religions was to mentally enslave the masses and make them weak-minded. They were targeted mainly at Africans, who they feared, and wanted to keep in a state of mental apathy.

Their new religion changed the Holy Trinity from Father, Mother and Son to a white god and his son, totally removing the Divine Mother from the Godhead. They stopped calling God by his name, and changed his holy day from Sabbath (Saturday) to Sunday. Knowing Africans are naturally spiritual and naturally *sexual* people, they created a false doctrine which separated sex from spirituality. When Europeans saw the high esteem African women held in their communities, they sought to destroy it; by blaming the woman (Eve) for the fall of humankind, they were able to use religion to make women subservient to men, just as their white women were to *them.* They changed all the characters who were originally black to white ones, including the Messiah. An artist named Michaelangelo was commissioned to paint the first image of a white Jesus, which was then heavily promoted by the Roman Catholic church. They knew the psychological effect this would have on Africans long term; that they would begin to view the white man as their saviour, who they would depend on. Over time, Africans forgot their *own* divinity.

An early Coptic Church painting of Jesus of Nazareth with his disciples

The new religion they had created was causing a lot of confusion. The different churches were teaching different things, so in AD 325 the Roman Emperor Constantine called the first *Council of Nicea.* Over 300 religious leaders from around the world met to finally put an end to the disagreements. In order for Christianity as a religion to be credible, they agreed that having one book they all referred to would prevent future discord. They used the manuscripts they had stolen to compile a 'holy book'. Over a 3 month period they deliberated on what information should be included, from what should be kept back from the masses. Once they had agreed on which texts to include, all other manuscripts were burnt, destroyed or hidden underground in order to prevent future heresy.

As she sat contemplating all of this, Suzanne recalled what Charles had told her about the missionaries using Christianity to gain control over the wealth of Africa, and to turn her people docile. Their new (white) savior had them believe they were powerless to save themselves, and to believe that earthly riches shouldn't be coveted. She could see how their plan had worked; Europeans were now living off the wealthy resources of the land, while the majority of Africans were living in poor conditions, mentally enslaved by their religions.

Worst still, none of these wealthy Europeans practiced the religion themselves! They were living the life they had told Africans to wait to get in heaven, when they die.

This reminded Suzanne of Britain's promise to her parent's generation; they were enticed with offers of well-paying jobs to leave their sunny Caribbean islands for England. Only highly educated people were targeted, but when they arrived in England, they could only get low-paying jobs that the British didn't want to do, such as nursing, cleaning, factory work, and bus driving. Suzanne's own mother had been an accountant before she arrived in England, but when she couldn't get employment in that field, she was forced to re-train as a nurse. They had invested all their savings into relocating, and their lack of finances prevented them from returning home. England had been painted as having 'streets paved with gold'. Who's to say that the promise of heaven in their bible wasn't also a deception?

Stolen His-story

Suzanne learned that Europeans had tried their best to suppress the rich African history which existed before they arrived on the Continent, including burning books, hiding manuscripts, tearing down buildings, vandalizing ancient monuments and re-writing history to credit *themselves* with ancient wisdom.

'*A people without knowledge of their past history, origin and culture is like a tree without roots'* ~ Marcus Mosiah Garvey

Suzanne thought back to her History lessons at school; she had never been taught of any Black Scientists and Inventors such as Garrett Morgan, Patricia Bath, Lewis Latimer, Granville Woods, and George Washington Carver. She had never learned about the Ancient Egyptians who built great dynasties, or the Moors who were instrumental in developing Europe. Instead, she was led to believe that the only history Africans had was slavery. She wasn't taught about great leaders such as Queen Nzinga, Harriet Tubman, Malcom X, Marcus Mosiah Garvey, Khalid Muhammed, or Martin Luther King. They had sacrificed their lives to save their people, yet there were no special days set aside in the year to honour *their* lives or deaths.

If Suzanne had continued to only study European literature and watch their 'programs' about Africa, she would have carried on believing that all indigenous Africans were starving and lived in mud huts. Europeans had tried to glamorize their own sordid history, while erasing African history and re-writing it to make it look as if it was their own, including claiming that Egypt wasn't in Africa! But as hard as they tried, African history, being the oldest and richest, could not be erased. There was too much of it, made obvious by the many sculptures, works of art, architecture, and ancient manuscripts left behind.

Mother Goddess

Suzanne's mother had never told the story of how her ancestors ended up in Jamaica. She had no remembrance of African traditions, had no Mother Tongue, no inherited land, and her African spirituality had been replaced with Christianity, a religion that rejected the Great Mother. She had simply passed down to her children what had been taught to her; that if they didn't accept Jesus Christ as Lord and Savior of their life they would spend an eternity in hell.

Never once had the history of the religion she was indoctrinated into been explained to her; it was all built on *faith* and *belief.* Knowing for *sure* didn't come into it.

One thing Suzanne *did* know for sure, was that she had a real relationship with her Creator; it was an *in*sperience, not *ex*ternal.

Her faith was shaken by her new revelations; she felt like she could no longer rely on the bible as her soul guide, without a spirit of discernment. Despite the religion of her ancestors being corrupted, she knew there was still a lot of Truth in it.

Suzanne discovered that in the *original* manuscripts which the bible had been constructed from, the Holy Trinity were Father, Mother and Son; Osiris, Isis and Horus. The Christian religion had been based upon this original story, but changed to suit themselves. She had always wondered how there could be a Father God and his Son, but no mention of a Mother? After reading from Proverbs 8:22, she realized there *was* a woman in the beginning with God! But why would they *remove* the Mother from the Godhead?

Suzanne went to bed with this question in her mind, and woke the following morning with the answer, which she wrote in her journal:

'Removing the Divine Feminine from the Holy Trinity allowed (white) men to place themselves as having almighty power. In Truth, both Masculine and Feminine Energies are needed to create an equal balance – equilibrium. The two energies are different, but *compliment* each other; men are more logical, women more intuitive. The two are supposed to work together; this is how it was in the beginning.

The male ego is a terrible thing; the woman was removed from the Godhead, and a white male god put in her place. The suppression of the Feminine Energy has caused all sorts of chaos in the world. It has allowed men to make women subservient to them, and caused an imbalance in nature, relationships, religion, education, business, politics, and agriculture which are now all male dominated. But the Feminine Energy is beginning to rise naturally, to bring about equilibrium again.'

Thinking of God as both masculine *and* feminine was going to be a challenge, since she was so used to viewing God as a Father figure only. Now she was going to practice viewing Father God as her Provider, Protector, Discipliner, and Director, and the feminine aspect of God as her Mother; Nature, Healer, Nurturer, and Wisdom.

Who Am I?

Suzanne realized that she didn't really have a sense of identity; was she African, Jamaican or British? Just because she was born in England didn't make her English; she had never felt 'at home' there, and could never get used to the cold weather. Even if she wanted to claim Africa as her roots, which part was she from? It was such a large Continent, and she had learned that Africans were captured from all parts and taken to the West Coast of Ghana before being carried away on the slave ships. How was she going to find where she originated from?

Up to this point, her strongest identity claim was being 'the righteousness of God in Christ Jesus'. She had no righteousness of her own – according to the bible, even her own righteousness was like 'filthy rags'.

She had no name with which to trace her roots; she had inherited a slave master's name. Africans put a great deal of effort into naming their children, even holding elaborate Naming Ceremonies, as they knew the spiritual effect it would have on the child in shaping the child's destiny. Europeans knew the devastating effect stripping them of their name and replacing it with their own name would have on them.

She pledged that when she found out where she originated from, she would change her surname to a name from that place, in honour of her ancestors.

Greatly impacted by everything she was learning, Suzanne was moved to write a poem:

Who am I?
I am a remnant of my ancestors,
Torn from my Motherland
By the rape of slave traders.

Who am I?
I am a watered-down version of an African Queen;
My blood is diluted, so mixed, that it's now in-between!
My skin is no longer its original color;
Rich, dark, like black gold;
The color of…tar.

Yet still,
I have Royal Blood flowing through my veins,
For my ancestors were kings, queens, rulers,
Inventors, scientists, leaders…

(Track 4 on the *'Seeds of Love'* CD)

She made a commitment that day to use her gift of writing poetry to help free her people from mental slavery.

Year Three: Mind...the Gap!

For eight months, Suzanne had no contact with Charles. She missed him terribly, but being the stubborn Scorpio woman that she was, refused to be the one to make contact first. The first few weeks were like being on an emotional roller-coaster; she didn't know if she could take much more of it...she felt sick.

But instead of wallowing in self-pity, she had thrown her Self into writing and recording her poetry, learning all about her African Ancestry and Spiritual Laws. There was so much to learn.

'Conversations with God Book One' had become Suzanne's second bible. She felt immense *joy* while reading, it resonated with *Truth*, and she experienced God's *Love* through it. She laughed, cried and said "Thank You!" with deep feelings of gratitude. She knew it was an answer to her prayers; every question she had asked God in her letter was answered. She learnt that where she was in life was a result of her *past* thoughts, words and actions. If she didn't like what she had created so far, she would need to change the way she *thought*, *spoke*, and *acted*, in order to get a better result in the *future*.

Suzanne had invested in her own copy before giving Charles back his book, and had begun putting into practice what she was learning, just as she had done with the bible. Her first lesson was that *thoughts are creative*. Before anything manifested in this physical world, someone first had to *think* about it, have the *idea*, *visualize* it, or *desire* it. Thought is the first level of creation. Speaking and writing down your thoughts is *second* level of creation. Putting *action* to your thoughts and words completes the creative process. Whatever you are *thinking* about, *speaking* about and putting *action* to with *corresponding feelings* will always manifest – whether good or bad. Suzanne realized that the reason she didn't always get what she wanted in life was because her thoughts, words and actions were not always in agreement with each other; she would find herself *thinking* one thing, *saying* something completely different to what she was thinking, and not *acting* on her initial thoughts and ideas.

She made a decision to become more consciously aware of her thoughts, words, and actions.

'We have over 60,000 thoughts a day – choose the good ones!'

'I'm not just a *human* being, I'm a *thinking* being! From the time I wake up in the morning to the time I go to bed, I'm thinking *all the time*; why was I never taught in church that my thoughts are creating my future?" Suzanne wondered incredulously.

Suzanne also learned that she had the power to create heaven or hell *right here on earth* with her thoughts, words and actions. She finally understood that by focusing on the negative, she was in fact attracting *more* negative things into her life. This is how she had been creating 'hell on earth' for herself. She thought back to her initial 'rant at God'; instead of focusing on all the things she could be grateful for, she had been focusing on all the 'bad' things going on in the world, and in her own life.

Suzanne continued selling her inspirational Christian posters at events, but never made as much money as she had done on that first occasion, when she met Charles. Sometimes, by the time she had paid for the stand, taken into account her travelling expenses and food, she might just about break even. But at least her words was getting out there, and the feedback she received on how much they inspired, motivated and encouraged people to 'keep the faith' kept *her* going.

She had tried getting them into the larger churches bookshops which would have made them sell like hot cakes, but the first questions Pastors always asked was "Are you a member?" and "How long have you been attending?" It was impossible to be a member of all the churches! Suzanne believed that if the church was indeed the 'body of Christ', she would be a blood cell, which would give her the ability to travel throughout the whole body (all the churches) with no restrictions. How was she supposed to reach all the people who needed the messages in her poems? It was impossible to be a member of every church – one Pastor had even demanded 60% of the sales! It made her think that churches were more about business than ministry nowadays.

So she focused on selling her posters at community events, where she could reach people directly.

At one of them, she was handed a leaflet advertising free meditation classes in Covent Garden. She decided to check it out. In the first class, she simply had to *observe* her thoughts and not try to do anything about them; just watch them to see how they were. Her thoughts reminded her of naughty children running around the playground of her mind, screaming, shouting, and behaving unruly. The next step was to learn how to slow her thoughts down by c*hoosing* the ones she wanted to entertain.

She learnt that thoughts are *energy*; they travel through the ether, and join with other similar thoughts. If she chose to entertain a thought, another thought like it would follow, then another, and before she knew it, a whole train of thoughts would have come her way!

She learnt that some of the thoughts she had were not even her own, but could even be coming from *other people's minds*! 'Ah, now I see how like-minded people are attracted to each other!' she thought.

If the thoughts she entertained were *positive* thoughts, she would remain in a state of bliss. But if they were *negative*, they could lead to sadness, stress, anxiety, fear, anger and melancholy. She now understood why she had often suffered from bouts of depression - wrong thinking! She learnt that 'depression' was just a fancy name for 'negative thinking patterns' and that if she didn't 'nip her negative thoughts in the bud' they would grow fast and spread like weeds.

Her meditation teacher taught her to think of her mind as a *garden*, and her thoughts as *seeds*. Her job was to keep the garden of her mind well cultivated by *uprooting* negative thoughts and replacing them with positive thoughts. If she didn't 'weed her garden' regularly, her mind would get cluttered and overgrown with weed-like thoughts, choking and even killing the positive flower-like thoughts.

Suzanne liked the metaphor of the garden; she had discovered first-hand from her own back garden how long flowers took to grow, compared to the weeds which sprang up quickly! It was the same with her mind; her job was to cultivate her positive thought-seeds so they could blossom into flowers, by uprooting the negative thought-weeds before they could spring up and stunt the growth of her flowers.

When a negative thought-weed sprung up, instead of watering (dwelling on) it, and letting it grow into *more* negative thoughts, she began practicing uprooting it and replacing it with a positive thought-seed.

Suzanne learnt that all thoughts are either rooted in *Love* or *fear*, so she began focusing on planting *seeds of Love* in the garden of her mind. A positive thought was rooted in Love, and a negative thought was rooted in fear – there was no other place for them to come from. Learning how to meditate helped Suzanne to control her thoughts, which in turn helped her control her *feelings*.

Thoughts Create Feelings

During a class, Suzanne learned that by focusing on her *solar plexus* or 'sun centre' (located at the back of her stomach) she would instantly be able to tell if she was thinking positively. Good thoughts created good feelings. If she had good feelings, like butterflies, she would be radiating *positive* energy. If she was feeling bad, she would radiate *negative* energy. Depending on how she was feeling, she would attract people, situations and opportunities on that same frequency.

Her *thoughts* were creating her *feelings*, but her feelings were the *fuel* which made what she was thinking about, saying, and acting on happen even faster. So her *emotions* were the real attractor factor!

Emotions are Energy in Motion

The reason 'bad' things had happened to her in the past was because of her own negative thinking. It was this vibration that had caused her to attract the negative situations.

She was now making a conscious effort to keep her Self feeling happy so she could remain on a good vibe. The way to keep her Self feeling happy was to think good thoughts, since her *thoughts* were creating her *feelings*. This reminded her of the bible verse:

'Whatever things are true, whatever things are honest, whatever things are just, whatever things are pure, whatever

things are lovely, whatever things are of good report; if there be any virtue, and if there is anything praiseworthy,

MEDITATE ON THESE THINGS'

(Philippians 4:8)

She began to learn how to be guided by her feelings instead of being *controlled* by them. If she felt bad, the way to make her Self feel good again was to change what she was thinking about. So she looked for ways to help keep herself feeling good all the time. She stopped watching the news as it *especially* made her feel down. She invested the time she saved watching 'programs' on the tell-lie-vision into developing her Self.

Suzanne found other ways to keep herself feeling happy; she created music playlists with positive, inspirational lyrics that she could play when she was feeling low, and chose to focus on *good* memories, rather than the bad ones from her childhood. She deleted all the music from her playlist that made her feel down when she listened to them, especially the doomy-gloomy love songs that spoke of broken hearts and unrequited love. Before, she had enjoyed wallowing in Self-pity listening to them but now, they were no longer conducive to her new way of thinking. As much as she loved them, they had to go.

She began attracting books, CD's, DVD's and free seminars that gave her a more in-depth understanding of how her mind worked, and how she could learn to control it, instead of *it* controlling *her*. None of them were Christian literature, but they often referred to the bible, which confirmed that the scriptures still contained Ancient Wisdom. She noted that most of the books she was attracting were written in the early 1900's by white men for white men, and had helped many of them amass great wealth.

Suzanne learned from one of them that it was the job of her *conscious* mind to protect her *subconscious* mind from negative influences, because the subconscious mind accepted everything that reached it as *fact*. For instance, if the news reported a recession or a new virus and she believed it to be true on a *conscious* level, it was more likely to affect her than if she didn't know about it at all, or if she chose to *reject* the idea.

Thoughts Become Things!

This was not so much because *she* believed it, but because thousands, possibly millions of others around the world believed it as well. It is the amalgamation of these like-thoughts that create things in the physical, material world.

As a result of everything she was learning, Suzanne decided to focus more on how she was feeling rather than how other people felt; her job was to keep her *Self* in a constant state of bliss – it was other people's jobs to do the same. How could *she* be responsible for how other people felt? 'If *your* thoughts create *your* feelings, surely it's everybody's responsibility to keep *themselves* feeling happy, and not expect someone else to do it for them?' she reasoned with herself. It was hard enough trying to manage her *own* emotions, without having to think about how other people were feeling as well! She decided that no matter what anyone said or did to her, she wouldn't take it to heart – that way, she couldn't be offended, and could remain feeling happy. Feeling happy was the ultimate goal, because to attract the 'good things' that she wanted in life, she had to be on the same 'vibration' as them. Was she becoming Self-ish and heart-less? She then remembered one of Jesus' teachings; "*Do unto others as you would have them do unto you*". Being kind, generous and helpful to others made *her* feel good too.

'If everybody learned to root all their thoughts in *Love*, this world would be a better place...but it starts with my *Self*,' she thought.

"Be the change you want to see!"
~ Mahatma Ghandi

Meditate to Create

Suzanne sat upright in a comfortable armchair with her eyes closed. Whenever her boys were at their dad's for the weekend, she looked forward to spending that time alone; she never felt lonely. To her, *loneliness* and *being alone* were two different things; being alone gave her time to connect with her inner Self.

As she sat poised in the chair, she consciously chose to ignore the thoughts that were always coming at her from different directions. She slowed her thoughts right down by taking full, deep breaths, and then focused on creating a space between each thought, making the gap larger and larger. She kept absolutely still as she did this. Before long, she had entered into the Silence. There, she was immersed in peace, Love, joy, and a kind of contentment she never experienced anywhere else. Sitting in the Silence for long periods of time helped her to take control over her physical body, and to hear the voice of her inner Self more clearly.

Some thirty minutes later, Suzanne opened her eyes. She felt refreshed and uplifted, as if she had just returned from a relaxing short break. She enjoyed sitting in 'the Silence'. It seemed to rejuvenate her somehow. On the odd free weekend, Suzanne would invite friends over, or go out for a meal. Occasionally she would spend an evening watching a DVD that she had chosen her Self, preferably a comedy or something light-hearted. This way, she was able to maintain her happy state. This evening, she opted to spend time alone, without the noise of anything external to interrupt her thoughts.

She ran a hot bath, adding some sea salt and the essential oil of lavender. As she relaxed her body and mind in the water, words came floating to her. She reached for her notebook and pen lying on the floor beside the bath. By now, she knew to always be ready for when those bolts of inspiration struck:

I am fertile soil!
When I plant Seeds of Love in the garden of my mind
They're gonna blossom...

Think of every thought you have as a seed
The thoughts you sow, you will reap;
Thoughts rooted in Love will grow into beautiful flowers
While thoughts rooted in fear
will grow into fast-growing weeds!

"Every day is a SEED to your future happiness, success and well-being, so plant the seeds TODAY for the FUTURE you want to see BLOSSOM!"

Just remember, you reap what you sow...

(Track 5 on the *'Seeds of Love'* compilation)

As Suzanne lay in the bath she marveled at how Mother Nature had taught the true nature of our thoughts!

By now she was aware that not all thoughts were produced from her own mind; some came from 'other sources'. In church, they said bad thoughts were from 'the devil'. She had often imagined this ugly little red figure sitting on her shoulder with horns, a pointed tail, and a dagger in its claws, trying to entice her to do things she knew were wrong. But the devil could only make suggestions to her; it was her choice to decide whether or not she was going to *act* on them. This reminded her of Adam and Eve in the Garden of Eden, being tempted to eat of the Tree of Knowledge of Good and Evil by the serpent.

When she thought about it, if she added a 'd' unto the word 'evil' she got 'devil', and if she took the 'o' out of the word 'good', it became 'God'. Was this just a coincidence, or was it a deliberate play on words? *God* and the *devil*. *Good* and *evil*. Good thoughts, bad thoughts. Right and wrong.... a pattern seemed to be emerging: What if they were simply opposite *forces*? If everything is energy, as she had learnt, then one was needed in able to experience the other. If there was no bad, how would she know what 'good' was? Both needed to exist in order to experience life.

The more she thought about it, the more it made sense.

It suddenly dawned on Suzanne that the Fall of Lucifer may well have been part of God's Original Plan.

This brought to mind another Spiritual Law:

You Attract What You Fear

In church she had been told to 'fear God', with Proverbs teaching that the fear of the Lord is the beginning of wisdom. From her *in*sperience, God was a force of pure, unconditional Love. 'If Love is the *opposite* of fear, why should we fear God?' she wondered. Her feelings of fear didn't resemble anything to do with Love. Besides, God's angels had always said 'FEAR NOT' whenever they showed up. So should we fear God or not?

Fear didn't feel like a positive thought or feeling to her. If her fearful thoughts made her feel bad, all she would do is attract negative things. She rejected the idea of fearing God, and chose to only *Love* God. It was her choice whether to focus on the positive or negative. She contemplated the fact that if she talked about the bad things going on in her life, she was actually giving glory to the devil. If she focused on the good, the wonders of nature, and all the things she could find to be grateful for, she would attract more things to *BE* grateful for. She suddenly remembered the poem *"Look to Me!"* which God had spoken to her two years ago. It was reminding her to focus on His Love and greatness, not her current situation.

She decided to spend some time right there, in the bath, in prayer and thanksgiving, singing and giving glory to God.

Metaphorically Speaking...

Suzanne began to realize that the stories in her bible were written in metaphors. Just as Jesus had spoken in parables, neither were meant to be taken literally. The Tree of Knowledge of Good and Evil in the Garden of Eden was a *metaphor* for the choice to think good or evil *thoughts*. If she allowed a thought to take root in her mind it would bear a harvest after its kind; *good* or *evil*.

Her *mind* was the metaphoric Garden of Eden, and her *thoughts* were the *seeds*. The Tree of Knowledge of Good and Evil were simply two *choices* that Adam and Eve could have made; they could have either chosen to entertain *good* or *evil thoughts*. 'The devil' could simply be a metaphor for the temptation to think 'evil' or bad thoughts. When she thought about it, all he could really do was make *suggestions* – it was down to her whether or not she *acted* on them.

If Adam and Eve had continued to eat freely from the *Tree of Life* by entertaining *good thoughts only*, they would have kept their thoughts pure. But they were tempted to think bad thoughts, and they did. The consequences of their actions were separation from God (Good), corruption, pain, disease, poverty, and ultimately, death.

Suzanne thought this through thoroughly; now she could see how we, Adam and Eve's descendants, were still under 'The Curse' – because we still insist on entertaining 'bad thoughts'! 'All we have to do to 'break the curse' is to focus on thinking *good* thoughts!' She considered.

'Good thoughts' are thoughts that make you feel good, put a smile on your face, a spring in your step, and that cause no stress to your body. When you think good (perfect) thoughts, it lifts your spirit, heals your body, and puts you in a positive vibration, which is the frequency you have to be on to *attract good things*. Suzanne decided make a conscious effort to reject the 'bad' thoughts that often came her way, and to only let *good* thoughts take root in her mind so that she could begin to create the life of her dreams – heaven on earth.

'So if the Garden of Eden is a metaphor for the *mind*, and our thoughts are the *seeds*, and the snake is a *metaphor* for 'temptation to think bad thoughts', then who, or what, are Adam and Eve?' she wondered. It was clear to her from Genesis 4:17 that Adam and Eve weren't the only two people God had made.

Re-United

Suzanne spent a lovely weekend with her boys; they spent Saturday morning cleaning the house and food shopping, then after the boys had done their homework, they settled down to watch a DVD together. At ages eight and ten, Micah and Elijah were into Sci-Fi movies, so as they watched '*The Matrix*'. Suzanne did her best to explain the symbolism used in the film.

On Sunday, they went to church, had dinner, and prepared for school the next day. After spending 'Quality Time' together and tucking the boys into bed, Suzanne curled up on the sofa sipping a cup of peppermint tea. Her mind ran across Charles; she wondered what he was doing right now. As she sat there thinking about him, she wondered if he ever thought about *her*.

"Why did I delete his number?" she questioned as she stared at her mobile phone, wishing she could call him.

Just then it started ringing – it was Charles!

"I don't believe it, I was just thinking about you!" she answered excitedly.

"Well, I must have sensed it," he replied calmly;

"You've been on my mind, too. It's been a while...how are you?"

"I'm okay."

She wanted to tell him how much she'd missed him, but the words just wouldn't come out.

"Just okay?"

"Well no, I'm *great*, actually. What about you, what have *you* been doing with your Self?"

"Well you're not going to believe this – I've been *painting*!"

Charles explained that the drawing *'Lace Seduction'* he'd done of her got his creative juices flowing, and he had dedicated nearly every weekend to painting since they had broken up.

"Can I come and see them?" she asked.

"I'd love you to!"

"When can I come?"

"Why not now?"

Charles had always been one to live in the moment.

Suzanne looked at the time. It was nearly 9pm. She knew the boys wouldn't wake up until at least 7am, and if they did, they would go to the toilet and go straight back to bed. If she left now, she could be back long before they awoke.

"...Okay, are you coming to pick me up?"

"Why don't you jump in a cab and I'll pay for it when you get here," he suggested.

That would give him time to tidy up a bit, and put clean sheets on the bed.

"Great! See you in about an hour then!"

Suzanne arrived at Charles' wearing a mini skirt, heels and a tight-fitting stretchy top.

As the cab pulled up outside his house, he opened his front door and waited as she strutted confidently towards him. He greeted her formally giving her a hug and kiss on the cheek, but as soon as he had her inside, he kissed her passionately. He didn't tell her how much he'd missed her, but his actions spoke louder than any words ever could.

Then taking her by the hand, he led her into his spacious living room.

On every wall hung a new painting, signed and dated by him Self. Suzanne walked around slowly taking in the colours and detail of each painting. She could see where all his sexual energy had gone these past eight months. Just by looking at them, she could tell something deep had been going on in his subconscious mind.

"They're *beautiful*...although I wouldn't have expected anything less, coming from you."

"Thank you. Choose one."

She thought she heard him wrong; "Did you just say *choose* one?"

"Yes, as my way of apologizing for not calling you sooner."

Suzanne knew straight away which one she wanted.

"Can I have that one?" she pointed to the woman emerging from a red tulip; it reminded her of everything she had been learning in her meditation classes.

"*Self Love*? Sure, it reminds me of you anyway."

"Well maybe I should let you keep it then!"

"It's okay, I'm thinking of putting them into print, so I'll just do one for myself and frame it."

"Well I'm glad to see you're finally taking your art seriously!"

"Thanks to you," he pulled her close to him in a small gesture of appreciation.

As they stood hugging and kissing, Charles could smell the essence coming from between her legs. He turned her away from him and started kissing her neck from behind.

'Self Love' by Cezanne (2009)

At the same time he reached under her top and fondled a breast with one hand, reaching slowly to lift her skirt with the other. To his delight, she wasn't wearing any panties. He reached between her smooth thighs to feel her moist, soft opening. Suzanne let out a sigh as his warm fingers began massaging her sensitive spot. Suzanne could feel the urgency of his passion, which intensified her own carnal desire for him. She turned around and began tearing at his clothes, which gave him permission to do the same to her. Kissing passionately, they stripped each other down, leaving a trail of clothes across the living room floor leading to the sofa, all the while keeping their lips locked and their tongues sensually wrestling. As they passed the dimmer switch, Charles masterfully reached over and turned down the lights. As he landed on the leather sofa, Suzanne straddled him. That was when he noticed that she was au natural.

"At last!" he commented.

"At last what?" (She thought he meant at last they were together again).

"You're in all your natural beauty!" he complimented.

"Oh, you noticed."

She had taken off her wig, taken her hair out of cornrows, and finger-combed it back into one just before she left home, knowing he preferred the natural look.

"Can I take it out of the bun?" he asked, already helping himself.

She didn't stop him. As soon as he had released her hair, it turned into a mass of wild curls. Suzanne tried to smooth it down, thinking it looked too messy.

"Leave it, it looks fine," he assured her.

She looked erotic, wild, and exciting in the dim light, while his magnificent painting *'Black Butterfly'* formed a calming backdrop on the wall behind her.

He couldn't wait any longer.

"I want to feel me inside of you," he murmured into her ear, searching for her opening with Pride. Suzanne raised herself unto her knees to make it easier for him. As she sat on him slowly, they both let out a sigh of relief.

Holding on as if for dear life, they began moving together rhythmically, slowly at first, then building up into a frenzy. Suzanne rode Pride as if she was at the races; she liked to think of it as her 'rod of correction', it sure whipped *her* into shape, anyway!

Talking to each other playfully and laughing, they changed into all their favorite positions.

"This is *real* Poetry in Motion!" Charles joked as he pushed her gently towards the arm of the sofa, forcing her unto her elbows. As he took her hips in his hands he slowly kissed one warm bum-cheek, then the other. She parted her legs slightly to make it easier for him to enter her garden. As he inserted Pride, he began gyrating his hips and waist as he moved back and forth. Suzanne could feel the bend in his organ massaging her g-spot; the sensation drove him wild too......as he galloped towards the finish line, he could feel the heat as he reached the centre of her yoni-verse;

"WHO AM I?" she demanded passionately as he drove deep inside her.

He didn't hesitate in reminding her who she was;

"You're my Queeeeeeeeeeeeeeeen..." he groaned as he came.

An hour later, his cock was still hard as a rock.

But Suzanne couldn't take any more. As they lay in his bed locked around each other's bodies, they talked about what they had both been doing while they were apart. Suzanne told Charles about the progress she had made 're-programming her mind', and learning Spiritual Laws. She also told him about some of the things she'd learnt in her African History class, and how it had helped to develop her *Self* and *racial* esteem. She told him that as soon as she had saved enough money, she was going to visit her Motherland.

"Which part do you want to go?"

"I'm not sure…I just want to go to Africa."

"Well I have family in Ghana, so if you're interested, we could go there? I've been meaning to take a trip back there myself."

"That sounds great! I'd want to take the boys as well, though."

"No problem…how much have you saved so far?"

"Just a little under £1,000 – that wouldn't even pay for all our flights, they go way up during school holidays!"

"When was you thinking of travelling?"

"It would have to be either during the 6 week holidays, over the Christmas and New Year period, or during their Easter break."

"Do you all have passports?"

"I have, but I'll have to do the boys ones…actually I'd better check to see if mine's still valid, I haven't been on holiday in years!"

"Well let's aim for next December; I'll pay for the flights, and you can use the money you've saved to pay for your passports and spending money."

"Are you serious?"

"Don't even think about it – I'm proud you've managed to save so much despite your circumstances – I'd be happy to contribute."

"Wow, thank you – now *that's* something to look forward to!"

"It sure is! We have 6 months to plan."

Suzanne had to get back home before the boys got up. He offered to run the shower for her, but she decided against it, preferring to keep the lingering scent of their love-making clinging to her body as a secret subtle reminder for as long as possible. She found her now crinkled skirt and top amongst the clothes strewn across the floor. After zipping up her skirt, with arms up, she squeezed back into her top. Charles watched her breasts disappear like a curtain at the end of an award-winning play. He called a cab to take her back home. As she left, she kissed him gently on the lips.

Even after she had gone, he could still smell her essence lingering in the air, on the sheets, and on his skin.

"This is going to be a long day," he thought, as he got ready to go to the gym.

He then decided against the gym as he'd already had a good work-out, opting to go straight to work instead.

That evening, Charles called as soon as he got in from work; he wasn't going to make the mistake of not calling her again.

"Can I come over?" he asked.

"I'd love you to – but I've got some work I have to finish tonight," Suzanne responded warmly. It was winter, and her body clock seemed to change around that time of the year; she would go to bed early, not long after the boys, then wake up around 4am and write until around 6am. There seemed to be a different type of energy at that time; inspiration flowed more easily, and she was able get a lot more done. If Charles was to come over they would go to bed late, and then she would wake up too late to write.

Plus, she was still a bit sore from the night before.

Charles reluctantly agreed. He had tasted her sweet nectar again, and now he wanted more.

"What about tomorrow evening?" he asked.

She paused before replying;

"...Okay."

As much as she enjoyed his company, Suzanne felt as if she was on a mission, other than pursuing their relationship.

As their conversation came to an end, Charles said he could still smell her scent on his sheets, and it was driving him crazy. He began telling her about all the things he was going to do to her next time he saw her – in detail. As he continued explaining all the positions he was going to put her into they both pleasured themselves, talking each other into a heated frenzy, until they both climaxed loudly down the phone.

Be Still...

Suzanne spent a two-hour long session sitting in 'the Silence'. She used the painting Charles had given her as a focal point.

Out of the blue, she received revelation of a scripture which she had heard so many times before in church, but *never* in this way:

'Be still...and KNOW that...I...AM...GOD!'

The thought shocked her. How could she go around telling people she got the revelation "I am God"?

But didn't the bible say God made man in His own image?

In the past, Suzanne had always heard the scripture interpreted to mean 'wait on God' to sort out her problems. But by 'being still', she had gained a new revelation that *she* was God – in the flesh!

She remembered what she had learned from one of the books she had read, written in the early 1900's called *'The Master Key System'*. It explained that 'I' is the creative force within. It wasn't her *flesh* that was made in God's image and likeness, it was her *spirit* which resided in her body!

Suzanne decided to become the *creator* of her future. She chose to no longer be the *victim* of her circumstances, but the *creator* of them. She was now living in the residual of her *past* thoughts, words and actions; if she didn't like what she had created so far, she had the power to change things, by changing her thoughts, words and actions. Her mistake in the past had been to conjure up all sorts of worst-case scenarios in her mind, then wondered why they happened, not realizing *she* was the one creating them.

She began using her meditation time to visualize her ideal life as if she was living it *now*, and then giving thanks with deep feelings of gratitude, as if she had already achieved it. She also gave thanks for every experience she had been through, whether she perceived them as positive or negative, as they had all helped to develop her character and personality, and make her into the person she was today.

She also used this time to focus on loving her Self from *within*.

Conversations Within

If prayer is time for talking *to* God, then meditation is time for *listening* to God.

As Suzanne sat in 'the Silence' her inner voice began to speak to her. In the Silence, it seemed much louder than usual;

"Who is *this*?" she questioned in her mind, in a surprised tone.

And the voice replied "It is I, me, YOU!"

"But…Who am I?" she asked incredulously.

*"You are a soul, living in this body. You are pure, creative spirit. You are the Source; everything comes from YOU (**Y**our **O**wn **U**niverse) and everything returns to YOU. You are a triune being; Mind, Spirit and Body, and you have the power to think creatively."*

Suddenly it was as if Suzanne remembered who she really was, and the voice inside was no longer a stranger to her. She realized that she had been looking in all the wrong places for the answers to her questions, when all she really had to do was look *within.*

(Track 6 on the *'Seeds of Love'* compilation)

Salt Fish

Charles asked Suzanne what she wanted to do on their next weekend together. She suggested they go to this all night spa she had been meaning to visit.

"Mmmm...sounds like fun!" Charles smiled broadly. He was already picturing her butt naked in the steam room.

They arrived at the spa at midnight. It was a Saturday, and very busy. People were walking around in the nude as if it was second nature to them.

Charles whispered to Suzanne "I'm not going naked!"

She laughed at him.

"Don't panic! Just wrap your towel around your waist if you don't want to go nude."

Charles looked around; there was a swimming pool, Jacuzzi, and a lounge area where you could lie down and relax, as well as the sauna, steam rooms and showers.

"This should be fun!" he thought.

Suzanne headed towards the women's changing rooms;

"Meet you back out here in 10 minutes, okay?"

"Sure."

They met up as agreed in the lounge area.

Charles was wearing a white towel wrapped around his waist, and flip flops. Suzanne had a large white towel wrapped across her chest, with a bikini underneath. She had taken her hair out of twists and wrapped her head with a smaller white towel.

"What do you want to do first?" she asked.

"I fancy going for a swim, you coming?" Charles asked.

"My hair will shrink!" Suzanne complained.

"Okay…what about the Jacuzzi?" Charles suggested.

"Alright then," she agreed.

They made their way over to the Jacuzzi, leaving their towels on the side. Suzanne got in first, lowering herself into the warm bubbling water, while Charles watched her cleavage disappear into the bubbles. They relaxed in the Jacuzzi for about 20 minutes, hardly talking, just enjoying being in each other's company. Although there were other women walking around naked, Charles didn't seem to notice.

Leaving the Jacuzzi, they headed for the showers.

They showered together and scrubbed each other's backs before entering the steam room. Once their pores had opened up, they left and showered down again. This time Suzanne un-wrapped the towel from her head and wet her thick, natural hair. Charles offered to shampoo it; he loved being able to play with her real hair. Pouring the shampoo into the palm of his hand, he rubbed them together and massaged it into her hair. She closed her eyes and enjoyed the head massage he gave her as he washed her hair with care. Directing her under the shower, He helped her rinse it out, then repeated the process. When he had finished, she towel dried it, then loaded it with conditioner and oil, and placed a plastic cap over it. They returned to the steam room so Suzanne could give her hair a good steam.

Suzanne opened the sea-salt, olive oil and essential oil mixture she had made up. Sitting on the warm tiles, she began scrubbing her arms and legs, feet, hands, torso and buttocks. She offered some to Charles, who did his arms and legs. She scooped a small amount into her hands and began scrubbing his back. He then did hers. They then relaxed and allowed the steam to do its job. Suzanne spread her towel on the tiles and lying down, allowed the mixture to penetrate her skin. Charles sat on the tiles opposite, watching her. Her skin glistened from the heat and oil. Admiring her perfectly toned body, he was unable to control Pride from rising.

Suzanne was unaware of the attention she was receiving, since she was lying on her front with her head on her folded arms faced away from him. He got up and sat beside her, and started caressing the small of her back.

"Mmmm….that feels nice."

Charles began massaging her back with more confidence. He undid the bow that was holding her bikini top in place, and applied firm pressure to his strokes. He ran his hands up her back and down her arms until he was almost lying on top of her. Kissing her on the cheek, he began the process again, starting from the small of her back.

"I feel dizzy," Suzanne said faintly.

By now, they had exceeded their time in the steam room, and coupled with their own body temperatures rising, the heat was getting too much. They left the steam room, and with Charles offering her support, they headed for the showers. Charles pushed the knob to start the shower running, then helped Suzanne in and stood behind her, becoming her wall so she didn't fall.

"Are you okay? I think we stayed in there a bit too long this time" he asked in a concerned tone.

"I'm fine, thanks," she replied, holding her head. "I just need some water."

He immediately reached for the bottle of water in his bag hanging outside the shower, and unscrewed the lid.

"Here honey, drink this."

She took a long swig at the bottle before handing it back to him. He had a few gulps, put the lid back on and placed the bottle back in his bag.

"Feeling better now?" he asked.

"Much better, thanks," she smiled up at him. Now she was feeling clear-headed, she took the plastic cap off her hair. It was almost shoulder length in its natural kinky state. Although she loved her natural hair, she still had the mentality that it was too much work to maintain. So she would plait it all down and put a wig on top. Sometimes she would get it hot-combed at the front and wear a weave, so the weave blended in with her own hair. It always looked great to start with, but after a few days her hair would start to revert back to its nappy state, and then everyone could tell she had a weave. But she wasn't going to relax it; she knew better than to put those chemicals on her head. She had done the 'big chop' and cut the relaxer out of her hair when she was pregnant with Micah, after researching the dangers of the chemicals used in them. Since then, she had slowly and painfully gone through the transition of growing natural, but not being brave enough to wear her hair short, she had been wearing the wigs and weaves ever since.

After washing out the conditioner, she towel-dried her hair.

"What am I going to do with it now?" She thought out loud as she stared at her reflection in the mirror. It looked ok in a big 'fro, but if she didn't take the time to comb, grease and twist it, by tomorrow it would be all dry and frizzy. Charles couldn't stand the wigs and weaves; he thought they looked like mops, especially when they got wet. He'd occasionally hint and drop comments but he'd never told her outright how he really felt, until now.

"Well you know where I stand on that – I don't care what you do with it, as long as you keep it natural..." he replied " ...with one exception."

"Oh? What's that then?"

"The only thing I'm not too keen on is locs."

"Why not?"

"I just think they look...untidy. And they can't be hygienic either"

For a long while, Suzanne had been considering growing locs, but hadn't quite made up her mind about them. She loved seeing them on other people, but wasn't sure if they would suit *her*. At the moment, all she knew was that she wanted to keep her hair natural – underneath her wigs.

Putting him to the test, she asked;

"Can you help me comb it out please?"

"I'd be happy to!" he obliged.

Moving to the lounge area, Suzanne sat on a chair and handed Charles her large plastic wide-tooth comb. He parted her hair into four sections, and then combed out each section individually, greasing it as he went along, as he remembered seeing his mother do with his sisters.

When he had finished, he stood back to admire his work. Suzanne looked in the mirror.

"Good job!" she said, smiling at his reflection.

Normally this is where she would plait her hair into small cornrows, cover them with a hair net, and put one of her wigs on top. But Charles seemed to enjoy playing with her hair, so she decided to leave it out.

"I think I'll just leave it to dry naturally" she said to him.

"Good – at least I'll be able to touch your hair!"

She paused to look him in the eyes, and finally realized how sincere he was being. She felt a sense of relief, happy to know that he was *supporting* her in keeping her hair natural.

When she thought about it; 'How much money do I spend buying these wigs and weaves every year? Probably enough for a holiday!' She laughed at herself.

They left the spa at 7am, arriving back at Charles's place around 8am; he couldn't wait to get her naked and explore her silky-smooth body. As he threw her down unto his sofa and spread her legs, he joked "There's nothing I like better than freshly-steamed fish!"

Today he was having *salt*-fish...

Life Path Number

Later that morning, Charles made Suzanne her favorite breakfast; porridge with banana and Manuka honey. He made himself porridge too, but without the honey. They spent the morning doing what they called 'twenty toes no clothes', chilling, relaxing, sleeping and listening to music. It was Sunday. Suzanne could have gone to church, but she was having such a great time with Charles. She no longer felt guilty about spending quality time with Charles when the boys were away for the weekend, as it seemed the natural thing to do.

In the afternoon, as they sat relaxed on the sofa, Charles suddenly started looking for a notebook and pen, and announced "Right, let's work out your Life Path number, shall we?"

"What's a Life Path number?" Suzanne questioned, intrigued.

"Well, according to Numerology, your Life Path number is the most important number relating to your birth. It reveals the road you're travelling, and gives a broad outline of the opportunities, challenges, and lessons you'll encounter in your life. It's simple to work out, so let's start with your date of birth; 5th of November…what year were you born again?"

"1974"

"Okay, so first we're going to reduce each unit of your birth date to a single digit, so we take the number 5 from the *day* you were born, the number 11 from the *month* you were born, then we reduce the numbers in the *year* you were born to a single digit. See?"

Charles wrote down all the numbers to demonstrate:

5

11

1+**9**+**7**+**4** = 21 (2+1= **3**)

"Then you add them all up": 5+11+3 = **19**

"Why haven't you broken down the 11 to a single digit?" Suzanne queried.

"Good question, you're on ball!" Charles commended her for spotting it.

"The number 11 is a 'Master Number'. The Master Numbers, 11, 22 and 33 are the only numbers you *don't* reduce to a single digit. But even if we did, in your case we'd *still* end up with the same Life Path number."

"How do you mean?"

"Well so far your Life Path number adds up to 19, but if we reduced the 11 to a single digit, we'd end up with 10. See?"

Charles added them up again:

5

1 + 1 = **2**

1 + 9 + 7 + 4 = 21 (2 + 1 = **3**)

5+2+3 = **10**

"So is my Life Path number 19 or 10?" Suzanne asked.

"Neither. We still have to reduce the two digits to a single digit. In your case, both the 19 and 10 reduce to a 1."

He showed her on paper what he meant:

1 + 9 = 10 (1+0=1)

1 + 0 = 1

"Suzanne, your Life Path number is **1**. Do you know what that means?"

"I have no idea!" she responded in anticipation, knowing he would enlighten her.

Charles reached for his Numerology book and flipped to the right section: "Being a number 1 makes you… *'A natural born leader; you insist on the right to make up your own mind; you demand freedom of thought and action. You have drive and determination. You don't let anything or anyone stand in your way once you are committed to your goal. You are exceptionally creative and original and possess a touch of the unusual. Your approach to problems is unique and you have the courage to wander from the beaten path. You perform best when you are left to your own devices. Ideally you should own your own business and be your own boss. Hold fast to your life's dream and work with the determination you possess to realize it'*."

He paused to look up at her before adding "It also says *'Don't let pride and over-confidence be your masters. Remember, your talents and abilities are a gift from a Higher Source, which should promote gratitude and humility, rather than pride and conceit. More often than not a person with a '1' Life Path will achieve much in life as long as the drive, creativity, originality and pioneering spirit are fully employed.'"*

"Wow, that's amazing!" Suzanne said in a surprised tone; "that sounds just like me – how does it work?"

"Pretty much along the same lines as Astrology; it's the same science," Charles informed her.

"Astrology deals with the way the planets were aligned on the day you were born, while Numerology deals with the numbers in your birth date. Both can give accurate descriptions about the potential your life holds, and what you came here to do – but you still have ultimate freedom to do with your life as you choose; you can fulfill its potential completely, or make some smaller version of your Self. It all depends on the effort and commitment you put in; however, the possible 'you' is contained within from the moment you were born."

"Gosh... *everybody* should know what their Life Path number is! What's *yours*?" Suzanne asked him.

"7"

"Read yours then!"

Charles proceeded to read about his Life Path;

'The 7 Life Path is the seeker of Truth. You have a clear and compelling sense of your Self as a spiritual being. As a result, your goal is devoted to investigations into the unknown, and to finding the answers to the mysteries of life. You possess a fine mind; you are an analytical thinker who is capable of great concentration and theoretical insight. You enjoy research and putting the pieces of an intellectual puzzle together. Once you have enough pieces in place, you are capable of highly creative insight, and of practical solutions to problems.'

"Oh, no *wonder* we get on so well – we're both Truth-seekers! So are 1 and 7 compatible?"

"They could be!" Charles replied cheekily.

He then proceeded to work out the rest of Suzanne's Core Numbers and explained them to her as he went along. He explained that the *day* she was born also held significant meaning, and reading from his book, explained to her what being born on the 5th meant: "*...Five represents change, non-conformity, individualism, travel and adventure –* "

"I like the sound of that!" she interrupted; "I've always wanted to travel!"

"Well it's written in your stars," Charles affirmed, looking at her intently. Going back to his book he continued; "*Five signifies opportunity, resourcefulness, and risk. 5 is extremely multi-talented and versatile, persuasive, sensual, magnetic, entertaining, scientific and analytical. 5 carries the magical mystique of quintessence that helps us experience the wonders of life. This vibration is the innate healer and teaches us to be flexible and adaptable.*"

Looking up at her he smiled as he added;

"I can vouch for that."

A Great Idea

In committing to be more attentive to Suzanne, Charles decided to spend more time doing things with her *and* her boys. So he started going to her house straight from work a couple of times a week so that they could all have dinner together, and plan their holiday together. He would also sit in and take part in 'Quality Time' before the boys went to bed. Whenever Suzanne had the boys at the weekend, Charles would spend it with them at her house, taking them to the 100 Black Men of London mentoring sessions on the Saturdays. Whenever she didn't have the boys, Suzanne would spend the weekend at Charles's.

They enjoyed being in each other's company, but also liked to pursue their own interests; Charles continued with his painting, and Suzanne with her writing. While he was painting, she would be sitting with her notepad, writing away. Sometimes she would just sit staring into space. They would be together, but in their own zones.

They would normally break from their individual worlds for lunch and dinner, and this is when they would engage in deep conversation.

"You must have so much stuff you've written by now," Charles questioned "What do you plan to do with it all?"

"I'm working on my first poetry collection, remember?"

"Oh yes, interesting…" and then as if a light had suddenly come on in his head, Charles blurted out; "I've got an idea!"

"What?" she asked in an interested tone.

"Why don't we go into *business* together – *my* artwork and *your* poetry – we could start a new range of inspirational Black greeting cards and prints!"

"Hmmm... that's a great idea – the only problem is, most of my poems are far too long to fit inside a greeting card!" Suzanne laughed.

"Well, I'm sure you can edit some down to fit?" he suggested.

Suzanne suddenly remembered a poem she had written, which went perfectly with the painting *'Self Love'* he had given her.

"I think you're right, some of my poems *do* go with your artwork!" Suzanne looked around at Charles's paintings, suddenly seeing how some of her poems *would* fit in with the themes of his artwork.

"YES!" she shouted excitedly.

They linked hands and started jumping around the living room together laughing as if they had just won the lottery, at the thought of how much money they were going to make.

Think 'Kink'

During her research, Suzanne discovered that a single strand of hair can hold a person's DNA for thousands of years even after they have died. This made her think more seriously about what she was doing, placing another person's hair on her head. Not only was she suppressing her *own* DNA, but she was taking on the DNA of someone she didn't even know!

Whose hair was it? Did she even know if the person was *alive* or *dead*? Apparently, it had been said that they were cutting the hair from corpses to fill the demand for the huge wig and weave industry. They were even getting hair from the temples in Asia, where people shaved off their hair to offer sacrifices to their gods. Before, she had taken pride in saying the hair she bought was '100% human', but now she wondered what had possessed her to stick or sew long straight hair belonging to someone else on her head and think that it's normal? The worst case of 'Self-identity crisis' had to be seeing her sisters wearing long, blonde weaves.

She also learned that energy travels in spirals, not in straight lines. Therefore kinky hair acts as a *natural antenna* for picking up frequencies from Mother Nature and the Universe. When the hair is straightened, it cannot pick up on frequencies so easily, making the person less in tune with the universe and the messages Mother Nature sends out frequently.

Knowing this, why would she want to remove the natural kink from her hair?

Suzanne began experimenting more with natural hair styles. It took a while for her to get used to the inconvenience of having to actually comb and style her hair every day, instead of just putting a wig or weave over it. Before, she had used the excuse that it was quicker and easier to manage, and that it was just a fashion accessory, like wearing jewelry. But now, she felt more confident about wearing her hair natural; it gave her a new sense of pride and identity. She wasn't trying to look Indian, or Brazilian or anything other than herself anymore. Her hair was naturally kinky, and she was going to love it and care for it as it was. She would just have to factor in an extra half hour in the morning to style it. The more she got used to it, the more she came to love it. She often moisturized and twisted it before she went to bed, then when she took it out in the morning, it would be all curly, enabling her to style it in various ways. Walking down the street, she began to get attention from the more conscious brothers would give her approving looks; one even commented that there needed to be more sisters like her. She found a hairdresser that could do bespoke hairstyles with natural hair, so whenever she had somewhere special to go, she would go to the gym, use the steam room to wash and steam her hair, then go to the hairdresser to get it styled. It could last a couple of weeks if she wore a head tie to bed.

She realized that she looked just as good, if not better, with her own natural hair rather than someone else's.

She began to embrace herself in all her natural beauty.

Year Four: Finding Her Self

"Do you ever get the feeling that there's more to this world than we're led to believe?" Suzanne asked Charles as they lay side-by-side in the park. They were enjoying a picnic together with loads of fresh fruit and water. Suzanne had taken off her shoes and had her feet firmly planted in the grass to ground herself, as she bent her knees while lying on her back, watching the clouds float by. Charles was resting on his left elbow with his arm around her waist.

"Definitely!" Charles responded, "My advice to anybody would be 'when contemplating life, remember that *nothing is at it seems'*. I often wonder how this world would change if everybody knew their thoughts were creative."

"Yes!" Suzanne agreed, "I'm *already* beginning to feel more in control of my life since finding that out. I'm well on my way to creating the life of my dreams."

"And what *are* your dreams?" Charles questioned, pulling her closer to him.

"Well, my main goal is to buy my house without a mortgage. I'd also *love* to have something that I can hand down to my children and my children's children, you know, like a family business."

"Wow, those *are* big ambitions! But what's wrong with getting a mortgage like everyone else?"

"Well, the idea has never really agreed with my spirit; I did some research on the word 'mortgage' and I bet you can't guess what it means?"

"Go on then, tell me."

"Well when you translate it from its Latin roots, the word 'mort' literally means *death* and 'gage' means *pledge*."

"Death...Pledge?"

"Exactly!" Suzanne continued excitedly; "The idea of committing to paying this large amount of money every month for the next 25 years or until I'm *dead*, just doesn't appeal to me. I mean, who knows what's going to happen down the road? I want owning my own home to be a pleasure rather than a noose around my neck. I see myself buying my house outright."

"Oh, okay," he replied, nodding his head in agreement, silently wondering how she planned to do that though – maybe she was hoping to win the lottery.

"So what would your ideal man be like?" he asked.

"Well, he definitely has to be business-minded, trustworthy, reliable, and know how to handle money, because I plan to make a lot of it!"

'She's living in a dream-world,' Charles thought, but decided to play along anyway.

"What else does this 'dream-man' of yours have to have?"

"Well he's got to be tall, handsome, have a good sense of humor, be spiritually grounded, and love children. Oh, and he needs to be financially stable, so that he doesn't feel intimidated by *my* financial success," she finally ended her list.

"A bit like you, really!" she added, smiling up at him.

He smiled back wryly.

"Well at least you know what you want out of life."

"What about you – what do *you* want out of life?" she asked him.

Charles sighed deeply.

"Just to be happy," he replied wistfully, staring up at an airplane streaking the otherwise clear blue sky.

"What does 'being happy' mean to you?" Suzanne pushed for something more specific.

Charles sighed again. Closing his eyes, he began;

"Being happy to me is a *state of mind*. You can be happy doing things you *want* to do, and you can also be happy doing things you *don't* enjoy doing, but which you know will lead to your ultimate goal."

"Give me an example," Suzanne urged.

"Well for instance, I may not like my job, but I know that the money I earn doing it will lead to my *ultimate goal* which is *financial freedom* – knowing that makes me happy doing it. But there's been times when I've felt pressured to do something, and even though there's something niggling away inside of me telling me I shouldn't do it, I do it anyway, just to keep other people happy. That's when I know

I'm not being true to my Self. I feel at my happiest when I'm being congruent with my inner Self."

"What does 'being *congruent* with your inner Self' mean?" Suzanne asked. She had never come across that word before.

"Oh you know, I just mean being in *harmony* with my Self – when my *conscious* and *subconscious* minds are working together."

"Wow, that's deep!" Suzanne commented.

"So how do you feel about *us*?" (She thought she'd throw that in since he was in the deep-talking mood.)

Charles took another deep breath before replying;

"Well, I love being in your company; you make me feel special, I feel at ease when I'm with you, like I can tell you anything. I get a warm feeling whenever I think about you, and whenever I'm away from you, what keeps me going is the thought of being back with you again."

Suzanne felt choked as she kissed him on the lips.

He continued;

"I'm happy when I'm with you; I *always* enjoy spending time with you, Suzanne. I want us to be together forever – why don't we try for a baby? I'd love you to be the mother of my child," he murmured, looking her deep in the eyes.

That was a bolt out of the blue!

'Hasn't he *missed* something?' she thought; 'he's jumped straight over the *marriage* part to having a baby!'

"A *baby*?" she ridiculed. "What, you think a baby will make sure we 'stay together forever'?" Suzanne had never imagined herself as a single mother. She thought her relationship with her sons' father was going to last 'forever', but here she was now, a single mum aged 35 with two young boys to raise, and here was Charles asking her to have a third! There was no way she was having any more children without proper commitment this time – marriage.

"It's a nice thought, but not one I can entertain right now," she replied tactfully. Stroking his face lovingly she added;

"What about this business we're supposed to be setting up? *That* can be our baby!"

"Fair comment – but don't you want any more?" he asked "You're a great mother, you know."

"I wouldn't mind having another one, but the time has to be right. Besides, I don't want to end up a single mother to *three* children!"

"Babe, no matter what happens between us, I'll always be here for you."

His words echoed those of her sons' father.

Suzanne's mind flashed back to the time her son's father had said that to her. He too had promised that he would 'always be there for her and the boys'. But where was he now?

Suzanne tried her best not to project her disappointment with her ex unto Charles, but it was difficult.

"I just want to make you happy," he said, kissing her gently on the forehead.

"I *am* happy!" She said, smiling up at him.

"She's always saying that', he thought.

In a way, he had learnt what it meant to be truly happy in life from Suzanne; it seemed to be something emanating from deep within her, not down to the things she owned (as she didn't have much), or how much money she had in the bank, or what people thought of her.

"I came into this world with nothing, I will leave with nothing, so why do I need to accumulate all these 'things' in between?" she often said. But in reality, Suzanne *did* want things: She wanted a nice house. She wanted a decent car. She wanted made-to-measure clothes. She wanted to be able to take a holiday at least once a year. She wanted to be able to buy the things that would help her fulfil her destiny, like build a recording studio in her house. What she *meant* was, she didn't want more than she needed; she didn't *need* 100 pairs of shoes lined up in the wardrobe, or more than one house to live in, or more money than she could possibly spend in her lifetime. However she *did* want to make a big difference in the world, and that would take money – lots of it.

Charles was different; he loved money, which is why he had chosen a career in Accounts. In fact he loved studying figures in *all* their forms, including women's, which he thought resembled the figure '8'. The number 8 was his favorite number. According to

Numerology, not only was it the *vibration* of money, but it also stood for infinity – no beginning and no end. Charles was busy building his property portfolio. He believed that the more houses he had, the better his financial status. He also bought himself a second car. Having two cars was like having two coats to Charles; one for everyday and one for going out. His second car was a flashy, black shiny convertible. He also upgraded his wardrobe to the best designer clothes he could afford, splashing out on colorful shirts, ties and sharp suits.

Your Own Universe

Charles noticed that since they had got back together, Suzanne didn't seem as 'needy' as before; she seemed to enjoy spending much more time on her own. She had explained that unless she spent time in what she called 'The Silence', she was not able to draw from her 'inner well'.

She would seize every opportunity to be alone. On the weekends that the boys were with them, Charles would often take them out to football matches, or to the cinema, or just back to his place where they would spend hours on the play-station together, leaving Suzanne at home to spend time with her Self. She knew she could trust Charles with her sons; he was a good role model for them and completely dependable. She suspected that he enjoyed *their* company as much as they enjoyed his. She had no doubt that he would make a great father one day. Whenever they returned, Suzanne would often look refreshed, and would have cooked a nice meal for them all. But Suzanne seemed to be becoming more and more of a recluse; she developed her own 'Self development' library, and seemed happy just spending hours reading, writing and 'meditating'. It was as if she was on some kind of a mission – her sole purpose (or should we call it her *soul* purpose?) became her writing. Her boys often commented that she had 'no friends', that she was 'no fun', and that she was 'boring'. Charles began to notice this too. It was as if she was cutting her Self off from the outside world. She didn't even seem to need *him* anymore. She would rather spend time alone in her 'inner world' – he'd never met a woman who enjoyed her own company as much as Suzanne.

Charles preferred to paint in the natural daylight, so come evening time, he was free to spend time with Suzanne, but that's when *she* seemed to want to retreat into her own little world. Not even *he* could follow her there. Suzanne had a habit of going to bed early during the winter months, as if she was hibernating. But then she would get up in the middle of the night to write. As soon as they had finished spending Quality Time with the boys, she would get ready for bed. So just when Charles was ready to 'get his freak on', Suzanne was only interested in going to sleep.

On this occasion, Charles decided to have an early night too. It was only 8.45pm, but Suzanne was already dozing off. He snuggled next to her under the thick duvet, pulling her close to him. Too late, she was already sleeping. As Pride rose, he slipped it gently between her thighs from behind, searching for her opening. Suzanne groaned as if not wanting to be disturbed, but positioned her body to make it easier for him to enter. As he slowly and gratefully began moving back and forth, he could feel her juices beginning to flow. She still appeared to be asleep though. As he built up a rhythm, he reached round and played with her breasts, kissing her gently on the back. She again let out a slight moan, as if not wanting her sleep interrupted. He paused for a moment, waiting to see if she would wake up and become responsive to his needs. Not a chance. Slowly, carefully, he carried on taking her from behind, until he finally let out a soft, deep groan as he came, falling asleep still inside her.

The Signs

It was ten o'clock on a Friday evening. Charles would normally have been at Suzanne's by now to spend the weekend, but she hadn't heard from him yet, so she called his landline.

"Hi darling, what time are you coming over?"

"Oh, I can't make it this weekend...I'm tired – plus I have some work I have to catch up on," he answered in a hushed tone.

"Shall I come over to yours then?" she volunteered.

"No!" He interjected, "…I think I'd just like to spend this weekend on my own, you know, get in touch with my inner Self and all that."

There was a touch of sarcasm in his voice which Suzanne didn't pick up on.

"Oh, great!" she commended him. "Well have a great weekend – and give me a call when you're free, okay?"

"I will," he said.

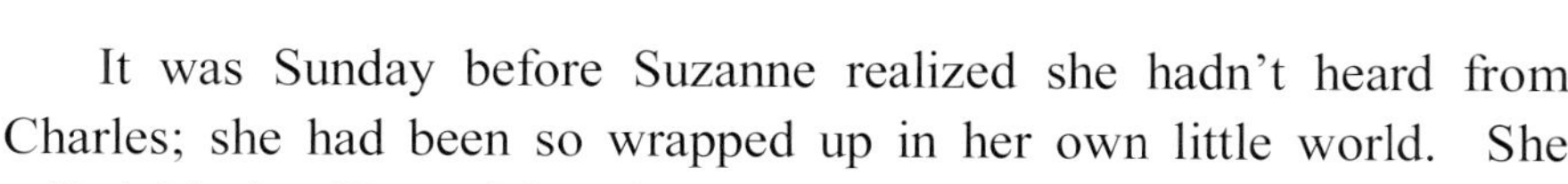

It was Sunday before Suzanne realized she hadn't heard from Charles; she had been so wrapped up in her own little world. She called his landline. The phone rang and rang before going to the answering machine. She called his mobile:

"Hi, this is Charles. Sorry I can't take your call right now, but if you'd like to leave a message..." She hung up.

'Why isn't he answering any of his phones?' she wondered.

She tried his landline again. It rang and rang. This time she left a message asking him to call her as soon as he received it. She sat wondering where he could be. Maybe he was at the gym? No, he always went early in the morning. What if he's ill? Maybe she should go round there. She decided to try calling one more time. It rang and rang.

Just as she was about to hang up, Charles answered.

"Oh! Hi babe…are you okay?" she asked hesitantly.

"Yes I'm fine – can't talk right now though, I'm kinda busy at the moment."

"Doing what?"

Suzanne heard what sounded like a woman cough in the background.

"What was that? Who's there?" she questioned him, trying not to sound panicked.

"It's just a friend...listen, I have to go, I'll call you tomorrow, okay?" he said hurriedly as he hung up the phone.

Suzanne sat in shock.

'He has another *woman* there? I thought he said he wanted to spend time *alone*? When did *this* happen?'

"She had been so focused on her Self that she hadn't even noticed Charles was feeling neglected.

"Bastard! He's gone and done exactly what I *thought* he would do! How *could* he?"

Should she go round there and explain to the woman that *she* was his girlfriend?

'No', her inner voice advised.

So she sent Charles a text asking him to call her as soon as he got her message.

Is This...Love?

The next few weeks were like a living hell. Suzanne couldn't focus on anything. She couldn't eat, she couldn't sleep properly, she could hardly *think* straight. Charles still hadn't called. 'Probably too busy having fun with his new girlfriend' she thought woefully.

Suzanne tried her best not to imagine him with this new woman. But she couldn't help picturing him walking down the street holding hands with her, driving in his car with her, relaxing on his sofa with her, making love to her, just as he had done with *her*. The pain was unbearable; she felt as if someone had taken a sharp knife and stuck it straight into her heart.

Trying to find a way to take her mind off things, she decided to put pain to paper:

Is this Love:
A yearning, burning feeling in my heart?

Is this Love:
The pain of knowing we're breaking apart?

Is this Love:
Feeling helpless, knowing we're dying,
But not knowing what to do?

Is this Love:

Not eating, not sleeping,
Not wanting anything, but you?

All I ever wanted, I found in you
But now I'm feeling blue
Missing you, so much
Wanting you, so near
Wanting you to appear
from nowhere...

Is this Love?
Is this how love's supposed to feel?
Oh, I wish I could heal my broken heart!

Is this Love:
The wrenching, tearing feeling at my heart?
The crying, crying, crying
As we slip further and further apart?
Oh the pain, it's too much for me to bear!

I'M CALLING OUT TO YOU
WITH ALL OF MY SENSES,
WHY CAN'T YOU HEAR?

But I need to move on,
Make a fresh start.
But it's so hard without you:
Is this...Love?

Be Happy NOW!

Once again, Suzanne threw her Self into her Self-development. She wasn't going to let the break-up send her spiraling into depression, as it might have done in the past. Instead, she focused on the now, and what she wanted to achieve for herself and her sons.

Suzanne believed that happiness is a state of *being*; not in *being in* a relationship, but being happy in her Self. To reach that state of happiness, all she had to do was *do* the things that *made* her happy.

Then doing the things that make her happy would eventually lead to her *having* the things she desired.

She made up her mind that she was only going to do the things that made her feel happy from now on; she was going to continue 'following her bliss'. She didn't particularly like doing housework, but she did it because having a clean, tidy house made her *feel* good, as she remembered Charles explaining to her. She loved writing, so she continued writing and recording her poetry in her free time, with a view to it eventually leading her to being able to *do* and *have* the things she desired. When she thought about it, being with *Charles* had made her happy, talking to *Charles* had made her happy, making love with *Charles*, had made her happy. But now she had to find happiness elsewhere...but the more she looked, the more she kept seeing bits of him everywhere; guys with his eyes, lips, nose, smile... 'Man, I've got it bad!' she thought to herself. She had to find a way to get him out of her system, but since she wasn't ready for another relationship, she threw her Self into her work instead. She put every bit of her free time and money into writing and recording her poetry. She had recorded 11 so far; only 2 left to go. She had collaborated with an acoustic guitarist and written lyrics to 8 of his compositions. A djembe drummer had accompanied two more of them, and a friend had added his vocals, while another brother played sax on a track – and Micah voiced the line 'Your Own Universe!' on her poem *'Conversations Within'*. It was all coming together very nicely!

She decided to stop doing stands at events for a while so she could focus on getting her poetry CD and Book of Lyrics finished.

Plus, her Christian posters no longer reflected where she was in life right now.

The Purpose of Relationships

Suzanne learned of a new way to look at relationships; she was to view them all as *opportunities* to decide who and what she was, and to create and experience greater and greater versions of her Self!

With this new outlook, she began to view all her relationships as *constructive*, regardless of how they turned out, since each experience, whether she perceived them to be good or bad, had helped her to grow. She thought back to her relationship with Micah and Elijah's father, and remembered how broken she had been when their relationship came to an end. She had made up her mind at that point, that she would never allow another man to affect her emotionally like that *ever again.* For two years, she had remained bitter and resentful, hating him and not allowing any other men close to her. Eventually she had to forgive him because *she* was the one ending up all bitter and twisted, while *he* was happily getting on with his life! Her negative thoughts towards him had only returned to hurt *her*.

> *"Holding onto anger is like drinking poison and expecting the other person to die"* ~ Buddha

She opted to forgive in order to alleviate her *own* suffering. This helped her to become a more forgiving person – for her sake, not the other person's. Having un-forgiveness in her heart blocked the flow of goodness from coming her way. This reminded her of a scripture which said *'...and when you stand praying, if you have anything against anyone, forgive, so that your Father in heaven may also forgive you'* (Mark 11:25)

It is impossible to receive God's blessings when you are holding on to bitterness and resentment for someone else.

Suzanne learned to just 'let it go'.

Honoring Her Feelings

In using her relationships as a *tool* to re-create her Self, Suzanne first had to admit honestly to her Self how she was feeling, before she could be honest with anyone else. This was going to be difficult, because although she felt emotions deeply, she rarely expressed them openly. Writing poetry had become a way for her to express her repressed emotions.

But now she was being challenged to honor her Self, by honoring her *feelings*. How did she really *feel* about her break-up with Charles? She had tried to push her feelings to the side by focusing on her work, but there was no doubt about it, she had been heartbroken – again! She thought that maybe if she had shown Charles more love and attention, she might not have lost him. Maybe if she had told him she loved him more often, he might not be with another woman now. She could count on one hand how many times she had actually told him "I love you" over the years.

But before she could understand and honor *his* feelings, she had to first honor her own. How did *she* feel now?

She was still hurting, but she was healing; even though a few months had passed, the wound still felt fresh. Before Charles, she had *thought* she'd been in love, but those feelings had been based on *needing* to be loved, not giving love unconditionally, regardless of whether it was reciprocated. Prior to him, the only other people she knew how to give and receive Unconditional Love with were her sons, and God. She realized Charles had been the only man she had really, truly been in love with. But she had lost him, because she was out of touch with her feelings. She hadn't had the opportunity to let him know how she felt about the break-up, nor did she believe she would have done a good job of it.

Maybe she should write him a poem, or a letter? She'd only just thought of it and it was a bit late now.

She decided to write him a letter but not post it to him, just to help get everything off her chest.

In it, she expressed her hurt and pain at the way he had suddenly ended their relationship, cheating on her with another woman. She asked how he could have got her and the boys hopes up about a holiday, but stated that at least it was his money that had gone to waste, not hers. She said she was glad she hadn't been stupid enough to have his baby, and asked him how he could have betrayed her trust after all they'd been through, and why he had bothered getting close to her boys if he had no intention of sticking around. She went on and on questioning him, crying tears onto the pages as she released all her pent-up anger and frustration. She wrote at least 16 pages before all the negative feelings began to subside. While writing she did her best to focus on asking her Self the questions *"Who am I, and who do I wish to be in relation to this?"* In the end she forgave him for the hurt and pain he had caused her, and thanked him for the time they had shared, wishing him a great life (without her). She ended the letter by coming to the conclusion that the relationship had been good, and had helped her to grow.

Suzanne knew that it was not in another person's *action*, but in her *re*-action that she would triumph, and that before reacting to any situation she should first re-mind her Self that she was patient, loving, kind and forgiving. Suzanne decided that in future, she would enter her relationships *not* with a view of seeing what part of another she could capture and hold, but what parts of her *Self* she would like to see show up.

Her intention was to become the master of all her thoughts and feelings, so that no matter what happened in her relationships, all possibilities of hurt, damage and loss would be eliminated. She no longer chose to experience feelings of rejection, failure, loss, or the pain associated with them.

As she lit the letter and watched it go up in flames, she felt a calm sense of relief.

Love-Sponsored Actions

Regardless of how other people treated her, Suzanne aimed to always ask her Self; *"What am I being, in relationship to that? Am I being loving, joyful, peaceful, forgiving, or am I being angry, argumentative, resentful, or bitter?"*

By choosing to make all her actions Love-sponsored (instead of fear-based), Suzanne knew it would always produce the highest good for her Self, and in doing so, would produce the highest good for others. Even where her children were concerned, she knew it wasn't her job to try and mould them into what *she* wanted them to be, but to teach them the basic Laws of Nature and allow them to experience life for themselves. They too were sacred souls on their own sacred journey; she didn't know what they had come here to do, or to experience. Her job was to allow them the freedom to develop into what *they* chose to be, with her guidance.

Even though both boys had the same mother and father, and had come from the same womb, ate the same foods, watched the same films, went to the same school etc, they were so different. Micah was strong-willed from birth, with a mind of his own. You could tell him to do the same thing over and over again to no avail, if it wasn't what *he* chose to do. Should she try and beat this 'stubborn streak' out of him, or should she see this as a positive determined attribute to his character? Despite his strong will, Micah had been a clingy baby, refusing to go to anyone but his mother and father. It was because of his clingy nature that Suzanne had been unable to return to her job. Elijah, the older brother on the other hand, was very independent from birth. Being the first child, Suzanne had expected *him* to be the clingy one, but no, he was a very independent child who went to people easily. He started nursery just after his first birthday, and Suzanne had returned to work, before falling pregnant with Micah. Micah had cried incessantly from the day he was born, and refused to take a bottle for the first nine months of his life, whereas Elijah had happily taken both the bottle and breastfed at night.

Elijah was of a more refined character, whereas Micah was 'rough and ready'. Elijah liked doing things by himself, whereas Micah always wanted to be around people, especially his mother. Even though they both had the same head-start in life, they were already two completely different characters and personalities, walking different paths. What worked with one, wouldn't necessarily work with the other.

'No wonder children don't come with a handbook!' Suzanne thought amusingly. Even the subject of teaching a child 'right' from 'wrong' seemed blurry to Suzanne. What is 'right', and what is 'wrong'? Right and wrong, as she had learnt, were only relative terms, depending on what part of the world you lived in, what religion you were indoctrinated into, how you were raised, what culture you were born into, etc. Suzanne had worked hard to instill good moral values into her boys from a young age; it is wrong to lie. It is wrong to steal. It is right to be on your best behavior as much as you can be. It is right to pray and think of all the things you can be grateful for when you wake up and before you go to sleep. It is wrong to be cheeky to an adult – this one was a bit hazy, as she had always encouraged her boys to ask questions if they didn't understand *why* she had told them to do something. She preferred to know what was going on inside their heads, instead of them just going along with whatever she told them to do, but secretly rebelling against her inside. She didn't believe that children should just 'do as they are told' with no say. Her mother (their grandmother) told her she was allowing them to 'back-chat' whenever they spoke back to her if she asked them to do anything. But she had learnt so much from her boys just from listening to their point of view. Sometimes it was as if *they* were teaching *her*. To think you cannot learn from a child is an adult's biggest error, she believed.

At ages ten and twelve, they were just beginning to come into themselves. Not quite teenagers, but 'young men' all the same, Suzanne admired and respected them, just as much as she expected them to look up to and respect her.

They had been the ones to comfort her and reassure her that everything was going to be alright, when Charles had disappeared out of their lives, being strong for her when they were obviously upset themselves. They stopped attending the mentoring sessions.

The Goddess Theory

Suzanne was developing a deep Love for her Self, something she had never experienced before; she had been too focused on her *outer* self. But now, she was coming into the realization of Who She Really Was. Based on what she had learned from *Conversations with God Book One*, she wrote in her journal:

- ♥ It is not true that I am nothing without a man in my life. The purpose of our relationship would not be for him to complete me, but for *me* to share my completeness with *him*!
- ♥ I love my Self: I do not seek Love for my Self through another.

- ♥ My goal in life is to know the highest part of my Self, and to stay centred in that. (Blessed are the Self-centred, for they shall know God).
- ♥ My most important relationship therefore, must be with my *Self.* I must first learn to honor and cherish and Love my *Self.* I must first see my *Self* as worthy, before I see another as worthy. I must first see my *Self* as blessed, before I see another as blessed. I must first know my *Self* as holy before I acknowledge holiness in another.
- ♥ I am becoming consciously aware of Who I Am (God in the flesh). My personal relationships are the most important element in this process, therefore they are *holy ground.*
- ♥ I see all those I am in relationship with as sacred souls on a sacred journey. I will always strive to see the god/goddess in every body, even when they are showing me less.
- ♥ In relationship, I will only ever be concerned about my *Self*; It doesn't matter what the other is being, doing, having, saying, wanting or demanding. It doesn't matter what the other is thinking or planning. It only matters what *I am being in relationship to that.*
- ♥ What am I being? What am I doing? What am I having?
- ♥ My grandest dream, my highest idea, and my fondest hope should never be centred on my beloved *other*, but my beloved *Self.*
- ♥ I will not lose my Self in my relationship. I will not give up Who I Am in order to be, or stay in a relationship.
- ♥ I am being the most loving person, because I love my Self!.
- ♥ I am now and forever centred upon my *Self*!

This sounded a bit radical! 'Put my *Self* first? Won't I be accused of being Self-ish and Self-centred?' She remembered Charles accusing her on more than one occasion of thinking the world evolved around her Self.

"Everything is always about me, me, *me*!" he once said.

But doesn't the bible say to 'put God first'? If she believed she was indeed made in God's image, then surely it was 'right' to put God first? Suzanne believed that this Self-ish attitude would ultimately serve others as well as her Self.

Even though it hadn't served her where *Charles* was concerned, she was sure she was on the right track. There was a much bigger picture emerging; this wasn't just about her and Charles anymore. She now 'innerstood' putting her Self first to mean that anything she did for her Self, she did for others, and anything she did for others, she did for her Self.

Charles had no idea; not only did the whole *world* revolve around her, but the whole *universe*! Yes, the whole *universe* was at her command!

God said "Let there be light!"

And there was light.

....A random bible verse popped up while she was contemplating this, but it took on a whole new meaning; being made in the image and likeness of the Great Creator, she too had the power to *speak things into being...*

Pray without Ceasing

One of the things Suzanne had earnestly sought God about was how to pray *effectively*. She was tired of praying, believing God that her prayer would be answered, and then nothing happening. But why would God hold back anything good from her?

Indeed, why.

So the issue had to be with the *way* she was praying, or what she was *thinking, saying* and *doing* while she was waiting for her prayer to be answered. The bible made it sound so easy;

'Whatever things you ask for in prayer believing,

you will receive' (Matthew 21:22)

'Whatever things you ask for when you pray, believe that you receive them, and you will have them' (Mark 11:24)

But this 'ask, believe, receive' process didn't seem so easy when she actually put it into *practice*. How many times had she asked believing, but hadn't received what she had been praying for? She'd asked for money, a husband, her own home, healing, the list could go on and on. And even though she thought of God as her spiritual Father, He certainly wasn't treating her like a spoilt brat; she *didn't* get everything she asked for.

Why not?

How did God decide who He was going to 'bless' from who was going to have to go without, or wait? Did God even *make* such decisions? If not, what was the deciding factor for getting her prayers answered?

Suzanne remembered the book '*The Master Key System*'. In it, she had learned that 'I' is the Creative Principle, so whenever she started a sentence with "I..." she had started the Creative Process. Every sentence beginning with "I..." is therefore an *activated prayer* – whether it's a *positive* or *negative* statement. Self-defeating statements like "I can't…", "I don't think...", "I forgot…", "I hate…", "I don't have…", "I'm sick and tired of…" etc, meant she was actually creating those circumstances in her future. Whereas Self-empowering statements like "I can…", "I have…", "I know…", "I remember…", "I love…", "I'm happy to...", "I will…" would help her attract the right situations, events, people, and opportunities to help her achieve her objectives.

If she found herself saying something negative, she could negate it by the 'power of three'; that is, she would say its opposite three times in her mind, or out loud.

She also learnt that the word 'AM' is *Present Tense*, so whenever she started her sentences with "I am..." she was powerfully bringing things into the *NOW*, instead of somewhere in the future. She realized that 'prayer' was simply what you *think*, *say* and *do*. It now made sense to her why the bible said to 'pray without ceasing.'

In Truth it is not necessary to 'ask' for anything, since everything is already available in the unseen realm. To bring things into the *physical*, Suzanne learnt that she had to keep her *thoughts*, *words* and *actions* in alignment with each other.

Looking at where she was in life right now, she could see the results of her past 'prayers'. On one hand she had lost the man she loved because of her incongruent thoughts and feelings about him. But on a more positive note she was well on her way to achieving her goal of earning an income from doing what she loved; she had taken the necessary actions towards her goal by writing and recording her poetry. However she hadn't been *thinking* or *saying* that she already *IS* a well-known poet – NOW.

'Speak those things that be not as though they ARE!'

...The way to make things happen is to *speak them into being,* with *EMOTION*!

Suzanne began visualizing her Self as an award-winning poet, and speaking it out into the universe.

She suddenly remembered the poem *"Look to Me!"* that God had inspired her to write the year she asked him for 'the Truth'. Part of it had said;

*"...**I Am** the Way that makes crooked paths straight,*

***I Am** the Key that unlocks the doors*

***I AM** the Great **I AM**!"*

It was as if God had been trying to tell her that she had the power to change her life, with the power of her *"I am..."* statements! Being made in the image and likeness of the 'Great I Am', Suzanne began to realize that she had the same creative power as the Great Creator, and her *"I am..."* statements were the *keys* to creating the life of her dreams!

She felt POW-her-full!

Believing in the Unseen

Now that Suzanne knew she could *be*, *do* and *have* whatever she could *imagine*, and that her *thoughts*, *words* and *actions* were powerfully creating her future, she decided to really push the boat out and take the limits off her imagination. She spent some time focusing on where she wanted to be in her future. She didn't know how she was going to get from *here* to *there*, but she believed that if she stayed focused on the *end result*, she would eventually reach her goal. If her current situation was the effect of her *past* thoughts, words and actions, then all she had to do to create 'heaven on earth' was to keep all her thoughts, words and actions in line with her desires from now on. The best way to do this would be not to talk too much, unless she had thought through what she was going to say properly.

Suzanne wanted to be recognized for doing what she loved, while at the same time making a difference in the world; if others listened to her poetry and learned something about Spiritual Laws, or if it inspired them to change the way they think for the better, her work would be almost done. Although she thought it was a bit far-fetched, she wanted to earn enough money from the sales of her CD's and books to buy her house with cash. Despite it being a distant dream, she spent time each day imagining the kind of house she wanted to live in. She had learned that when going through the 'visualization process', everything must always be pictured in the NOW, as if it is *already achieved.* So she built a clear image in her mind, and focused on herself and her sons already living in the house, and felt deep feelings of gratitude. Giving thanks *before* seeing her desires manifested showed her unwavering faith in the process, and helped her get on the right vibration to *attract* her desires.

This is where her faith had to come in. She was to believe *without a doubt*, that she had *already received* what she had asked for, *before* it had materialized.

'Faith without works is dead'

Then she had to 'act as if' she had already received it. This was the most difficult part. She didn't think she was that great at performing her poetry; sometimes nerves would grip her and ruin her performance. Left to her, she would have been happy to record her poetry and stick to selling her poetry online. But how would they sell unless she actively went out and performed them? She would have to sell a *lot* of CD's to buy her house with cash! But she believed in the process, and trusted that every time she went out to perform, she would get better and better. Just before each performance she would tell her Self *"I am a first-class performer!"* The better she got, the more CD's she would sell. The more CD's she sold, the more money she could save towards buying her house. In the meantime, her job was to visualize herself doing a flawless performance, and selling enough CD's with their Book of Lyrics to buy her home.

How would she *feel* if she had already achieved her goals? Once she was able to feel the feelings of having it *now*, she gave thanks to her Source, sometimes with tears streaming down her face.

Perfect Peace

Every time a 'vain imagination' popped up (one that was not in line with her desires) her job was to 'cast it down', and stop her mind from conjuring up images of things she *didn't* want to happen.

On one occasion, she received a letter through the door from the bailiffs. They were threatening to come and take away all her possessions if she didn't pay the bill within the next 7 days. As feelings of fear and anxiety overwhelmed her, Suzanne began to imagine men banging on her door and forcefully removing her goods. She knew that she had to take control of these negative thoughts before they got out of hand. If she continued with these vain imaginations, she could certainly *create* the event.

Suzanne sat in a chair, closed her eyes and quieted her mind.

Instead of projecting her thoughts into the future, she focused on her breathing; nothing else. In the past her thoughts would have wandered all over the place but now she was able to slow them right down by bringing her full attention back to her breath. As she inhaled deeply she noticed how her abdomen expanded. Once her lungs had filled, she held her breath for a few moments, before exhaling slowly, fully and consciously.

After repeating this a few times, she no longer needed to focus so intently on her breathing; her mind had become a peaceful void free of thoughts. Suddenly she opened her eyes as she received a flash of inspiration. Grabbing her notepad and pen, intuition kicked in as she penned a poem:

Equilibrium

When the pressures of life get me down,
And the stresses of life make me frown
I've got to find a way to get my peace of mind
And create equilibrium.

In order for me to keep my sanity
I must find the balance between my mind, spirit and body
Let go of all the things causing strain on my brain
So I can keep my mental and emotional stability.

So I rise early with the morning sun
To give thanks for all the Lord has done
Take time out to meditate and pray before I start my day
When I focus on all the positive things in my life,
I realize I'm too blessed to be stressed
There are so many things for me to be grateful for!
So by taking a few minutes to switch focus away from
I put my Self in a positive vibration...
I let anxiety drop from my mind
I let all fear slip away from my heart
I release all feelings of guilt and condemnation
I am free from all burdens; mental, physical and financial.
I am now light,
Thank You!

(Track 7 on the *'Seeds of Love' CD*)

'*Blue Lotus*' by Cezanne (2010)

Suzanne finally knew where to find peace, no matter what the circumstance. If she wasn't happy with anything she was experiencing, the way to change it was to go *within*. Everything she desired, she could find within. If she desired to be loved more, she had to first find love within, and learn to love her *Self* more. If she desired more peace and harmony in her life, she had to first create it *within*. If she desired to know God more, she had to find God *within*.

"I Am What I WILL to Be!"

Suzanne came to the conclusion that 'prayers' and 'affirmations' were actually the same thing.

Affirmations are powerful "I..." statements spoken in the *Present Tense*, that when repeated often enough, reach the Subconscious Mind. The job of the subconscious mind (amongst other things) is to *make those things happen*. She had learnt that the subconscious mind *only* deals with 'NOW', and that she could programme anything she desired for her future *into* her subconscious mind as long as she kept it in the *Present Tense*. The thing about the Subconscious Mind is that it can't tell the difference between what is *real* and what is *vividly imagined*. Nor can it tell the difference between what's happening *now*, what is *past* or *future*, which is why Affirmations have to be spoken in Present Tense. In order to stop the critical conscious mind from analyzing the statements and saying "No you're not!" she had to put her Self in a state of *deep relaxation*. She was good at that by now.

She made long lists of Positive Affirmations beginning with "I am...", for example;

"I am in perfect health; mind, spirit and body"

"I am whole, perfect, strong, powerful, loving, harmonious and happy!"

"I am abundant" (there is enough/I am enough/I have enough)

"I am the master of all my thoughts and feelings"

"I lam loving"

"I am peaceful"

"I am limitless"

She recorded her Affirmations and played them to her Self first thing in the morning and last thing at night, when she was in her Alpha state. This made it easier for them to go straight into her subconscious mind, which was connected to her Source.

Now it made sense to her why the bible advised;

Let the weak say "I am strong"

(Joel 3:10)

Let the poor say "I am rich" (Rev 2:9)

She knew that by constantly repeating 'Positive Affirmations' to her Self despite what the circumstances looked like, she could eventually reprogram her mind. She became more consciously aware of the "I am..." statements that she thought and said about her Self. When a Self-defeating thought-weed came to mind, she would uproot it and replace it with a positive, affirmative thought-seed.

So she would replace "I can't...." with "I can....", "I haven't..." with "I have...", "I'm not good at..." with "I'm great at...", "I don't feel well" with "I'm fine," and so on.

She categorized her lists of Positive Affirmations into 'health', 'finances', 'career', 'relationships', and repeated them to her Self daily. She also wrote long lists of all the things she intended to BE, DO and HAVE, and compiled them into one long poem which she entitled *"I Am What I WILL to Be!"* (Track 8 on the *'Seeds of Love'* CD)

'...Tell Us what the future holds,

...so that We may know you are gods!'

(Isaiah 41:23)

Year Five: Be Careful What You Wish For!

Suzanne finally completed her first collection of poem-songs. As most of them were quite long, deep and meaningful, she had also recorded them to music, so people could read and listen at the same time. The acoustics, drumming and percussions coupled with her lyrics were very powerful! Now all she had to do was get the CD duplicated, and get the Book of Lyrics published, and she would be ready to share them with the world!

She wanted to use the painting Charles had given her to illustrate the front cover, as it complimented her poem *'Fertile Soil'* nicely. She was sure he wouldn't mind, and the painting was technically hers to do with as she pleased now, anyway. If he hadn't defaulted on their relationship, they would have been doing this together, she reasoned.

She had enough money saved to pay for the duplication of the CD's, but had spent some of the money on 'retail therapy' and a Butlin's holiday with the boys after her break-up with Charles. She decided not to worry about *how* to publish the Book of Lyrics; she would just focus on the end result, and visualize seeing them both together as a package.

She imagined her Self going out performing to large crowds, then long queues of people lining up waiting to purchase her CD's and to get their books signed. She figured that if she sold enough, she would be well on her way to accomplishing her goal of buying her home without a mortgage. On one hand it sounded unrealistic, but on the other, what other option did she have?

She also began attending open mic poetry nights one evening a week, and on the weekends she didn't have the boys. This gave her the opportunity to perform her poetry in front of a non-judgemental crowd, which helped build her confidence. She always returned home with a buzz, which fuelled her desire to perform on stage even more. On the weekends that the boys were with her she would take them too, if children were allowed. Suzanne was following her bliss, and it seemed to be taking her in the right direction...

"I Wish..."

Suzanne had learned from *'The Secret'* DVD that she could 'order' things from the Universe, much like ordering from a catalogue, and as long as she believed in the 'ask-believe-receive' process, the things would be delivered.

The first stage was to put her desires 'out there', while being grateful for what she already had. The second stage was to 'act as if' she was already in the process of receiving what she had asked for, and to act accordingly. The third stage was to be open to the abundance of the universe, and realize that it might look a little different to what she had requested, but to trust the process. So she had ordered a beautiful four bedroom house, bought and paid for with cash. She visualized thousands of people around the world benefiting from listening to her poetry, and in return, it providing a way for her to buy her home. She also ordered the necessary people to help grow her business.

She imagined taking her boys abroad on holiday during school breaks, and being able to buy the things she needed to express her Self fully, like her own recording studio.

She spoke 'Divine Order' over her finances, business, relationships, and health, and prayed for health, wealth and happiness for all her family, friends and potential customers as well.

Since Suzanne had always had a weakness for dark men with locs, she decided to 'order' one. Adding to that, she ordered a Piscean brother, since according to Astrology (and judging by her experience with Charles) she believed Piscean men were her best match.

"Dark, with locs, and a Pisces, please!" she put it 'out there'.

R U 'The One'?

Whilst out performing one night, one of the organizers of the event told Suzanne about a poetry competition that was open for submissions. They were looking for poets of African descent to include in an Anthology, and the overall winner would get their poetry collection published for free. Suzanne eagerly took down the website details, and the following day, went online to get more information.

This was it! This was just what she needed to get her book published; she was sure to win – she could just feel it in her guts!

She called the number. A baritone voice answered.

"Hello, Black Independent Publishers, Solomon speaking, how can I help you?"

"Oh hi Solomon, my name's Suzanne; I was just calling to get some more information about the competition you're running."

"Okay...what would you like to know?"

"Well, I've been on the website and viewed the criteria, and, well I just wanted to find out what type of response you've had so far?"

"We're really pleased with the quality of submissions we've received so far – are you trying to weigh up your chances of winning?" he asked in an amused tone.

"Well, kind of," Suzanne confessed.

"Well you've got just as good a chance of winning as anybody else – but you've got to be in it to win it, so the sooner you enter the better! What type of poetry do you write?" he asked.

"Love poetry mainly; anything to do with relationships."

"That always goes down well, I'd say go for it! You can recite one for me now if you like, I *love* poetry," Solomon requested.

"Really? Well most of my poems are quite long, so I'll just give you a snippet of one, okay?"

"Okay…"

"This one's called *'Ode to My King Part 1'* and it's written in the style of ancient Egyptian poetry, okay?"

"Sounds great so far…"

Suzanne began: *"Beloved, what shall I compare you to? Spiritually, you are like a tree standing tall and strong, with roots that go much deeper than our wrong: You remember the richness of our history before slavery, when we ruled as Kings and Queens, scientists and inventors, building empires! And now, you bear the mark of our ancestors; you are strong both physically and mentally. You have the Genius Gene; man, you don't know how much you inspire me!* ...Shall I stop there?"

"No, no, keep going!"

"Okay... *Let me study YOU and get my degree from Mother Nature's university, for there is nothing more I'd like to achieve: Your eyes are like two pools, sparkling and watery, and in them I see the perfect reflection of...me. Your nose resembles the ones cut off the great statues in Egypt; too defined for the white man's mind, but I like it!"*

(Solomon laughs)

*"Your lips are like two juicy mangoes, and your kisses, sweeter than honey. Your voice is like a deep, dark river, carrying me away to ecstasy...*I think I should stop there."

"Why, is it ex-rated?" Solomon asked, "I was just getting into that!"

"No, it's not ex-rated – that comes in Part 2!"

"Well go on then, give me some more!" Solomon urged.

Suzanne sighed.

"Okay...*Your neck is like a tower, strong and sturdy, and around it you wear a reminder of our history...*"

Solomon interrupted; "*I'm* wearing a reminder of our history!"

"Are you? What is it?"

"Some cowrie shells!"

"Oh! Well you'll like the next line then;

"Your teeth are like a string of cowrie shells, and when you smile, you light up my world!" (he laughs again)

"Sorry Solomon, but this poem is six pages long - I couldn't *possibly* recite it all to you over the phone!" Suzanne concluded.

(Track 9 on the *'Seeds of Love'* CD)

"Well I'd like to hear the rest of it – why don't we meet up, then you can give me a personal performance?"

Suzanne huffed.

"When my first collection is published, *then* you'll be able to read – *and* listen to it all," she replied matter-of-factly.

"Oh don't be like that, you sound like just the kind of sister I'd like to get to know. In fact there's an event going on this Saturday you might be interested in coming to – the Ma'at Market; we sell all kinds of African-inspired things; books, clothing, jewelry, carvings, natural hair and skin care products, all sorts – *and* they do live performances, I might even be able to get you a slot to perform one of your poems."

"Hmmm...Sounds interesting, what time?"

"It starts at 11am. If you give me your email address I'll forward you the details."

"Okay..."

After Suzanne had obliged, Solomon ended the conversation;

"Try and make it if you can, I'd really like to meet you."

"I'll do my best," Suzanne promised. ?"

He sent her the email straight away with the added message;

"I'll look out for you!"

The Ma'at Market

That Saturday, Suzanne attended the Ma'at Market with Micah and Elijah. It was a beautiful event; Suzanne got there just in time to see the djembe drummers do the opening Drum Call, and to witness libation for the first time; this is where they pour water and make an offering to their ancestors. It moved her spirit.

It was an indoor market, filled with stalls of quality African-inspired garments; Pan-African books, hand-made natural hair and skin care products, hand-painted ceramics, elaborate wood carvings, soft furnishings, jewelry, greeting cards and prints, spiritual oils...

"Our community is *so* creative!" she thought.

She felt at home.

She enjoyed walking around with the boys, looking at all the different stalls. Micah and Elijah soon found other children to go and play with; there was a real community spirit in the place.

Suzanne got talking to some of the stall-holders; she was thinking that when her poetry CD and Book of Lyrics was ready, this is just the type of place she'd like to promote it. She bought her Self some hand-made cowrie shell drop-earrings, and bought the boys each a leather bracelet with cowrie shells on them.

All of a sudden, she heard her name being called out over the loudspeaker; *"Is Suzanne the Poetess here?"* the host asked. That *had* to be her – when Solomon had asked for her surname, she had said "Just put *'Poetess',*" as she didn't want to use her inherited slave master's name. She suddenly felt panicked…she felt the fear but raised her hand anyway.

"Ah, you're here! Make your way to the stage, please. And next up we have..." as he introduced the next performer Suzanne made her way to the stage, looking for her boys as she went. Spotting them, she called them over;

"Stay in this room, don't go anywhere, okay? I'm just going up to perform."

They said okay and ran off again.

When she reached the stage, the host asked a little about her while she handed him her backing track on a CD. She hadn't been 100% sure Solomon was going to get her a slot, but she had prepared just in case.

"What's the title of the track you're going to be performing?" the M.C. asked.

"R U The One."

"Mmmm...sounds interesting!" he replied with a mischievous grin.

Suzanne retreated behind the stage and took a minute to go into her Self. She closed her eyes and took some deep breaths as she re-affirmed to her Self who she was;

"I am a first-class performer, I am bold like a lioness, I can do this..." she repeated her affirmations to her Self, and just as she was opening her eyes, she heard her Self being introduced to the crowd.

As the backing track began to play, Suzanne took centre stage and asked "How many single sisters do we have here today?" (raising her hand as well). Quite a lot of hands went up. She then asked "How many single *brothers* do we have?" A fair number of hands went up, but not half as many as the sisters. She dedicated the poem from all the single sisters to all the single brothers, and told the single sisters to keep their eyes peeled towards the end of the poem:

R U 'The One'?
Can you make my heart <u>beat</u> like an African drum?
(du-dum, du-dum, du-dum)
Are you the star I've been hoping, wishing and praying upon?

Is it YOU sending ME positive vibrations,
Letting me know that I'M the one?
Do you love me, the Black Womban,
And will you put me on a pedestal where I belong?
Will you hold me in high esteem and treat me like a Queen?

Can I look up to YOU,
And give you the respect you want from me?
Do you conduct your Self with honesty, dignity, and integrity?
R U 'The One'?

Suzanne worked the stage and put her all into the performance;

"...You are my brother and a King,
So don't deny me my rightful position as your Queen,
I'M The One you need; no other race can take my place –
I am your spiritual and intellectual equal!"

Engaging with the crowd, she singled out four of the brothers who had raised their hands earlier;

(Pointing at the first one she asked) *"...Do you know your history?*
(Pointing at the second) *Are you mentally free?*
(At the third) *Do you know where you're coming from?*
(And at the fourth) *Are you like a tree, standing strong?*
You must know these things for you to be 'The One'!"

She could see the crowd was really enjoying her performance. The sisters had big smiles on their faces as if she was speaking on their behalf, while the brothers seemed unsure of how to react. Only a few looked like they were confident enough to respond;

"...I know this is a tall order, but brothers, if you think you fit the position, show me by the raising of your hand –
That is, ONLY if you're 'The One'!"

(Track 10 on the *'Seeds of Love'* CD)

Sure enough, only a few hands went up at the end. But one hand was raised sky-high and the brother was even approaching the stage!

He took Suzanne's hand and helped her down the steps as he introduced himself.

"Hi Suzanne I'm Solomon, I'm so glad you came!"

"Oh, hi Solomon – I should have guessed it was you!"

"Were you expecting someone else?"

"No – and thanks for giving me the opportunity to perform by the way, I really enjoyed myself."

"Don't even mention it, it was blessed – and that poem…*I am 'The One'*!" he asserted, smiling confidently.

His teeth were crooked, but he had a personality like dynamite; he was full of positive energy. He wasn't much taller than Suzanne, maybe two inches, but he was dark with locs.

"Don't tell me – you're a Pisces," Suzanne suggested.

"How did you guess?" Solomon asked, looking surprised.

"Oh, I just had a feeling..."

"Let me get you a drink – that was a long poem, you must be thirsty!"

"I did warn you!" Suzanne laughed.

"But it was well worth listening to. I'd like to hear it again."

"As soon as my CD's out, you can be my first customer!"

"Sounds great – when's it due out?" he asked.

"I don't have a *date*, but soon."

"Well I wish you all the best with it – *and* with the competition! Have you submitted your poems yet?" he asked as they made their way over to the vegan café.

"Not yet, I'm still deciding which ones to submit."

"Well you should definitely submit *that* one, *and* the one you recited to me over the phone the other day – I think they'll both go down really well."

"Thanks, I will!" Suzanne smiled at him thankfully.

She didn't know that the organizers of the poetry competition were also the organizers of the Market. They had been bowled over by her poem, *and* her performance of it.

Flashback

I woke up thinking 'Damn, I wish I had a woman here right now to relieve me of this stiffie!'

A text came through from Sharon. "Do you fancy meeting up today?" it said. I like Sharon, but she's not the one for me, and I'd rather not lead her on; I know how emotional women can be. Besides, there are so many other options that I haven't even tried yet. I don't know what I *want*, but I know what I *don't* want.

"Sorry, I'm busy today," I rep-lied.

Then my mate Dave called to tell me about this Caribbean Expo taking place in the Docklands. He said there would be loads of sisters there, so we should go. I didn't want to; I wasn't looking for anyone right now, I was quite happy being single after the break-up of my long-term relationship. But Dave, he was *always* on the look-out. He insisted he'd pick me up at 12pm, so reluctantly I agreed to get ready and go with him. He was right; when we got there I'd never seen so many Black women all in one place, except in church.

"She's nice," Dave commented as this beautiful sister passed us by, smiling at me. But I wasn't interested; nothing really caught my eye. So here was me and Dave having an in-depth conversation as we headed towards the 100 Black Men of London stand, when all of a sudden I heard someone call out "EXCUSE ME!"

When I looked in the direction of the voice, all I could see was colours – that's what caught my eye at first, the colours of the posters she was selling. Then, I noticed her eyes; amazing, large, deep, intense, dark eyes, beckoning me to come. "Come to bed" eyes some might have called them, but honestly, I wasn't thinking along those lines at the time. All I was focused on was the deepness and intensity with which they drew me in. They were magnetic, and I was powerless to resist. I veered off to the right involuntarily, leaving Dave to carry on heading towards the 100 BMOL stand by himself. I didn't even hear him call out to ask me where I was going. As I reached her stand, I couldn't understand the strange feeling that came over me. Her eyes were still fixed on me and I began to feel all weak, light-headed, hot, warm inside, all at the same time. "What's going on?" I asked my Self. I may be 6' 3", but in that moment I felt 3' 6".

She asked me if I'd be interested in buying one of her posters. I pretended to read one, but I couldn't really focus on the words properly. It was as if my mind and body were somewhere else, but my consciousness was locked into this person. Exhilaration, fear, anticipation, and confusion all mixed together – it took my breath away. I could see her lips moving, but all I could hear were muffled words. It felt as if everything around us became a blur, and it was just me and her in the room....

Once the noise came back, all I was interested in was how I was going to speak to her again. I just *knew* I was going to have to see her again, that's all that was on my mind. I chose three random posters and asked if she had a business card. After she handed it to me, I introduced myself and began walking back to meet Dave. As I crossed over to the stand opposite I was thinking "I've got to look back – but I'm a guy, I *never* look back!" I could feel her eyes piercing into me, and sure enough, when I turned around she was looking. She smiled and waved, and in that instance, we both knew something special had just happened.

I spent the rest of the Expo walking around in a daze. I kept looking at her card and smiling to myself, thinking "I can't wait to call her!" I wasn't interested in anything else anymore. I found what I'd been looking for.

Newborn

Charles held his newborn baby for the first time.

"She's beautiful, just like you," he said as he kissed his fiancée on her forehead in reward for all her hard labour.

"Well done."

They had decided to get married when they found out she was pregnant, but hadn't got around to it yet. It had all happened so fast; from the time she announced she was pregnant, to him moving in with her, and now, the birth of their daughter. He felt proud; a father at last! At forty-one years old, this was something he'd dreamed about, but never thought would actually happen. Okay, so it wasn't with the woman he would have *liked* it to have been with, but still, 'I have a family!' he thought. Charles had been the only boy in his family. His two sisters were older than him, and although they were very close to each other, they weren't so close to him. Growing up, they thought he had been spoilt, being the only boy and the youngest, *they* had to do everything while Charles was treated like royalty. As a result, sibling rivalry had built up towards him. So when his nieces and nephews were born, his sisters hadn't involved him with them much. The only person he was still close to was his mother. He didn't really know what to expect now that he was a father, since he hadn't had any experience with looking after babies. But he would do his best – that much he did know. No-one and nothing would harm his baby girl.

"Charlie, can you call my family and give them the news please?" Maria asked.

"Sure, no problem."

He carefully handed his beautiful bundle back to her mother and reached for his phone inside his jacket pocket.

"And can you get me something to eat please?" she added.

"Of course, I'll do that right now," Charles responded, making the calls as he made his way down to the canteen.

The Ones

Suzanne chose 3 poems, the maximum allowed, to submit to the competition; '*Who Am I?*', '*R U The One?*', and '*Ode to My King Part One*', all of which reflected her African ancestry.

As she collated the poems with the application form, she again visualized her book of poetry as a finished product, along with its CD. She had every intention of winning. She imagined seeing her poetry book and CD on shelves in bookshops and libraries, being bought whenever she performed, being ordered from the internet, and she even imagined herself doing book signing events with long queues of people waiting to get their books signed. She could see, feel, taste, touch and hear the sounds of sweet success.

She gave thanks with tears streaming down her face.

No Chemistry

Suzanne began dating Solomon.

To look at, he was the weakest-looking man she had ever been out with, but mentally, he was the strongest. It was as if the universe was playing some kind of cruel joke on her. After all, he was dark, had locs, and was a Pisces. That's what she'd *asked* for. She had been sure with that combination she couldn't go wrong. Yet, his most attractive characteristic was his Positive Mental Attitude; he didn't do negativity; she'd never met anyone quite like him in that sense. He was always starting his sentences with things like "The beautiful thing about it is..." or saying "I'm happy!" and he always *was* happy! Solomon was also loving, caring, and generous. He had three daughters, one a year older than Elijah, one the same age as Micah, and another in between, so they were all in the same age group. Solomon was a family man; although he was no longer with either of the two mothers of his daughters, he played a key role in his daughter's lives. He had them *every* weekend, and *every* school holiday. They came first, as far as he was concerned. Suzanne had met the girls briefly at the Ma'at Market, as they had been in the group of children her boys were playing with, so they were already familiar with each other.

She loved the way he interacted with his daughters as well as with her sons, and he was hard-working; not only did he work at the Publisher's during the week, he also taught Black History classes to the youth on a Saturday morning. His daughters already attended, so Suzanne started taking her sons.

Every weekend, Solomon planned something different to do with his girls; swimming, shopping, cinema, eating out, he always had a schedule. Suzanne and her boys became part of their weekly planning. It was fun going out together, and it also gave them all time to get to know each other better.

For the first few weeks, they only met up with the children. Solomon had his girls every weekend, so the only time they could spend alone was during the week when the boys were in bed, or on the weekends when Suzanne didn't have her boys and the girls were in bed.

Suzanne admired Solomon; he was a great guy. He was always telling her he loved her, and was constantly showering her with praise, and encouraging her with her poetry. He wasn't always able to accompany her when she went out to perform, but he was like the wind beneath her wings; you couldn't see him, but he was there, supporting her invisibly. Suzanne and Solomon got along really well; they laughed a lot together, they liked doing the same things, their children got along together, they made a great team, as he always said.

"I am 'The One'!" he would often say confidently.

She'd never met anyone quite like him before. He didn't do 'negativity'. He knew nothing about the Law of Attraction, yet seemed to operate in it effortlessly. He was the type of person who could attract anything he desired, because he was on the right *vibration*, one of those 'natural' Law of Attraction 'magnets'.

But still, something was missing.

Suzanne couldn't quite place her finger on what it was; she had gotten over the height restriction; he made up for it in so many other ways. But their first night together left a lot to be desired. Solomon had been celibate for a lot longer than Suzanne could have been herself – six years. When he had split up with the mother of his youngest daughter, he had decided to focus all his energy on raising his daughters and working to provide for them. He was a great father but not such a great lover. Or maybe it was just that Charles had raised the bar. What was Suzanne to do?

She decided there was more to a relationship than good sex.

Locs?

Solomon finger-combed her thick hair.

"Why don't you grow locs?" he asked.

"I've been thinking about it," Suzanne responded, looking in the mirror at her afro. She loved the way locs looked on other people, but wasn't sure if they would suit *her*. Right now she was just happy that she was finally able to wear her hair natural and feel good about it.

"I think you'd look *great* with locs," Solomon tempted her.

"Do you?" she asked, looking at her reflection, trying to imagine herself with a head of locs.

"Yeah, what are you waiting for? You've got a good head-start there!"

7-8 inches of hair *was* a good start.

"I'm not sure..."

She remembered Charles' comment about them looking untidy and hard to keep clean. Solomon's ones always looked clean and tidy though. He almost always kept them under a big wooly hat, unless he was indoors, or going out somewhere special. If she *was* going to grow locs, the rebellious streak in her probably wouldn't allow her to keep them looking neat and tidy though.

"Mmmm...maybe I will," she said.

"Then you'll *really* be my Queen," Solomon urged, hugging her from behind as he admired her reflection in the mirror, imagining them *both* with locs.

"Well, you're *my* king" Suzanne replied, turning around and kissing him on the lips.

She said it, but she didn't *feel* it.

:

'My King' by Cezanne (2009)

Lucid Dream # 2

Suzanne woke from another lucid dream. She was getting married (again). But as they were saying their wedding vows, it was as if the 'camera' zoomed into the groom's mouth. His smile wasn't Charles's. His teeth weren't Charles's. It wasn't Charles. Suzanne woke with a tear streaming down each side of her face.

"I *am* marrying my soulmate – whoever it is!" she re-affirmed to her Self.

You Won!

A letter came through the door for Suzanne. She picked it up and turned it over. It was stamped 'Black Independent Publishers'. She closed her eyes and took a deep breath before opening it:

'Dear Suzanne,

Thank you for submitting your poems into our competition. We are pleased to tell you that you are the overall winner of our competition, and that your poem ***'Ode to My King Pt. 1'*** *has been selected to be included in our Anthology...'*

Suzanne could hardly believe her eyes. She'd won, and they were going to publish her whole collection of poems as well! She hurriedly read the rest of the letter, before excitedly calling Solomon and her sisters to tell them the good news...

Year Six: Trust the Process!

The Anthology sales were going really well, partly due to Suzanne's efforts. She was one of the few contributors who actively went out and performed their poetry as well. BIP had also published her own poetry collection, and both books were selling very well; Suzanne's idea to include a Book of Lyrics with her poetry CD was paying off; people seemed to like the idea of being able to read the words as they listened to her poem-songs. Not only that, she had worked out a deal with the publishers, to earn a commission on each of the Anthologies that she sold. Whenever she went out to perform, she always took a batch of both books with her, and her performances helped to sell them both. Suzanne was making quite a name for herself. She would wake up every morning thinking *'I love my life!'* She was finally doing what she loved, inspiring others in the process, and making a good living from it too. She set up a website where people could listen to her poems and buy the CD with its Book of Lyrics.

As Suzanne began her rise to stardom, her relationship with Solomon began to decline. They were seeing less of each other because she was out most weekends performing; she didn't expect him to bring his girls to every event she performed at, and lately they had been starting to act up because they were used to having their dad to themselves. They didn't seem to want to share him with her. This wasn't a problem for Suzanne, she preferred to spend her free time writing new material and going to the studio to record them.

NOT 'The One'

It was Thursday. Solomon called...again.

"Is it alright if I come over?" he asked.

Suzanne hesitated before answering. "...Okay"

She really wanted to carry on with her writing, but she couldn't put him off any longer. This was the third time this week he'd asked if he could come over, and it would be weekend starting tomorrow. She couldn't even think up another excuse. So she reluctantly cleared her bed of all her papers, books and pens, and made way for the king.

They watched a DVD, talked for a while, and then it was obvious Solomon now wanted what he'd come for. As he rode her in the missionary position with his face buried in the pillow, she thought about how the title *'My King'* just didn't seem to fit him anymore, much like an ill-fitting crown.

After he had come, his penis slithered between her legs, leaving a slimy trail like that old serpent, the devil, trying to tempt her with his lies.

"You are *not* the One!" a random thought escaped from her lips.

"What was that?" Solomon jerked his head up, a surprised look on his face.

She couldn't lie to her Self anymore.

As she got off the bed, he watched his life-force trickle down her inner thigh, then he watched her wipe it away with a tissue as if trying to erase his memory.

"I need some time alone." Suzanne stated bluntly.

"Are you asking me to leave?"

"Don't put it like that, I just need to be alone," she replied without looking at him.

Without another word, Solomon picked up his clothes, got dressed, and left.

Suzanne ran a bath, scooping a handful of Aziza's *Lavender, Rose and Orange Body Scrub* into it. The Dead Sea Salt and essential oils softened the water, while the rose petals floated on top, adding a touch of luxury.

As she immersed herself neck-deep into the water, she let out a sigh-prayer; "Please let him finish with me!"

He hadn't given her a reason to finish with *him*, so she felt she had to wait for *him* to make the decision.

Twenty minutes later, her mobile phone started ringing.

"Hi Suzanne, it's me."

"Hi Solomon..."

"Listen, I think it's best if we call it a day; I can see your heart's not in it anymore, and I don't want you staying with me out of obligation. I want all of you, not part of you."

Suzanne remained silent. She knew she couldn't give him what he wanted.

"You know I love you and I always will..." as he continued she could hear his voice breaking; "...But I know it's for the best."

"Thank you for understanding," was all that Suzanne could say without sounding too heartless.

As she pressed the 'end call' button on her mobile, she breathed a sigh of relief.

Second Time Lucky?

Suzanne decided to try again. Maybe she should focus more on his *physical* attributes this time. So she ordered a tall, dark handsome Piscean brother with locs.

Believe it or not, a few months later Suzanne *did* meet another Piscean brother.

She had first seen him at one of the 'black conscious' events she attended. She hadn't spoken to him at the time, but spotted him again while shopping in her local supermarket (dark with locs always caught her eye). She'd smiled at him and continued shopping, not really giving him a second thought. The next thing she knew, he was walking beside her, asking if she needed help with her shopping. He was carrying a basket while she was pushing a trolley so if anything, *she* should be helping *him,* she had joked. But it broke the ice anyway, and they got talking. He introduced himself as Malachi. Nice biblical name, Suzanne liked it, but she wasn't sure about his yardie accent. They continued talking while doing the rest of their shopping. Malachi finished way before her, as he'd only come in for a few things, but he accompanied her while she finished hers, making a mental note of everything she put in her trolley. At the checkout, they paid for their things separately and Malachi help Suzanne with her bags.

"Yu have cyar?" he asked.

"No, I just live around the corner."

"Mi wi gi yu ah lif'," he announced.

Suzanne checked her gut feeling before replying "Okay then."

He seemed like a nice enough brother; good looking, nice smile, and polite enough in his Jamaican way. As they took the short ride to her house, conversation flowed easily. When they reached her 'yard'(as he called it), they sat in the car talking for another 20 minutes before Suzanne suddenly remembered the ice-lollies she had bought for the boys.

"I have to go, but thanks for the lift," she said gratefully.

"But wait! Ah so yu ah gwaan?? How yu mean, 'tank yu fe de lif'? Yu naah gimme yuh numbah den? he replied with a smirk on his face.

Suzanne was attracted to his cheeky charm, but wasn't about to fall for it.

"Me ah play out dis Sat'day y'noh, you wan' come?" he added.

"Playing out? What, you mean like in a band?" she asked interestedly.

He kissed his teeth.

"Cha! Which band? Ah sound system me deal wid!" he replied, pulling a flyer from his car door and handing it to her.

"Oh..."

His sound system was called 'Jah's Blessings'. The gig was all the way over the other side of the river in South London. Suzanne wasn't sure if she wanted to travel all that way just for a night out.

Sensing her hesitation he offered "noh worry yu'Self, if you wan' fe come, jus' gimme a call, mi will come pick you up. Mi numbah de pon de flyer, seen?"

"Okay," she answered, getting ready to head towards her door.

"So yu naah gimme yours?" Malachi asked again.

Suzanne finally gave in and gave him her mobile number. He smiled happily and said he would call her.

"Is who you ah cook fah wid all dat shopping in a de bag dem? You need me fe help yu carry dem in?" he asked.

"No, no, it's alright, my boys will help."

She called the house phone and the boys came out.

"Boys, this is Malachi," she introduced them. They said 'hi' without even looking at him and headed back indoors with the shopping.

"Okay, thanks again for the lift," Suzanne waved him goodbye.

A couple of hours later, she received a text from Malachi saying how blessed he felt that they had met, and how he really hoped she would come on Saturday. The boys would be at their dad's that weekend, so she would be free, but did she really want to start anything with Malachi? No.

She sent a text back saying 'We'll see.'

'If you come, I'll make it worth your while.'

'I'll let you know by Thursday.'

'Ok, but can I call you tomorrow?'

She replied 'Ok.'

His last text said 'I look forward to it princess.'

Suzanne couldn't stand it when men called her 'princess'. That title suited someone a lot younger than herself, she thought. If she had a daughter she would call her 'princess', but a grown woman? She didn't bother to reply. Still, she was amused by the fact that his texts didn't sound like how he spoke.

Sure enough, Malachi called the next day. He asked if she had made up her mind about Saturday yet.

"No, I'm still deciding."

"Oh, okay...well I was thinking, have you ever recited any of your poetry to music before?" he asked.

"Yes, I've recorded quite a few of them to music actually," she informed him.

"Well I would love to create a track for one of your poems," he offered.

"Really? What, a reggae track? I haven't done a poem to reggae yet!"

"It could be reggae, could be jazz, could be soul, whatever you want," he practically sung.

"Really?" Now Suzanne was getting excited.

"Yeah, you name it, I can do it!"

He told her that he had a home studio, and invited her over to see it whenever she was ready.

"Sounds great!" she replied enthusiastically.

It was only *after* the telephone conversation that she realized he seemed to have lost his Yardie accent.

Malachi's Date

Suzanne decided to go and see Malachi and his sound system play out that Saturday. He seemed like a good person to keep in touch with.

Malachi arrived to pick her up almost an hour late, by which time she had almost changed her mind about going. He made no apologies for his bad time-keeping either. He looked fine, in a neatly ironed khaki-colored shirt, army trousers with a red, green and black belt, and Timberland boots. His waist-length locks were neatly tied back away from his face, accentuating his smooth dark skin, goatie beard and moustache.

Although Suzanne was attracted to him, she had her reservations.

She felt over-dressed in a tight knee-length black dress and high heels.

She already knew before he confirmed it, that he was a Pisces.

All the way across London, Malachi played loud reggae music created by his sound system and shouted above it to inform her of all the places they had toured to play at, including Europe, the West Indies and parts of Africa.

They eventually arrived at the venue.

It wasn't really her scene; more loud reggae music pumped forcefully against her chest, while the M.C.'s took it in turns to 'toast' on the mic.

Malachi's charismatic presence and animated performance captivated the audience. He toasted about the injustices of 'the system', how Babylon was going to 'bun', and how Black people needed to unite. It was good. But after two hours, Suzanne couldn't take anymore; she left the dark basement to head upstairs for some light refreshment. She bought herself a drink and found a comfortable sofa to relax on. It was only 11.45pm and she'd already had enough.

Malachi came upstairs looking for her.

"But wait! You need fe res' a'ready?" he asked.

"I just thought I'd rest my feet for a while," she said wearily.

She noticed his Yardie accent had returned.

He sat beside her admiring her smooth brown legs; her dress had ridden up, revealing quite a lot of thigh. Suzanne tried to pull it down, wishing she'd worn something longer.

"Come mek we go back downstairs fe ah dance nuh? Is a long time I man no get fe rub up an' love up an' wine up an' grin' up an' bump up fe mek me trousers lump up!" Malachi sang.

Suzanne looked at him incredulously. She wondered if he had been smoking something, because this didn't seem like the same man who had come to pick her up. Besides, she didn't know how to dance to reggae, especially the slow dub tracks, and had never been interested in 'rubbing up' Lover's Rock style. It just wasn't her thing.

"I'll be down shortly, I just want to finish my drink," she said, encouraging him to leave without her.

As he headed back downstairs, a striking sister with a head-wrap entered the front door. She was wearing a colourful ankle-length flowing dress, and flat shoes. She and Malachi started talking and laughing as they headed downstairs together.

Suzanne waited another 20 minutes before venturing into the basement again. She could see Malachi in the crowd, dancing with this sister as if they were in a world of their own. They appeared to be moving in slow motion as they held on to each other, foreheads locked together as they moved up and down, in time to the lover's rock music filling the hall. They might as well have been making love on the dance floor.

She felt betrayed.

'How could he invite me out and then go off dancing like that with another woman?' she asked herself.

Enough was enough. She decided to leave. How was she going to get home now? She was all the way over the other side of the river. She asked at the bar if they had any cab numbers. They did, so she called a taxi and asked if she could stop off at the cash machine on the way back. By the time she got home, she wasn't just angry at *him*, but upset with herself for not trusting her gut feelings.

Suzanne came to the conclusion that since she didn't know what was best for her regarding relationships, she would leave the choice with the person who knew her best – her Creator. So she stopped trying to attract what *she* thought she desired in a man because surely, God had prepared (or was preparing) someone just right for her. She ditched the idea that Pisceans were her best match; she had now been out with *three* Pisceans, and none of them had been 'The One' in the end!

Now that she had released her will to God where her soul-mate was concerned, she decided to focus on her goal of buying her house with cash instead; she had always believed that if she sold enough of her books and CD's, she could reach her goal, but so far, it had been a slow process. Most of the money that came in from the sales had to go back out to market them to get more sales. So far, she had only managed to save £3,000.

One day she found herself backsliding into her old ways of thinking as she sat alone at home;

"I wish I could just *win* £1,000,000 on the lottery or something, then I wouldn't have to worry about selling anything, I could just buy my house with cash!"

'Instead of focusing on the money, why not focus on your *mission*?' her inner voice advised.

Her mission was to help millions of her people break free from mental slavery, and to inspire others to live an authentic life and discover their true purpose, just as she had.

"You're right," she reasoned with her Self, "If I stay focused on my *mission*, I will reach my *goal*."

Her inner voice also advised:

'LET GO AND LET GOD'

Suzanne decided to let go of her need to know *how* her house was going to manifest. She should just be open to the abundance of the universe. After all, she was limiting herself by thinking that it could only come from the sales of her poetry CD's and books.

She recognized that the more she worried about money, the more she was sending messages to her subconscious mind that she didn't *have* money, and her subconscious mind could only act on the suggestions made to it. She had to plant *new* seeds in the fertile soil of her subconscious mind; ones of abundance and plenty. She registered with some estate agents and told them what type of house she was looking for, and (window) shopped for furniture that she would like to put in her new house, right down to new cutlery, crockery and bathroom accessories. Now that she had planted the seed, her job was to keep watering and nurture it with positive thoughts, words and actions.

The 'problem' with the manifestation process is that it takes *time*...time is neither here nor there in the spiritual realm, but in the physical world where we reside, 'time is of the essence'. Its fundamental nature is like a seed; once planted in the dark soil, it remains hidden from view, underground. Yet all the time it is growing, splitting and germinating, until the shoot breaks out and begins heading upwards towards the light. When the seedling breaks through the soil, it doesn't look like the beautiful flower on the packet, so do you dig it up and throw it away? No, you leave it to continue growing. Soon enough, leaves and buds begin to appear on its stem, and then the buds begin to open; eventually you see the full beauty of the blossom.

– But it doesn't stop there; after the flower has bloomed and it *dies*, it bears thousands of *new* seeds, which in turn grow into millions of *new* flowers!

Now what would have happened to that seed if you kept digging it up to see if it was growing?

Suzanne learned that words of doubt, 'negative affirmations' and disbelief in the process 'dug up' the seeds she had planted.

'Black Orchid' by Cezanne (2009)

The dark soil represented her *subconscious mind*; it was the job of her *conscious* mind to protect her subconscious mind from negative suggestions.

Suzanne made a conscious effort to keep her thoughts, words and actions *positive*, regardless of what her situation looked like.

She decided to take heed to the little voice inside that was always telling her "Trust the process! Trust the process!"

Attitude of Gratitude

Every morning before getting out of bed, Suzanne would think about all the things she could be grateful for, and express thanks with deep feelings of gratitude. This set her on the right vibration for the rest of the day.

She would then speak her Positive Affirmations and Declarations out loud, referring to her notebook where she had written them in long lists. Pacing the floor, she spoke them out with power and authority. She had even recorded some of them to play to her Self just as she was about to fall asleep at night, and first thing in the morning, when she was in her Alpha state.

She spoke *life* into her finances, relationships, health, business, family, home, and every area of her life. She also prayed for her community, and for help to do her part in healing the world.

She prayed over her son's lives, and reminded God of the promises He had made to her regarding them, giving thanks.

Suzanne made sure she only thought good thoughts about her sons, especially when they were away from her. With all the gun and knife crime prevalent within her community, she knew that if she imagined it happening to her sons it could become a reality. So instead, she used scriptures like *'a thousand shall fall at their side, and ten thousand at their right hand, but it shall not come near them'* to keep them safe, and always pictured them coming home safe and well. She taught them never to fear, and that they will always be safe because they have their angels to protect them.

Now that she knew she could *think* her life into existence, Suzanne no longer chose to be poor. Why be poor when you can be rich? She was done with the poverty mentality.

As Wallace D. Wattles had put it:

'Whatever may be said in praise of poverty, the fact still remains that it is not possible to live a really complete or successful life unless one is rich. You cannot rise to your greatest possible height in talent or soul development unless you have plenty of money. For to unfold your soul and to develop talent you must have things to use, and you cannot have these things unless you have money with which to buy them'.

Instead of focusing on the *money*, Suzanne thought about what she wanted to *do* with the money; buy her home, set up a studio, create professional poetry videos, hold retreats in exotic places around the world, get her clothes made to measure, take the boys on holiday at least once a year, and have the *time* to write and record her second poetry CD. She also wanted to travel to the USA to attend events where she could perform. The poetry scene was much bigger in America, and she felt she could do really well over there with her products.

Those who are 'spiritual' might argue that you don't need plenty of money to 'unfold your soul' or to develop your talent, but judging from her *own* experience, Suzanne knew that the more money she had, more she was able to do. So she started uprooting her negative programming about wealth and replacing it with positive thoughts; she would tell her Self *"I am NOT poor, I AM rich!" "I am NOT in lack, I AM abundant!" "I am NOT limited, I AM unlimited!"*

Sacred Woman

As Suzanne continued her journey of Self-discovery, she attracted another book entitled '*Sacred Woman*' by Queen Afua. She wrote the 12 Principles of a Sacred Woman into her journal:

1) "As a Divine, Sacred Woman I am the highest physical and spiritual projection of woman-consciousness; I represent the abundance of life in health, wealth, love and beauty".

2) "I embody grace, dignity and majesty at all times"
3) "I nurture my Self through the nurturing of others"
4) "I manifest the highest principles of spirit, mind and body, through transformation of thought, word and deed".
5) "I can never be abused by man, woman or child, for I represent the active presence and power of the Almighty Creator".
6) "I have the power to heal with a glance, smile or word".
7) "I am the Original Healer, who calls upon the Creator's creation (the elements of air, fire, water and earth) to heal physically, mentally and spiritually, for I am the great grand-daughter of Mother Nature Herself!"
8) "I beam and radiate my inner divinity, by adorning my outer being with garments befitting my royal form".
9) "I am a vegetarian-fruitarian by nature; my foods contain the breath of life..."
10) "I endeavor to transform my domestic atmosphere into a PARADISE!!! My environment radiates my inner tranquility..."
11) "I am ever striving to resurrect and exalt the divinity of my mate and counterpart..."
12) "I epitomize the highest aspect of the feminine principle in my great love of being a *woman*!"

Suzanne began incorporating these principles into her daily living, and learned to respect her Self above everything, because she realized that to love and respect her *Self*, was to command love and respect from others.

'Shine, You Brilliant Woman,
First Mother, Healer, Lover of the Universe!'

Year Seven: Love Attraction

Suzanne settled down for a quiet night in with a glass of red wine and one of her favorite DVD's. She spent most of her spare time reading, meditating, listening to audio books or 80's and 90's soul music, R&B and Rare Groove – that is, when she wasn't writing.

She hardly ever watched 'programs', preferring to watch films she had chosen her Self. That way, she felt more in control of what impressions might be made on her subconscious mind. She also preferred watching films with characters reflecting her own colour, and there weren't too many on mainstream tell-lie-vision. Tonight she was watching *'Dreamgirls'*. She identified with the main character Effie White; Effie was a single mother. All she could do was sing, and that's all she wanted to do. Her dream was to become a famous singer. All *Suzanne* wanted to do was to write and perform her poetry; her dream was to put out a best-selling poetry collection and help make 'Poetry' a popular genre. Just as the film was about to start, Suzanne's message alert went off on her mobile phone. She glanced to where it was lying on the armrest, and was surprised to see a text from Charles. She hadn't even been thinking about him. She smiled as she opened the message;

'Hi Suzanne it's Charles, it's been a while, how r u and the boys?'

Suzanne pressed the pause button on the remote control.

'We're all fine thanx, u?' she texted back.

'Very well thank u. How's the poetry going?'

'Great! My first collection is finally out!'

Suzanne waited for the next text from him, but instead, her mobile phone started ringing. Composing herself, she answered it.

"Hi Charles."

"Hi – I hope you don't mind me calling?"

The sound of his deep, seductive voice gave her butterflies.

"Not at all, why should I?"

"After the way we broke up, I wasn't sure you'd want to hear from me again."

"That's in the past. Let's forget about it, shall we?"

"Well, it's not as easy as that…"

"What do you mean?"

Charles paused before replying; "...I'm a father now."

Suzanne sat in silence for a few moments....after the initial shock of his revelation had passed, she asked "So is it a boy or a girl – and are you still with the mother?"

"She's a girl, and no, I'm not with her mother anymore. We broke up a few months ago."

"Does *she* know that?" Suzanne asked in a patronizing tone.

"Suzanne I tried to make it work, I wanted more than anything for us to be a family, but it just didn't...*couldn't*...work."

"Why not?" Suzanne quizzed him. She was on the woman's side on this one. Here was another brother walking out on his responsibilities as far as she was concerned.

"Don't make this hard for me, Suzanne."

"Well if you'd rather not talk about it..."

"She wasn't *you*!" he blurted out "...That's what it boiled down to. As much as I tried to put my feelings for you to the side and concentrate on my family, I realized I just wasn't being true to my Self."

"Well were you being 'true to your Self' when you pissed off and left me for her?" Suzanne couldn't help shooting out. Her Scorpio sting wasn't in her *tail*, it was in her *tongue*.

"No...it was a big mistake." Charles replied quietly.

"Well you've made your bed, now lie in it!" Suzanne pressed the 'end call' button and threw down her phone as the wound of the break-up re-opened. As she sat there heaving with tears brimming in her eyes, another text came through from him. She picked it up and opened it.

'Please, we really need to talk,' it said.

'About what? U have a family now.' she responded with shaking hands.

'We're not a family. I love my daughter dearly and I'll always be there for her, but it's u I want.'

Suzanne sat staring at the last phrase in his text. She didn't know what to say in reply. Just hearing his voice again after all this time had set her emotions off again. And a baby! 'He not only had *sex* with another woman, but fathered a *child* with her! And now he wants to come back to me! How *dare* he?' she thought self-righteously.

But her inner voice was urging her to give him a chance. Five minutes passed, then another text came through from him.

'Can we meet up? I'd really like to talk to you in person.'

Since she was learning to be guided by her inner voice, she decided she would hear what he had to say. 'But he's not coming here, if that's what he's thinking!' She knew that the chemistry between them would be just as strong as ever, so if they were going to meet up, it would have to be somewhere public. She was performing that Saturday night, so decided to invite him to meet her at the venue.

'We can meet on Saturday at *The Phoenix*...' she sent him the address, but told him to meet her there after 11.00pm, by which time she estimated she would have finished her slot.

Love Attraction

Suzanne often used her poems to express her deepest feelings and wishes, the ones she found it hard to verbalize.

Every time she went out to perform, she noticed the amount of single sisters in the crowd. Perhaps some of them had a man who would turn up later that night, Suzanne imagined, while others were patiently waiting for 'Mr Right'. Suzanne was also hoping to attract *her* perfect partner, so she had sat in 'The Silence' one day, and asked for guidance to write something that would help them *all* to attract their soul mates. She would be performing it for the first time that Saturday, so she rehearsed all week in front of the mirror to get it right. When she arrived at *The Phoenix*, once again she noticed that the amount of single sisters in the audience outnumbered the men by 5-1. Some she knew personally from the poetry circuit, so she sat with them and enjoyed watching their performances. Soon it was her turn. As she began singing, she tried her best to emotionalize the words, which wasn't too difficult:

I've been on my own too long
And I'm tired of spending my nights alone

I'm looking for a love that's true
Someone to call my very own.

Lord can you help me please
To attract the man of my dreams?
Tell me what I have to do
To attract a love that's true
Please...

(Inner Voice)
First, I must heal myself
from the emotional damage caused by past relationships
The hurt, the pain,
The wounds that keep opening up again and again
Each time I'm reminded of a negative experience
it starts a chain reaction;
I lash out, shout and scream, say words I don't mean
And before I know it, I'm alone again!

Oh Lord, show me the way
What steps do I have to take
To find the perfect One for me
Who'll give me the commitment that I seek?
(Inner Voice)
I must learn to drop the emotional baggage
I've been carrying around for years
Let go of all my insecurities and fears
Releasing bitterness, hurt and pain
Forgiving, so I can heal from within
And learn to love and trust again...

Even though the poem-song was over six minutes long, Suzanne had memorized it so well, she made no mistakes. It was a teaching tool to help women *prepare* to meet their soul-mate. It hadn't so much been written *by* her – it had more come *through* her; the words were just as much for her as for anyone else. She recited the last lines;

Now I trust and let go because I know that...

DREAMS DO COME TRUE!

(Track 11 on the *'Seeds of Love'* CD)

As Suzanne left the stage to a resounding applause, a familiar figure approached her.

"You again."

"Me again."

They hadn't seen each other in over two years. He couldn't believe how much she'd changed.

"Damn, you look good enough to eat!" he exclaimed impulsively.

She smiled, thinking that all her efforts had paid off. Suzanne had by now gone from wearing the wigs and weaves, to wearing her own natural hair. It was more work to maintain, but somehow, it gave her a new sense of pride and self-identity. For this occasion, she was wearing it in a Bespoke Hairstyle; cornrow twists going up off her face into an elegant bunch on top. Her clothing style had changed, too; she no longer wore jeans or dark, dull-looking clothes, but long, flowing dresses in bright colours. She tended to avoid understated clothes, preferring bold prints with an ethnic feel, which made her look more daring and exciting in appearance. There was grace in her movements, reflecting her keen sense of harmony and refinement. Her makeup was natural-looking, enhancing her features rather than changing them completely.

'She definitely seems to be going through some sort of transformation' Charles thought – 'for the better'.

"Can I buy you a drink?" He asked, taking her by the arm.

"That would be nice," she replied, thinking 'Why did he have to touch me? He *knows* what his touch does to me!'

It sent an electrical current right through her whole body.

As they stood by the bar talking, invisible sparks were flying everywhere. They couldn't really hold a proper conversation because of the noise, so Charles asked if they could go somewhere quieter. Suzanne suggested the lounge area upstairs.

She left her books and CD's with her sister Janice who she was sharing the stand with, saying she would be back soon. Janice smiled at Charles and said "Good to see you again!" and gave Suzanne an approving wink.

As they sat on the comfortable leather sofas, a waiter handed them both menus.

"Would you like anything to eat?" Charles asked.

"No thanks," Suzanne responded "...But I wouldn't mind a cup of peppermint tea, if they have any."

He looked through the menu, then said "Yes they do, I think I'll have one too."

Charles signaled to the waiter to come back over, and ordered two pots of peppermint tea.

"Okay I'm ready, fire away." Suzanne stared him straight in the eyes.

Looking back at her regretfully he held her gaze as he began; "Suzanne, I'm really sorry for any hurt and pain I may have caused you."

"May have?" Suzanne replied sarcastically.

"*May* have?" she repeated.

Sarcasm is the lowest form of communication, and it failed to help the situation. Ignoring her remark, he continued;

"I know I did wrong, but all I'm asking for is another chance. I now know that it's *you* I want to be with."

"What about your baby mother?" Suzanne asked; "How does *she* feel about this new arrangement of yours?"

"I don't want to talk about her too much or put her down in any way, but all I can say is, it's over. I'm never going back. It's you I want." He added; "I've missed you so much Suzanne, all the time I was with her I was wishing it was *you*. I thought I could make a life with my new family, but I was only lying to my Self. As much as I love my daughter, I have to take my own needs into consideration as well. I don't just *want* you Suzanne, I *need* you…I was wrong. I'm sorry, please forgive me?"

His words played with her heart strings, but Suzanne did her best to stay in control.

"What about the mother of your child?" she asked again.

"Look, we'd only known each other about six weeks and before I knew it, she was telling me she was pregnant. I tried my best to do right by her, but it wasn't long before I knew I'd made a big mistake. But does that mean I have to suffer the rest of my life for it? I'll always be there for my daughter, but I'm not interested in a relationship with her mother anymore. I want *you*. I'm still madly in love with you Suzanne."

This was the first time Charles had told her he loved her out of his own free will, not before, during or after sex, or with the influence of alcohol egging him on.

As she looked at him from across the table, he smiled sheepishly with that boyish grin, and a pleading look in his eyes.

"When did you break up with her?" she continued questioning him.

"I moved out a few months ago. She was making my life a living hell – I couldn't do anything right!"

"Well it's your daughter I feel sorry for. *She's* the one who has to suffer in all of this," Suzanne stated bluntly. "How old is she?"

"You're right. She's sixteen months old. I love her to bits and I *will* be there for her, and have her as often as I possibly can," Charles claimed.

"Do you have a photo of her?" Suzanne asked.

Charles brought out his mobile phone and showed Suzanne the picture on his screen-saver.

"Oh, she's beautiful!" Suzanne exclaimed.

"How's your relationship with her mother now?"

"Maria? Not good. But it hasn't been for months, even before Ebony was born. She seemed to switch on me the minute she got pregnant," he answered sulkily.

Suzanne remembered how she had been when *she* was pregnant. Her hormones had played havoc with her emotions; she recalled the time she ripped her son's father's waistcoat clean off his back.

"Are you sure it's not just her hormones?" she asked in defense of Maria.

"What do I know? All I know is, I'm not in love with her – I'm in love with *you*."

As they sat staring at each other from across the table, Charles reached over for her hand. She knew that if they got too close, touched skin-to-skin, she would lose control. She withdrew her hand before he reached it.

He looked down at the table, feeling deflated.

"Please Suzanne, give me the chance to make it up to you. Whatever the consequences of my actions, I'll do anything to have you back in my life. Just name it, and I'll do it."

This was too much for Suzanne. Getting up she replied "This situation was not caused by me, and it's not for me to try to fix it."

As she walked away, he rushed after her.

"How are you getting home?" he asked.

"My sister has a car."

"Let me drop you home – come on, that's the least I can do."

Suzanne exploded.

"The *least* you can do? You go off and make a baby with another woman then come telling me the least you can do is give me a f***ing ride home?"

She turned and stormed off.

Charles caught her by the arm to slow her down. She stopped, spun around and glared at him.

Trying again he pleaded;

"It would give us a chance to talk some more. Look Suzanne, *We Belong Together* but if you're too angry to see that.....I mean, if you're prepared to let your anger and hurt at my mistake keep us apart forever then I'll have no choice but to walk away and we'll spend the rest of our lives wondering what could have been...or we can take this opportunity to examine what's in our hearts. Let me drive you home and we can just...... talk."

Suzanne huffed before replying "...Okay."

By the time they returned back downstairs, the event was over and Janice was packing up the stand.

As they walked to the car, Charles tried to put his arm around her shoulder to protect her from the frosty breeze blowing, but refusing his gentlemanly gesture, she pulled her coat tightly around her instead.

They drove in silence for the first five minutes before Suzanne asked if he could put some music on. As soon as he pressed the play button, one of the CD's Suzanne had compiled for him years earlier began to play. They looked at each other and smiled. Memories flooded back to her.

"I must admit, I *have* missed you," Suzanne said to him reluctantly.

Charles reached over and took her hand. He placed it on the gear stick *of the car* and put his hand over hers so she could help him change gears, like they used to. Silent tears began to fall down her cheeks. Turning to look out of the window, she wiped them away before he could notice.

As much as she wanted to be strong, she knew she was powerless to resist him.

Re-united

They arrived at Suzanne's house. She turned the key and opened the door gently, hoping the boys would have gone to bed by now. At 11 and 13, they were now old enough to stay at home by themselves, but whenever she was going out, she always told them to be in bed by 10pm the latest. Sometimes they stayed up late playing video games. It was half term, so there was no school the next day, and no reason for them to go to bed early. It was dark and quiet, so they had obviously been obedient. She checked in on them just to make sure. Charles asked if he could take a peek too; he had been like a father to them, and felt guilty about his sudden exit from their lives.

He followed Suzanne into the living room.

"Would you like a cup of tea or anything?" she asked.

"I've had a cup of tea, so I'll take the 'anything' if that's okay with you," Charles replied with a smirk.

"Ha ha, very funny," she scoffed.

As she joined him on the sofa, they sat staring at each other from opposite ends for what seemed like ages. He was thinking about how beautiful she looked - even more so if anything - and she was thinking about how stupid he'd been for going off and making a baby with another woman.

"I can't believe I'm actually here with you again – I didn't think it would happen," Charles finally said.

"Yes well don't get any ideas, I'm not jumping back into another relationship with you, if that's what you're thinking!" she retorted.

"I know I hurt you Suzanne, but I'm going to do everything I can to make it up to you," Charles promised, reaching for her hand again.

She withdrew.

"It's like you said, it's not as simple as that – you have a baby and a baby mother to think about now," she reminded him.

"I know...but can you forgive me?" he pleaded.

"I've *already* forgiven you. I did it for *my* sake, not yours."

"That's one of the things I love about you Suzanne; you find it so easy to forgive," Charles eased himself slowly over to her side of the sofa.

"*Forgiveness is the fragrance that the violet sheds on the heel that has crushed it,*" she recited.

He paused, taking in what she had just said.

"Beautiful, is that from one of your poems?"

"I wish...no, it's Mark Twain."

As he continued to shift his way over to her she asked anxiously "Where do we go from here?"

After 8 months, her body had ceased to let her know she desired a man, but she could feel the passion re-awakening again.

"Well I've never been one to beat around the bush, so I'm just gonna lay my cards on the table," Charles asserted, placing his arm on the back of the sofa behind her.

"I want to be with you, Suzanne, I don't want anyone else. I know I have my daughter to think about, and that's complicated matters, but I've never been more sure about anything in my life."

Suzanne still wasn't sure if she should give in to him. It had been a long time since they were last together; she hadn't even told him about Solomon yet, and she wasn't sure how the boys would feel about seeing him back here again, as suddenly as he'd disappeared. "We really need to talk before deciding whether this would be a good idea," she said. "...It's not just about me and you, there's your daughter, and my sons to consider, and your baby mother..."

"I know, I know…" Charles whispered, laying a finger on her lips.

He kissed her gently.

If she hadn't been sitting down, her knees would have given way.

She kissed him back, wholeheartedly.

As they embraced passionately, their tongues played with each other while their hands re-discovered each other's bodies. She could feel her temperature rising; there seemed to be a ball of fire between her legs.

"I don't want to have sex with you, not tonight," she said weakly.

He kissed her on the neck, and as he slid her top up, he slipped his hands around her back and expertly undid her bra to expose her bare breasts. Cupping them in his hands, he slowly began sucking each of her nipples. She writhed underneath him; by now she was wet, but it didn't put out the fire.

He slipped his hand up her skirt, stroking her inner thigh as he searched for the elastic in her knickers. Finding it, he pulled it to one side and began massaging her wet clitoris with his finger while he continued sucking her nipples.

"Oh my god, I've missed you!" Suzanne whispered.

"I've missed you too," Charles mumbled between mouthfuls.

Suddenly, she pounced on him like a lioness, tearing at his clothes.

He willingly helped.

As he sat on the sofa naked with Pride standing to attention, Suzanne stripped off too, saying "I'm starving, so you'd better know what you came here for!"

She stood on the sofa with her feet either side of him looking like a Nubian Queen, and his *face* was her *throne*. As she sat on it, he grabbed hold of her bum cheeks, pushing her deep into his mouth. He ate her yoni like it was his favorite fruit. As she looked down at him and he looked up at her, in that moment, they re-connected again.

When he had finished, Suzanne re-acquainted herself with Pride; kneeling in front of him, she sucked as if it was her favorite ice-lolly, trying to finish it before it melted in the hot sun.

When she had finished, she stood in front of him between his legs; he buried his face between her breasts and let out a deep sigh, as if he had just arrived home from a hard day at work. Suzanne took his head in her arms, and held him as he held unto her around the waist. Slowly, he directed her to lie on her back on the sofa, before lying on top of her in the missionary position. As he entered her slowly looking into her eyes, they both exhaled deeply.

"You're just as I remembered," he murmured into her ear, as he picked up the pace.

It was pure lust as they laughed, joked, and talked openly, re-enacting some of their favorite positions.

"Go deeper!" she commanded.

He didn't think he could *get* any deeper, but upon her request, he found another half an inch to put inside her.

As they approached the finishing line, he made his signature deep-throated groan of gratitude, while she let out her signature sigh of relief.

Just as they both climaxed Suzanne was sure she heard the sound of the door creak shut, and the boys sniggering to themselves as they ran back to their bedroom.

Reflections

The following morning Charles told Suzanne that he hadn't had sex with Maria since the day she found out she was pregnant. She believed that if she had sex, she might lose the baby. And then after the baby had been born, she was always 'too tired'.

He had been starved.

"So what attracted you to her in the first place?" Suzanne asked.

He was about to tell her that it was her beautiful half-Jamaican, half-Asian features, long, wavy hair and golden, flawless skin, but thought the better of it. Sometimes, when conversation dried up – which was quite often – that's what he would focus on. But instead, he told her that they didn't have as much in common as he had originally thought. They were both professionals (she was a barrister), they both owned their own properties, they both liked going to the theatre, and doing things 'buppies' liked to do. But they didn't have *chemistry*, like he did with Suzanne, and he didn't feel like he could talk with her about anything, like he could with Suzanne.

Suzanne told Charles about Solomon. It didn't seem to bother him, especially as Solomon had decided not to keep in contact with Suzanne, saying it would be easier for him to get over her.

As they lay entwined in bed, they talked about the events that had led to their break-up. Charles explained how he had felt shut out, like she didn't need him anymore. Suzanne explained to him that there were going to be times when she needed to spend time on her own, in order to do what she did.

"Relationships have their seasons," she explained, "Mother Nature has shown us this; just as there is Summer, Autumn, Winter and Spring, relationships go through their seasons too; it can't always be Summer. There are also the cold winter months, when it seems as if everything has died, but in Spring, everything starts to blossom, and before you know it, it's Summer again! The problem is, most people give up during their winter period, thinking the relationship has died. That's what *you* did, Charles. If you had just hung on, you would have seen it start to blossom again."

Charles thought about what she had just said;

"You're right. I must remember that next time we go through our 'winter season'."

Suddenly he got up, swung his legs round and sat on the edge of the bed, as if he had just remembered something. Placing his elbows on his knees and his head in his hands, he closed his eyes, looking as if he had just taken the weight of the world on his shoulders.

Suzanne knelt behind him and wrapped her arms around his shoulders, pressing her bare chest against his back. Slow, silent tears began to fall down his face. Turning to look her in her eyes, he gently whispered "I'm sorry." She began to cry too. In that moment they both realized their relationship would never be the same again. Now there was a baby and a baby mother who would always come between them.

Just then, his mobile phone started ringing in his jacket pocket, which was hung on a chair across the room. He looked at her as if seeking approval to take the call. She nodded, un-embracing him as he got up to answer it. Suzanne could hear the woman's raised voice from where she was sitting.

"Is Ebony okay?" he asked anxiously.

He relaxed at her reply, then attempted to calm her down as she appeared to be ranting and raving down the phone. As he ran his hand from his forehead to the nape of his neck, Suzanne knew that the woman was transferring her negative energy unto him, and that *she* was going to have to be the one to remove it again.

"She wants to go out tonight, and she wants me to babysit," Charles stated.

"Why don't you bring Ebony here?" Suzanne suggested.

"She said its better if I look after her at *her* house, that way she'll be settled."

"That's ridiculous!" Suzanne exclaimed. "You're her father! Tell her you want to take her to meet your family."

"I'd rather just keep the peace."

"Are you sure she's not just trying to get you to sleep over?" Suzanne asked suspiciously. "What if she wants you back?"

"Well that's not going to happen, is it?" Charles assured her, taking her by the hand and pulling her close to him.

"It's *you* I'm in love with, just remember that."

"Well you're going to have to let her know that you have a partner and that you can't keep staying over there – you should start having your daughter at weekends so she can have her breaks too."

Introduction

It was a warm, sunny Saturday morning. It was Charles' first time having his daughter for the whole day without her mother. Maria hadn't agreed to him taking her for the whole weekend, instead insisting that he needed to 'build up' to it. It was now 11.25am. He had dropped Suzanne off on the High Road to do some 'retail therapy' while he went to collect his daughter. It took a while before Suzanne's mobile phone started ringing.

"Hi babe, I've got her, where are you?" he asked.

"I'm in the indoor shopping centre."

"Oh good, I've just parked in the car park, can you meet me there?"

"Okay."

By the time Suzanne reached the car park, Charles was already approaching carrying his daughter on one arm, and the bag her mother had packed for her on the other. She was wearing a yellow sleeveless floral print dress with frilly ankle socks and pink sandals. Her hair was styled in two big puffy bunches with colorful bobbles to keep them in place. She was the spitting image of her father. She had taken most of her father's rich melanated skin tone, and her eyes, nose and lips resembled his. No doubt, she was a daddy's girl.

Suzanne felt nothing but love for the little girl.

"Suzanne, meet Ebony, Ebony meet Suzanne," Charles introduced them.

"Hello Ebony!" Suzanne cooed.

Ebony reached out her hands for Suzanne to take her.

"Oh, my goodness!" Suzanne exclaimed, taking Ebony from her father while he took her bags.

They took to each other straight away.

"She's adorable!" Suzanne said to Charles.

"Yes...sometimes I find it hard to believe I helped create something so beautiful," he replied, looking at his daughter lovingly.

They spent the next two hours shopping for clothes and toys for Ebony. Suzanne enjoyed picking out little dresses, cardigans and hair accessories, almost as much as she enjoyed shopping for herself – and it made a change from buying boys clothes.

They found a nice restaurant to have lunch in. While Charles ordered their food, Suzanne looked in the bag that Maria had packed for Ebony. Finding her lunch, she asked a waitress if she could warm it up. She put a bib on Ebony, and watched in amusement as Charles fed his daughter. By the time he was finished, Suzanne was glad they had bought another dress she could change her into. After Ebony had her juice, Suzanne took her into the women's changing room and changed her nappy and dress. By now, Ebony was tired.

Carrying her back into the restaurant she asked Charles "Where's her pushchair?"

"Oh...I left it in the car," he replied, looking embarrassed.

"Never mind, just remember it next time, okay?" she said laughing.

Suzanne wanted Charles to do right by his daughter just as much as he did, and she supported him in spending as much time with Ebony as he possibly could. So twice a week, Charles would go to Maria's straight from work and spend a couple of hours with his daughter, returning to Suzanne's after Ebony went to bed at 7.30pm.

Maria would often offer him dinner, but he always made sure he had a snack before he got there, and waited until he got back to Suzanne's before having his dinner. He didn't want Maria to getting used to him eating there, besides, he often felt sleepy after his evening meal.

Sharing Space

Charles and Suzanne decided to move in together, for practicalities sake more than anything. If Charles was going to start having Ebony at weekends, he would need Suzanne's help. Plus, he spent most of his time at her place anyway. He had a three-bedroom house already, so to him, it made sense for Suzanne and the boys to move in with him, but when he suggested it to her, she objected.

"It's too small. Micah and Elijah are getting big now and will soon need rooms of their own. Plus Ebony will have to have her own room, and we need to set up an office if we're going to start this business. We need more space."

Charles thought more carefully before replying "You're right. Five of us in a three-bedroom house *would* be a bit cramped. Right, I'll sell my house and buy something bigger."

It didn't take long for Charles' house to sell; it was in perfect condition, and in a desirable location. Everything seemed to work out for the good; he had a cash buyer so there was no long chain. In three months, the sale was complete. During that time, Charles, Suzanne and the boys spent most weekends and some evenings looking for a house that they all liked. They finally found one in Croydon near a park and good school. It was slightly over Charles' budget, so he took the equity out of one of his investment properties to put towards the house, and towards setting up their business.

Suzanne gave back her council property and sold or gave away most of her possessions, advising Charles to do the same. This was going to be a new start for them all, she stated.

Wings of an Eagle

Charles woke from a vivid dream. Suzanne had been watching him sleep.

"What were you dreaming about? You seemed all jittery," she asked, stroking his face.

"Oh, man...I was having this weird dream...I was standing on the ledge of this high-storey building," he closed his eyes, reliving it;

"I looked down...I must have been at least 100 floors up, and my feet could barely fit on the ledge – I was scared shitless. Then I noticed a guy standing to my left on safe ground, watching me. He had these huge wings, like eagles. My foot slipped, and just as I started falling, next thing I knew, he was right there, catching me. He placed me where he'd been standing – then he was gone. I didn't even get a chance to thank him."

"...Then another scene; I was looking for him. I really wanted to thank him for saving my life. As I walked down a busy high street, I met another man. I instinctively sensed that he was another angel. He gave me a cheque for a large amount of money – then he disappeared too."

'Wings of an Eagle' by Cezanne (2009)

"Wow, what do you suppose it means?" Suzanne asked.

"I don't know...but I've been thinking a lot lately about giving up my job and pursuing my art instead. That's a BIG leap of faith. I guess subconsciously, I'm afraid I'll fail."

"You won't fail, Charles! We're in this together now; two heads are better than one," Suzanne tried her best to convince him.

"Yes but it's not just me now; there's the mortgage to pay, Ebony, you and the boys to support as well. How will I manage?"

"Trust the universe Charles, you are abundant, everything you need will be supplied – come on, I learnt all this stuff from you!"

Suzanne reminded him. "...And the sooner you get off the plantation, the better!" she added.

He laughed.

"You're right, I should know better. I'm seriously going to work out the figures and see if it would be a viable option to give up my job."

"Well you don't have to do it straight away – let's get this business off the ground first!"

"Yes that sounds like a plan… I was in a financial session with an Asian client last week, we got comfortable in our conversation so he said 'Charles, may I ask you a question? I don't mean to be offensive, I'm just truly curious, and I feel like I can ask you this.' So I said "sure, go ahead." He asked 'when you all (meaning Black folk) move, why is it that the first thing you do is look for a job, or move for a job?' I paused; that seemed like a dumb question to me, so I replied "We have to provide for our family, so we have to have a job." He then said 'Oh, because when *we* move, we look to start a business. And we always look in *your* part of town first.'

That changed my life."

Friends?

The house phone rang. Suzanne answered; it was Maria.

"Is Charles there?" she asked.

"Hi Maria, how are you?" Suzanne replied pleasantly.

"I'm fine thanks."

"Is everything okay?"

"Yes, I just need to speak to Charles – is he there?"

"No, he's gone out, can I take a message?"

"Yes, can you tell him to call me as soon as he gets in – actually don't worry, I'll just call his mobile, thanks."

Suzanne caught her before she hung up;

"Maria?"

"Yes?"

"I think it would be really nice if we could at least be friends. Ebony will be spending time here, and it would be much better for her if we both got along, don't you think?"

"*Friends*?" Maria sneered. "You steal my man and then come telling me you want to be *friends*?"

"I didn't steal your man, Maria. Charles and I had a history long before he met you. The fact that things didn't work out between you both, isn't because I *stole* him from you."

"Well as far as I'm concerned, we were still together when he started seeing you, so what do you call that then?"

"But I thought he'd moved out?"

"He had, but that doesn't mean we weren't *together* anymore."

"Oh...so you *were* still together?"

"Yes!"

"You mean (whispering now) you still had a sexual relationship?"

"What business is that of yours? Is sex everything?" Maria stated bluntly.

"Oh, so you *weren't* still having sex," Suzanne breathed a sigh of relief.

"Whether we were or we weren't, you still stole my man!"

"Maria, somehow we have to get past that. Charles and I are back together again. He has a daughter with you. I love Ebony just as much as I love Charles, and I'd like us all to get along, if possible."

Maria hung up.

'Well at least I tried,' Suzanne thought.

Settling in

Charles began having Ebony every other weekend. They arranged it so that Ebony came on the same weekends the boys were at home. That way, they would have alternate weekends with all the children, plus a weekend together without any children. Suzanne and the boys looked forward to the weekends when Ebony stayed; she was a great addition to the family. She had her own room which was decorated in pink and purple, and the boys each had their own rooms as well. On those weekends, they did things together as a family. Due to the age gap between the boys and Ebony, it was difficult to decide what types of films to watch at the cinema, but they enjoyed doing things together like going to the monthly *Kemet Market*, eating out, going to the park, and swimming. The boys doted over their 'little sister' as they called her. Everywhere Ebony went, one of the boys would follow, to make sure she didn't hurt herself.

Suzanne enjoyed having a little girl to dress and comb her hair, and to play dolls with. It was definitely different to having boys! They had bought her some little black dolls with wooly hair at the *Kemet Market*, so that she didn't develop an identity crisis as she got older.

Some weekends the boys would go to their cousins, so Suzanne and Charles would do things with Ebony on their own, and sometimes Suzanne left Charles to spend Quality Time alone with his daughter.

All of them settled into the new routine easily. The only thing Suzanne had a problem with was the extra laundry, cooking and cleaning.

"Do you think we could get a cleaner?" she asked Charles.

"Even if it's just to clean the kitchen, bathroom and toilets once a week – that would really help!"

"I don't see why not. The time we spend cleaning could be put to better use – we have a business to set up, so go right ahead and find one."

Planting the Seed

When Suzanne woke it was still dark, but Charles had already left the bed. She looked at the clock; it was 4:10 am. 'Where could he be so early?' She wondered. 'Maybe he's gone to the toilet'. She waited five minutes. When he hadn't returned, she got up to look for him.

Bleary-eyed, she headed downstairs, as she could hear what sounded like chanting coming from the living room. As she approached, she realized it was Charles; it sounded like he was saying his prayers and affirmations out loud.

When she opened the door to the living room, he stopped and turned to greet her.

"What are you doing up so early babes?"

"Looking for you," she said, making her way towards him;

"I didn't realize you were into doing Affirmations as well!" she added.

"Of course, how do you think I make progress in life? I speak it into being!"

"Well maybe we should start doing it together," she suggested.

"That's a great idea!" he agreed.

Suzanne locked the door.

Taking him by the hand, she led him to the sofa, before pushing him gently unto it. He was already hard in anticipation.

She was wearing a short night dress and he was wearing loose-fitting pyjama bottoms, so when he sat down and she straddled his lap, it was easy for her to slip Pride in. Once he was all up inside her, she told Charles to keep still, close his eyes and focus on his breathing. She did the same. By focusing on their breathing, she informed him that they would be better able to control their natural desire to begin thrusting.

Sitting upright, she placed her left hand over his heart, and instructed him to do the same to her. As their breathing slowed right down, they reached a state of deep relaxation and entered the Alpha state, where their subconscious minds were in touch with their Source. Following her in-tuition, Suzanne began riding him slowly. She took Charles through a guided visualization, asking him to describe *in detail* his ideal work situation in the Present Tense, as if it was already happening now.

"I'm running my own business."

"Doing what?"

"Working with you; we're creating products using *my* artwork and *your* poetry."

Suzanne encouraged Charles to paint a clear picture in his mind of how the business would run by asking him the relevant questions, while slowly gyrating on Pride to keep him up.

Charles tried to stay focused as he shared his dream of running a High Street shop with offices above it. They would sell greeting cards and prints and other inspirational products featuring original artwork and poetry, starting with their own. They would also 'buy in' artwork and poetry from artists of African descent, and would sell their products around the world via their website. The high street shop would also offer a personalized greeting card, print and framing service to walk-in customers.

Suzanne reminded him to keep his vision in the *present*, before asking what type of people he employed.

He had to fight hard to resist the temptation to flip Suzanne unto her back and drain his seed into her – her dominating position was a big turn-on for him. But instead, he took some deep breathes and allowed her to carry on guiding him. He explained that it would be a *creative* business, not a *competitive* business, and explained the difference between the two. He said all their employees would be able to climb the ladder to success, and feel as if it was just as much *their* business; they would get out as much as they put *in*. Micah and Elijah would be trained to help run the business, so that they always had employment. He was offering monthly bonuses for sales targets reached, and yearly bonuses based on annual profits. He believed these incentives would keep their employees work-playing at their best. His aim was to attract the best employees and *keep* them. Charles created flexible office hours, especially for working parents, whose obligation should be to their children, not their employer, he said. Parents didn't have to start work until 10am, which would give them time to take their children to school or nursery first. He believed this would prevent them arriving at work feeling stressed before they even got started. He created greater flexibility in working hours because he understood that some people are *day* people and some are *night* people. So instead of the office operating from 9-5, it would open at 8am and close at 10pm for those who wanted to start earlier or work later. Suzanne agreed; Micah, who had been born at 7.30am always rose early, whereas Elijah who had been born at 12.20am seemed to prefer staying up later the older he got. She could already picture them working there when they got a bit older.

Charles also shared his dream of setting up a Benevolence Fund to help those in need. He said he wanted to provide a way for people in his community to set up businesses, schools, and community centers. Suzanne asked him how he planned to do this.

"10% of all the businesses profits go into the Benevolence Fund. I am setting it up as a charity, so I'll get a tax allowance for it."

Sharing his vision with Suzanne helped her build a clear image in *her* mind too. She got excited at the prospects and began sliding up and down on Pride with added zeal. Charles took a peek at her face; her eyes were still closed and she had a big smile on her face, as if she could see it all in detail. He was about ready to come, but Suzanne sensed it and slowed right down. The aim was to channel their sexual energy upwards, and bypass the lower animal instincts of lustful sex. Once Charles was in control again, Suzanne continued in a slow and rhythmic voice;

"What effect do you see our business having on the masses?"

"I see our greeting cards, art prints, poetry CD's and other products inspiring millions of people all over the world to connect with their inner Source, live an authentic life, and live their life 'on purpose'. Our products leave a lasting impression, and they in turn tell others about them."

"Can you see our business sustaining this family?"

Charles thought about the mortgage, and his other commitments.

"Yes, I'm following my path in life, and everything I need to fulfill my purpose is being supplied."

"Do you believe it's possible for you to have an unlimited income from running your own business?"

Charles thought for a moment before replying "Yes!"

"Then let's say that together!" Suzanne said excitedly.

Together they chanted "Yes, yes, yes....!" as they focused on Charles' vision, with Suzanne riding him like a cow-girl.

Just as they were about to climax, a sudden surge of sexual energy rose up their spines, bypassing the lower four chakras, heading straight to their crown chakras…

Charles orgasmed without ejaculating and a spiritual seed was planted *in her*.

"I can see it!" Suzanne exclaimed as the gateway opened.

Neither of them even realized it was a New Moon.

'Thoughts impregnated with Love become invincible'

~ Charles F. Haanel

The Joy of Co-Creating

Suzanne and Charles began working on setting up their business together. They kept Suzanne's logo but changed the slogan to *'Touching the Heart...through Art!'* While Charles was at work, Suzanne wrote a Business Plan based on what he had shared with her, leaving him to do the Cashflow Forecast and Budgeting Plan at the weekend.

With Charles' accountancy skills and Suzanne's admin skills, it didn't take long to have everything in place. He paid for a website to be built and they worked together to create products using his artwork and her poetry. Later on, they would add to the range by 'buying in' artwork and poetry from others in their community.

It all came together very nicely!

Micah and Elijah also got involved in the business.

At ages 12 and 14, they were old enough to take personal responsibility for certain jobs. Micah was assigned the job of helping Suzanne with any paperwork, filing and setting up templates for invoices and letters, and Elijah had the job of helping Charles with the bookkeeping. Charles started teaching Elijah basic accounting with a view to him working in the office when he was older.

The boys seemed happy that their mum and Charles were back together; they had missed him more than they had let on to their mum. The four of them carried on where they had left off – the only difference was that they now included Ebony on alternate weekends. Micah and Elijah adored her, and enjoyed playing the 'big brother' role.

Over the next year, things progressed at lightning speed.

By combining *Faith, Love* and *Sex*, the irresistible force of the Law of Attraction was formed. Suzanne was a force to be reckoned with on her own, but when she joined forces with Charles, they became immutable – there was nothing they couldn't accomplish! Suzanne had written inspirational poems for each of Charles' paintings, and designed posters for each of them in Photoshop. They were soon earning enough money from their business for Charles to be able to work part-time, so he could focus on painting more. They advertised in various newspapers and magazines, and took stands at events where Suzanne was performing, to promote her poetry CD and books, along with their greeting cards and prints. All their products complimented each other.

Suzanne had also set up a website where people could listen to her poetry, which helped sell her CD and Book of Lyrics.

By visualizing their desires in detail, speaking *life* into them, and taking positive *action*, Charles and Suzanne were surprised at how quickly things were beginning to manifest.

Suzanne was grateful to be with someone like Charles. Two like-minds seemed better than one.

They developed a following of repeat customers, who in turn recommended their products to friends and family. Orders flooded in from all over the world.

Within a few short months, they had found the perfect location to set up shop and offices, right on the busy high street in Brixton.

'When LOVE and SKILL work together,
Expect a MIRACLE'
~ John Ruskin

Year Eight: In Deep

Within the space of one short year since launching their business, Charles and Suzanne made their first million. It wasn't about the money for them, they were on a mission of Love; the positive energy they put into their work simply came back to them in the form of money.

They had a set 'formula for success' which they repeated every day, which went something like this: *"I give thanks to Infinite Intelligence which inspires me daily. I easily tap into the field of Infinite Wisdom through my subconscious mind, where all knowledge and possibilities lie. I am One with my Creator and all living things; I am here to serve humanity; I help create the greatest success and good for all humankind; as I help others, I help myself. I am connected to all the right people and resources to help me fulfill my destiny and higher purpose. Through my work, I remind my Self and others that we are One with the Great Creator and each other... As I share my wholeness, it comes back to me in a multitude of ways. I am unlimited, I am abundant, I am fruitful; I spread LOVE through creativity, and whatever I put my hands to prospers! And it is so!"*

It was their *combined* forces of thoughts, words and actions that helped to catapult their business into success so quickly – and this was just the beginning! Their plan was to build a large Black-owned Corporation that would not only help them gain financial independence, but would help others in their community who had been impoverished by 'the system' to benefit from their God-given talents.

After paying off their mortgage and taxes, they looked for ways to make their money grow and share their good fortune, so they began planting money-seeds. Charles set up a Benevolence Fund where he put 10% of all their profits. This would help those who couldn't find work to set up their own businesses, learn new skills, and use their natural God-given talents for their financial benefit too. This was one way they could 'give back' to their community.

They also began buying-in original artwork and poetry which enabled the contributing artists and poets from their community to earn an income from their creativity, while at the same time it helped them to increase the diversity of their designs. As their range of products increased, so did their reputation for producing high-quality, inspirational, motivational greeting cards and prints using original artwork and poetry, which left an indelible impression on their recipients.

Neither Charles nor Suzanne believed in 'profit without purpose' and both were clear that their business wasn't just about making money; its purpose was to help heal their community, and the world.

Building an Empire

Their high street shop was an immediate success; their products sold to walk-in customers as well as to people all over the world, via their website. They employed two staff to work in the office, and another three to work in the shop below. Before recruiting, Charles and Suzanne sat down together and wrote out Job Descriptions for each of the positions they wanted to fill. They discussed what type of person would best be suited to each job, and used their knowledge of Numerology and Astrology to decide what *type* of person would best fit each position.

Once they were clear about the type of person they wanted to fill each position, they then advertised, believing they would *attract* the right people. And they did.

Their employees were selected by their birthdates, gender (as they wanted to achieve an equal balance of masculine and feminine energy in the office), heritage, whether Charles and Suzanne 'took to their spirit' when they came for interview, whether they were spiritually-minded, and lastly by their skill level, since they were prepared to train the right person for each role.

Being on the same wavelength mentally made a big difference not only to the smooth running of their business, but to their home life. There were no big arguments, no long silences (unless of course, they were meditating) and there was generally a good vibration in and around them both. This feeling of unity flowed from their home into the office, providing a peaceful and nurturing working environment.

They agreed to focus on the business during the week, but every other weekend when they had the children, they would switch off. That was Family Time. The only exception they made to this rule was if Suzanne had a paid performance to do, in which case they would all go as a family, or if it was too late in the evening, Charles would stay home with the children, while Suzanne went with a girlfriend or two.

They agreed that even though they were now living together, they should still take time out individually to continue their *personal* development, so that when they came together, they would be stronger.

Suzanne trusted Charles implicitly. Even when he returned home late from visiting Ebony during the week, she never questioned him. She had by now learnt not to entertain worst case scenarios, imagining the things she *didn't* want to happen. The more she trusted him, the more he was determined not to break it.

Occasionally, they would reach a point where they both had a build-up of sexual energy, and relished the weekends when they didn't have the children. Every other Saturday evening to Sunday was their special time together, and they looked forward to them with anticipation.

Her Own YONI-verse!

It was Charles who taught Suzanne about the sacredness of her Yoni – in fact, he even named it for her.

He told her that her Yoni was the milky way to her personal solar system – her Yoniverse, and that he, the Black Man, was the gatekeeper.

He explained that the man plants the seed, but it's the *womban* who nurtures the seed, and brings forth life. He said babies are *souls* that come from the spiritual realm through the *womb*man, into this physical dimension – but her womb also has the power to create *other* things, not just babies. Suzanne didn't have a clue what he was talking about so she meditated, focusing her attention on her Yoni and womb. Gaining *in*sight, she discovered that her womb was a *powerful dynamic creative force* similar to the universe. It was able to bring forth *anything* from the Unseen Realm into the physical, and her Yoni was the *gateway* that connected the inner womb of gestation with the outer world of human life. The liquid that came from her Yoni held within it a strong transference of power; it is therefore sacred. Charles was aware of this, which was why he happily and gratefully engaged in cunnilingus. He told her that whenever he opened her gateway and their fluids infused together, he was *also* taking on the ability to bring things from the spiritual realm into the physical, which is why he had a deep love and respect for his Queen/goddess and the *inher*ent powers of her Yoni and womb.

Suzanne did some research online and discovered that some Eastern cultures believe that if a man focuses on the Yoni while meditating upon his desires, it has the power to grant his wishes – but this all depended upon the woman the Yoni juice was coming from. If a woman was *aware* of her powers, her flower would naturally emit a 'fragrance' which provided the attraction inherent in it.

Suzanne was grateful to have Charles as her King. She realized that many gods and Kings didn't understand the importance of finding their goddesses and Queens, for the gateway that leads to paradise with*in her*. And many goddesses didn't 'innerstand' the power they had *inher*ent within them.

All men are gods, but not all men are *Kings*. To reach Kingly status, the god must raise his level of consciousness to his *crown* chakra, located at the top of his head. This is the same for the goddess; for her to become a *Queen*, she must also raise her level of consciousness to her *crown* chakra. If a god has reached his highest level of consciousness and becomes a *King*, he has the ability to use his 'key' to open the goddess's gateway during their Sex Ritual, even if she isn't a Queen. Unfortunately, it doesn't work the same for the goddess; unless the god has become a King, the two can only go as far as *his* level of consciousness. If he hasn't reached a high enough level of consciousness, he may not be able to open her gateway for them to be able to bring things from the non-physical realm into the physical. *It is therefore imperative that all gods raise their level of consciousness to their crown chakra, and become Kings.*

Once a god has achieved Kingly status, he should then find his goddess or Queen. Without her feminine energy, it would be difficult for him to manifest his desires on the physical plane, since the gateway to bringing things from the spiritual realm into the physical world is found *in her*.

In finding, protecting and serving her well, she will in return love, nurture, protect and heal him, opening the gate to infinite possibilities.

It is therefore necessary for the Black Man to understand that before he can lead, he must first allow his Queen to sit on her throne...in allowing her to do so, his own immortality will be heightened.

'Above the yoni is a small and subtle flame,
whose form is intelligence'.
~ Shiva Samhita, 15th century

Melanin in the Skin

Suzanne was now able to only work part-time in the business. This enabled her to achieve a more balanced lifestyle of devoting more time to her writing, research for her writing, and family. Most of what she needed to do could be done from home anyway, like choosing which poems submitted were going to be used for the greeting cards. So she left Charles to manage the day-to-day running of the business, only checking the books and financial reports with him on a monthly basis, and attending the office every Monday morning to do staff appraisals. So with Charles in the office and the boys at school and college during the day, she had more time for her Self.

It's funny, because now that she could afford to 'shop 'til she dropped' she had no desire to do so. Designer clothes, expensive handbags and hundreds of shoes could never validate her worth. She much preferred to get her clothes made-to-fit with fabrics that she had chosen, anyway. She wasn't willing to be a walking advertisement for high street brands.

She attended yoga classes twice a week, went for a steam/sauna once a week, exercised daily at home, and spent the rest of the time focusing on her writing. Today she was doing research, and became fascinated when she learnt about what makes Black people Black: MELANIN.

This biochemical pigment, she discovered, was actually a *blessing* to people of colour!

She learnt that Melanin is secreted from a small gland in the middle of the brain called the Pineal Gland, also referred to as the 'third eye'. The Pineal Gland is a known link between the *physical* and *spiritual* worlds, and provides the connection to higher consciousness, creativity, spiritual awareness and being able to manifest in the physical world. An *activated* Pineal Gland creates a stronger connection between the individual and the Creator, increases the body's ability to hold more light, and expands clarity.

Brown to black in color, Melanin is more evident in darker-skinned people and Caucasians with brown eyes and hair. It plays an important part in the function of the brain and nervous system, and is said to help elevate consciousness; it is the thing that makes Melanin-dominated people more spiritual. In dark-skinned people, Melanin is concentrated in the genitalia. Suzanne wondered if there was any particular reason for this.

She learned that Melanin can also be found in nature e.g. plants, springs, lakes, soil, animals and in the air (ether) as well as the dark matter that permeates the universe. It is therefore Melanin that causes a person to be more in tune with nature. Suzanne considered that perhaps that was why those who were Melanin-deficient were causing the most amount of damage to Mother Earth.

She also learnt that Melanin provides a natural barrier from harmful UV rays reducing the risk of skin cancer, and because it maintains moisture in the outer layers of the skin, it prevents long-term signs of aging, which is why dark-skinned people generally look younger than their age.

The darker you are, the more Melanin you have.

Melanin also has the ability to *absorb* all types of energy including ultraviolet rays, electromagnetic waves and music, and turn them into *energy* for the body to use. She smiled as she thought '*that* must be the reason why we like to play our music so loud!'

She wondered how it had been possible for those who lacked Melanin to convince everyone else that the lighter or *whiter* you are, the more superior you are!

Suzanne also learnt that Melanin is kept healthy by the sun's energy, and by what is taken into the body through the *mouth*, *eyes*, *ears* and *skin*. When a Melanin-dominant person is deprived of natural sunlight (vitamin D deficient), eats unhealthily e.g. junk food, listens to music with un-natural frequencies, and watches 'programs' on the 'tell-lie-vision', it has an adverse effect on their psyche. Skin-bleaching creams also affect the mind, since they go into the bloodstream through the skin.

Suzanne could see this all being played out in her community, and it was having a devastating effect on the psyche of her people, causing them to act in ways contrary to their true nature. However, in Dr Llaila Afrika's book *'Melanin: What Makes Black People Black'* he explained that vitamin B helps keep Melanin clean. He explained that a natural diet for a Melanin dominant person is the food that Mother Nature provides; fruit, vegetables, herbs, water, nuts, seeds, beans, sprouts etc. Depending on your Blood Type, meat should or should not be consumed, and should not make up the largest part of your diet.

Up to this point, Suzanne would occasionally 'treat' the children to takeaways, but now she was becoming more aware of the effects of food on the brain, she decided to cut out unhealthy foods like burgers, fried chicken and chips, and incorporated more foods provided by Mother Nature in her cooking. When she told 'the family' she was going to stop buying meat and include more fruit and veg in their diets, there was practically an uproar! The boys said they needed meat to get their protein. Even Charles said he had to have chicken. So she agreed to cut out red meat but continue buying chicken, opting for organic rather than the processed chemically-filled ones. It was hard trying to get the boys to eat greens or seeds straight off the plate, but she found that if she blended them and added them in to the sauces or gravy, they hardly noticed.

From Suzanne's point of view, there seemed to be a psychological war going on with Melanated people. She believed the issue wasn't just because of the richness of their *skin*, but the richness of their *land*.

This brought Suzanne right back to Adam and Eve. She'd read somewhere that the Garden of Eden was in Africa; it had been scientifically proven that the hue-man race originated in Africa, so surely Adam and Eve must have been *African*? 'They certainly wouldn't have been walking around naked in Europe!' she thought.

On her Black History course, she had learnt that Cauc*asians* originated from Nubians (Blacks). From Nubians came Asians, and from Asians came Caucasians. The process took millions of years, with the migration of Africans into Europe, surviving the Ice Age, the lack of sunlight and cold environment calcified their Pineal Gland. This caused them to become Melanin deficient and cold in nature. In Suzanne's mind however, this still didn't account for the change in their eye colors or hair textures. Perhaps there was more than one type of Original Nubian, she reasoned. Maybe there were Nubians with *straight* hair and Nubians with *woolly* hair? There were even theories that Cauc*asians* evolved from Albinos (Nubians born with no melanin in their skin). They had been ostracized from their community because of their 'leprosy', and had migrated to Europe where they ended up living in the Caucasian Mountains becoming 'cavemen'. Suzanne wondered if this was the reason why the Black race had been revenged by Europeans. 'There has to be a *reason* why they hate, or *fear* us so much,' she believed.

Suzanne wondered how Europeans managed to turn everything upside down, making themselves to be the superior race, stealing the inheritance of her people, and claiming Nubians were the minority.

She recalled the way Europeans had treated Africans during the Transatlantic Slave Trade, as if they were less than animals. They had justified their actions by saying that 'niggers' had no soul, when it is *Melanin* that makes a person spiritual. They had in fact demonstrated their *own* lack of spirituality by treating other hue-man beings in such a barbaric way, with no conscience.

When Suzanne meditated on the word 'Spiritual' it was revealed to her as;

'Spirit-ritual'

...in other words, to be 'Spiritual' is to perform ceremonial *ritual with Spirit.* And whose tradition is it to perform rituals? Africans.

Yet Africans have been told that their traditions of making offerings to their ancestors and to Mother Nature were wrong; they were given a new religion, which acknowledged and made offerings to a new, white god. This new religion cut them off from knowledge of their true Self, power and spirituality.

Suzanne wondered how her ancestors would be feeling if they were looking down and watching their descendants. Would those who had shed their blood be happy to see their descendents although *physically* free, were still in *mental* slavery, and worse still, didn't even realize it?

'The worst type of slave is the slave
who believes he is free' ~ Harriet Tubman

The Black Womban

The more Suzanne realized her own divinity, the more she carried her Self with virtue, dignity, grace and Self-discipline.

She discovered that the Black Womban carries The Mother of All Genes –Mitochondria DNA; mDNA is only found in *women* and since it has been *scientifically proven* that all races can trace their DNA back to the Black Womban, she is rightfully known as the Mother of All Nations.

She also learnt that ancient African cultures were matrilineal, meaning that one's lineage was traced through the *mother,* not the father. Women were the most important element of society; queens didn't become queens because they were the daughters or wives of kings, they had queens that succeeded queens. And **inher**itances weren't passed down from the father, they were passed down through the *mother*;

In Ancient Kemet (renamed Egypt by the Greeks) Pharaohs often ruled equally with their queens. It was the custom among Nubians that when a king died and only left a son, if his *sister* had a son, his nephew would reign instead of his own son. In other words, *inher*itance came through the *woman*, not the man.

Yet somehow this had all been turned upside down. The Divine Feminine had been removed from the Holy Trinity, and the first woman (Eve) was accused of causing the downfall of humankind, which had resulted in women generally throughout the bible and other religious texts being forced to become subordinate to men. The genealogy of Jesus and other prominent men in the bible didn't even acknowledge women. It was even said that the Gospel of Mary, who was the closest 'disciple' to Jesus, was omitted from the scriptures.

Suzanne learned that the original Christian cross originated in Ancient Kemet and was called the Ankh cross. It had a loop at the top which represented the *womb*, and an elongated bottom part which represented the *phallus*. The line in the middle symbolized the two coming together to create *Life*. The Ankh was a symbol of life.

When the religion was hijacked by Europeans, it became a *patriarchal* religion, the loop (representing the Feminine Principle) was removed and replaced with another (smaller) phallus. It then became the symbol of *death* instead of Life. Throughout various forms of religion, the masculine energy became dominant, forming a patriarchal mindset which allowed men to dominate women. This masculine energy grew until it not only dominated religion, but politics, law, education, business and agriculture, causing extensive damage to Mother Earth and her inhabitants. The *cause* of all the problems in the world today was the lack of Feminine Energy, which had created an imbalance; an equal balance of Masculine and Feminine energies creates *equilibrium*.

Suzanne remembered what she had been inspired to write a while back regarding the Feminine Energy rising naturally, and considered that those in power were trying to harness it by turning men *feminine*, and women *masculine*.

She decided to write a blog about it.

She put that women are generally more intuitive than men and more in touch with their *feelings*, while men tend to act out of *ego* rather than *emotion*. Their need for power, status, and control causes them to oppress the one thing they cannot live without – the woman.

To be fair, it wasn't *all* men who had this mindset; it was a small group of white supremacy elitists who wanted to rule the world. The only way they could achieve their goal was by causing the Black race to forget who they are and the power they have innately. They knew that when the Black Man and Woman come together in a high state of consciousness, they can accomplish anything, so their strategy was to break down their psyche using the things the loved the most; music, entertainment and food – especially chicken.

As Suzanne sat thinking about all of this she heard the key turn in the door, and in walked in Charles. She glanced at the time; it was nearly 10.30pm. She hadn't realized it was so late; the boys had already gone to bed.

"Hi babes, what are you doing?" he asked as he hung up his jacket.

"Well I thought I'd have a go at writing an article for a new blog I'm starting, so I'm just doing some research for it," she answered cheerfully.

"Oh! What's it about?"

"Adam and Eve."

"Okay…" he sat down beside her.

"What about Adam and Eve?"

"Well, the whole Adam and Eve story never really sat well with me. I didn't like the way Eve was blamed for tempting Adam to eat the forbidden fruit which brought a curse on the whole of the human race, and ever since then, women have been oppressed by men, especially in religions. So I decided to write an article to show how the story is flawed."

"Yes, well don't forget to mention the X and Y chromosomes."

"What's that got to do with it?" Suzanne asked with a puzzled look on her face.

"Well you just said it your Self – the *story* of Adam and Eve. I'm sure we've had this conversation before babe? Adam and Eve aren't literal people, they're *metaphors!*"

"Yes I know…but for what?"

"I'm starving, can I eat first?" He knew this was going to take some time.

"Your dinner's in the oven honey. The salad's in the fridge."

Charles headed for the kitchen and seeing his covered plate of food in the oven, set the timer and switched it on. Returning to the living room, he carried on the conversation.

"If I remember correctly, Adam is a metaphor for the XY chromosome and Eve for the XX chromosome."

"Really…Where did you learn that?" she half-laughed sarcastically.

"Think about it; the bible says Eve was made from Adam's rib, right?"

"Yes…"

"Well look at the X and Y letters," Charles grabbed a piece of paper and pen and jotted the letters down.

"Okay…" Suzanne watched intently. She loved learning from him.

"Now the XX is a female chromosome, and the XY is a male chromosome. Two XX's make a girl child, and an XY makes a boy child. You following this?" he continued to draw the letters on the paper to prove his point.

"Yes…"

"Well according to the bible, God took a 'rib' from Adam to create Eve, right?"

"That's right…."

"Now watch this; Adam is a male, so he must be an XY, right? If you take away a 'rib' from the X or the Y, you'll either end up with YY, or XV (he scribbles out the bottom right branch of the 'X' and the bottom part of the 'Y' to illustrate). But if you take away a 'rib' from the XX, what do you end up with?"

"Oh my god, XY!...but what does this prove?" Suzanne looked up at him, still perplexed.

"That it is *scientifically impossible* for women to be created from men. Men come from women, women do not come from men! So many things are hidden in the English language, and this is just one of them."

Suzanne sat in astonishment. But why was she even shocked by this revelation? She suddenly remembered her poem *"I Am What I WILL to Be!"* Some parts of the poem had come as a 'download', where she felt all she was doing was taking dictation. She believed the ancestors spoke through her sometimes. In a part of the poem she had written *'The ancestors speak through me, so listen carefully...'* She remembered waiting to see what they were going to say.

The next lines were;

"I am the Original Woman – I was here first!
***MAN** came out of **WOMAN**,*
***HE** came out of **SHE**,*
MALE** came out of FE**MALE
*and **HE** came out of **HE**R,*
See it's hidden in the words!"

She thought about how far she and her sisters were from re-member-ing themselves, and wondered how they were ever going to regain their positions in the world.

The timer went off on the oven.

Be the Source

Suzanne, Charles, and their three children spent a lovely weekend together. On the Friday night, Charles had suggested they go to the cinema, but Suzanne had told him to take the boys, as little Ebony wouldn't be interested in anything they wanted to watch, plus she would only fall asleep. While they were out, Suzanne corn-rowed Ebony's long, bushy hair and seasoned the fish for dinner the next day.

On the Saturday they held their usual stand at the monthly *Kemet Market* where they sold their products. Suzanne performed, and afterwards enjoyed walking around with Ebony looking at all the other stalls. She stocked up on natural hair and skin care products, and also bought some beautiful African-inspired soft furnishings and carvings for their home, some jewelry for herself, and a little African print dress for Ebony. Whatever money they had made on their stand, Suzanne spent it supporting the other Black businesses!

On the Sunday they entertained family members; Suzanne's two sisters came over with their children and her mum, and Charles picked up his mum and brought her over too. Each family member brought a dish or dessert, while Suzanne cooked the rice and peas, organic chicken, and salads. The boys played video games with their cousins, and the adults caught up with the drama in each other's lives. Before they knew it, it was time for Ebony to go home. Everyone kissed her goodbye, and since Charles decided to take his mum back home too, the rest of the family started getting ready to leave as well.

When everyone had left, Suzanne sat thinking about how great her life was now. She had the perfect partner (for her), two lovely boys who gave her no trouble, a successful business, an adorable step-daughter, and they lacked for nothing.

Charles was by no means perfect, but by focusing on the positive things about him instead of the negative, she seemed to be able to draw more of that out. The more things she found to love about Charles, the deeper her love for him grew. It worked the same with the boys; she found that if she rewarded them with praise anytime they did anything 'good', they wanted to do more good things.

Looking back at her life, she recalled how not so long ago, she had been struggling to make ends meet, waiting for 'The One', and experiencing mental frustrations because she believed she needed more in life to be happy. It was only when she learnt to 'let go' of all her striving to be, do and have, and learnt to just 'follow her bliss' that things began to flow her way. She had stopped subconsciously telling her Self "I don't deserve this" or "I'm not worthy" and simply allowed her good to come to her, and received it gratefully.

She had realized her life was not about acquiring 'things' but to simply *experience* who she was, and that was when life began to open up for her. She began to feel joyful just because. She began to love her Self unconditionally for the first time. The secret was in learning that she was not here to acquire anything, but to *give*. She had learnt that if she desired to experience more love in her life, she had to *give* more love. If she wished to have more money, she was to demonstrate that she already *had* it, and give. If she aspired to have more wisdom, she had to share the wisdom she already *had*. She was surprised at how quickly things had begun to change for her once she began to 'be the Source'.

When Suzanne began showing her divine Self by demonstrating Who She Is Right Now, there was nothing else for her to do. Instead of believing that she was 'born in sin' and that she had to achieve some state of perfection, she believed that she came *into* this world in a state of perfection. Every time she looked into a baby's face, she knew this was true. Now all she had to do was simply *experience* who she was:

"I am loving. I am peaceful. I am joyful. I am patient. I am kind. I am whole, perfect and complete, in each moment called NOW"

It was only when she began showing more love to her Self and to others that love came back to her in abundance. It was only when she chose to be happy all the time, that experiences came to *keep* her in that state of bliss. When she decided to remain in perfect health, she began to learn about the right types of food to eat and exercises to do to help her stay healthy. So whenever she found herself wishing for more, or wanting more of anything, she would ask her Self "I wonder if there's anyone else out there who wants more of this too?" She would then choose to be the Source in *their* lives; it could be a friend, family member or complete stranger. She would think to her Self 'What if I had *so much*, that I could afford to give some away?' It didn't matter what it might be, she began giving away anything and everything that she thought she didn't have enough of. Whether it was patience, love, wisdom, compassion, money or friendship; when she wanted some, she found other people who wanted more of the same and gave it to them. The feeling of giving to another and making *their* life better gave her such an energy lift, that her whole life purpose changed. She no longer began trying to get things for herself, but began having things so that she might give them away!

She discovered that the more she gave, the more she received. As she began to fulfill her life's purpose of *giving*, the universe began to open up an unlimited supply, because the universe knew that there were a lot of people now depending on her to be the Source of it.

Sharing the Love

Even though she and Charles were now affluent, they didn't see themselves as better off than others in their community; as far as Suzanne was concerned, they were all in this together. She wanted to do whatever she could to help her brothers and sisters rise above their circumstances, starting with the way they thought about themselves. When they raised their levels of Self-esteem, Self-belief, and raised their vibrations, they would be better able to progress in life.

Luckily for her, Charles felt the same.

Being a Nubian brother, as he preferred to be called, Charles had experienced first-hand how difficult it was to navigate through 'the system' and come out whole. From school, college, university, to finding work, he'd had to fight the subliminal messages which suggested to him that he would never be as good as his white counterparts. But he had received a strong foundation in the home, and was able to fight the system all the way – to the top. Now he was in a position to make a difference.

Charles was sympathetic towards his brothers who were still fighting the system daily. He had often seen images on the tell-lie-vision of angry black men, or heard stories of them being jailed for dealing drugs. What had *not* been explained was how they had been forced into these positions due to a lack of jobs, and to jobs not paying them enough money to support themselves *and* their children. He empathized with his brothers; what were they supposed to do? Of course they were angry – at a system which was against them!

Suzanne empathized for her sisters who longed to meet a Nubian brother but couldn't find one. All the media portrayed was negative images which made them believe that their brothers were either in prison, unemployed, gay, violent, in mental institutions or with white women, so you might as well 'Try Something New.' If all sisters were to start believing this, where would that leave the Black race in generations to come?

And the message being sent out through mainstream media to her brothers was that their sisters were angry, bitter, unattractive, h**s and b****es, only good for sex, and that white women were prettier, had nicer hair, and would give them better-looking children and 'status'. They didn't take into consideration that the women offered to them were of lower class, not desirable to the elitists themselves.

Suzanne and Charles discussed what they could do to help their people heal, and agreed to start putting on their own events, aimed at helping Black singles to meet, and Black couples to stay together. Now that they had achieved love, peace and harmony within their *own* relationship, they were better able to spread it to their community.

Year Nine: Another Level

It had been over a week since Charles and Suzanne last made love, but they had been so busy, they had hardly even noticed.
Charles was in the office when he received a text from Suzanne;

"Tomorrow's the night X" it said.

Charles smiled.

"The night for what?" he texted back.

"It's a surprise ;-)"

She knew she had to give him advanced notice because he wasn't as spontaneous as she was, although he sometimes made the effort to be. Tomorrow would be Saturday night and it was their free weekend without the children. She didn't really have anything planned; she'd just sent the text on impulse – now she had to think of something!

She called her hairdresser to see if she could get an appointment for the following afternoon, and also arranged to have a manicure and pedicure. Tomorrow was going to be a busy day, so she did the food shopping, and returned home in time to help the boys get ready to go to their dad's for the weekend.

"So what do you have planned?" Charles asked the following morning.

"We're going out this evening," Suzanne responded casually.

"Oh! Okay, where?"

"It's a surprise, remember?" Suzanne smiled mischievously.

"Okaaaay...so what's the dress code?"

"Traditional."

"Wouldn't you rather have an early night in?" he asked with a glint in his eye.

"Mmmmm....there'll be plenty of time for that when we get back!" Suzanne replied, jumping out of bed.

"Hey, where're you going so early?"

"To the gym for a quick sauna and steam, then I have an appointment at my hairdressers!" she replied, unwrapping her silk scarf from her head.

"Oh alright...I might as well come with you then."

Charles had been hoping they were going to have a lie-in. He stumbled out of bed and dragged on a pair of jogging bottoms. He still looked good, but he'd put on a bit of weight around the middle as he wasn't going to the gym as regularly as before. On top of that, he was eating better. A work-out would be good for him.

On the way to the gym, Suzanne informed Charles that they had to be ready to leave home that evening by 6.30pm. They agreed to meet back at home by 5.30pm the latest.

Charles did his workout then came straight back home, had a shower and spent the rest of the day relaxing, reading and sleeping. He'd had a busy week at the office, and was grateful for the peace and quiet.

Suzanne arrived back home just before 5pm. Charles greeted her at the door with a hug, kiss and a stiffie.

"Put that thing away!" she laughed.

"Come on, we've got time for a quickie before we go," he murmured in her ear.

"No we don't, look at my hair – I'm not messing it up!"

"It's lovely..." Charles said, turning her around in a full circle.

"I had my nails done, too!" She showed him her French-manicured fingernails.

"Mmmm...nice!" he commented. But really he only had one thing on his mind.

"Right, I'm going to have a quick shower and then we'll be off – are you hungry?" she asked.

"Starving."

He didn't know what she had planned, so he'd been saving his appetite since lunchtime.

"Good, because there's food where we're going."

"What kind of food?"

"Oh...you'll see."

Suzanne carefully placed a plastic cap over her hair and had a quick shower. When she re-entered the bedroom Charles asked "What are you wearing?"

He always liked to match the colour of his shirt or tie with her dress when they were going out together. They even had a few matching outfits. Suzanne walked into her wardrobe and chose one of them; a Vintage 70's Dashiki Tunic dress with intricate, bold patterns. Laying it carefully on the bed, she unwrapped her towel and began oiling her body. Charles stood watching with a huge bulge in his pants as she lovingly caressed the herbal oil over her skin, admiring herself in the mirror. Seeing his reflection behind her she turned and asked "Aren't you going to get ready?"

Walking towards her he replied "Yes, in a minute."

He took the bottle from her and began oiling her back.

"Oh, thanks!"

He pressed himself against her from behind so she could feel his hard-on.

"Charles...." she warned, "...If we don't hurry up, we're going to be late!"

"Okay okay," and like a scolded school-boy, he sulkily made his way to the bathroom.

When he returned from his cold shower Suzanne had already dressed, and was carefully applying her make-up. She only wore enough to enhance her features, not to change them completely. She applied lime green and gold eye-shadow to match the colors in her dress, then applied red lip-gloss to accentuate her lips. She placed small hairclips with little red roses attached to them to jazz up her hair.

"You look stunning!" he commented.

"Thank you darling!"

Charles went to his walk-in wardrobe and chose his matching dashiki top, chino jeans, a brown belt and shoes. He un-wrapped the cellophane sheet from the dry-cleaners, laid them on the bed and pulled his tight white boxers on.

"I'm thinking about starting a martial arts class," he announced as he got dressed.

"Really? Which one?"

"Well I was coming out of the tube at Seven Sisters and someone handed me a flyer for Mashufaa classes."

"Mashufaa? Is that a form of martial arts?"

"Yes, it's *African* martial arts. It sounds really good, I'm thinking of taking the boys for the free taster session next Friday. D'you think they'd want to come?"

"I'm sure they'd love to!"

"The only thing is, the classes are on a Friday evening so if we *do* start going regularly, you'll have to look after Ebony – is that okay?"

"That's fine by me – it's a good swop actually!"

Dance in Trance

They arrived back home in high spirits from the evening's entertainment.

Suzanne had taken Charles to an African restaurant called 'Black to Africa' where they had sat on mats on the floor eating pounded yam, egusi soup and other African delicacies with their hands, while watching the live African bands playing. The Kora player had been the highlight of the evening for Suzanne.

The djembe drumming, African dancing and singing had gone straight to the core of their beings, reminding them of their roots.

They had bought the band's CD and played it all the way back home, and by now, Suzanne was beginning to feel something awakening that had been buried deep within her DNA. Taking off their shoes at the door, they headed straight for their bedroom. Suzanne brought the CD with her, put it in the stereo, and pressed the 'play' button before lighting some candles. Charles took off his dashiki and jeans and sat on the bed, watching her enter her wardrobe again. He knew Suzanne well enough by now to know that he was in for a treat. He thought perhaps she was going to re-appear in some sexy lingerie, so wasn't mentally prepared for what he saw when she *did* finally emerge.

Suzanne seemed to have transformed her Self into some kind of Exotic Dancer/Sexual Healer/Temple-Priestess. She was wearing a white see-through flowy dress-thing which plunged into a V-shape at the neck-line right down to her navel. It was fitted at the waist, with long, embroidered sleeves. The skirting dropped in multiple folds down to her ankles. He could see right through it – and she wasn't wearing anything underneath; her nipples jutted through the sheer material, begging for his attention. Around her forehead, she wore a gold chain with various symbols hanging from it – he'd never seen it before. She was barefooted, showing off her pedicure.

As she began moving her body to the rhythm of the drum beats still playing on the CD, the spirit of her ancestors seemed to take over. With arms swaying like leaves in the breeze, she twisted and twirled, gyrating her hips in a sensual, sexual manner, as she sent forth her Inner Womb Message. The whole atmosphere in the room changed.

Charles became aroused, moved almost to tears, and concerned all at the same time. The look on her face was unlike he'd ever seen before. She wasn't focused on him; she looked as if she was in a trance, totally caught up in the moment. The elongated shadows on the walls behind her created by the candlelight looked like spirits dancing along with her. Perhaps she was calling on the spirits of her ancestors...or was it the Holy Spirit? He couldn't tell – all he knew was that it was a force of Love. He felt at peace as he watched her; he'd never seen her move that way before. 'Where did she learn to dance like that?' He wondered.

When she had finished, she gracefully walked towards the bed where Charles was sitting propped up on one elbow.

"Is there no end to your talents?" he asked, awestruck.

"I can do whatever I put my *mind* to!" she replied, smiling as she sat next to him on the bed.

Charles stared at her intently as he watched her come back to herself. As they sat in silence Charles appeared to be in deep thought. He finally asked "If there was anywhere in the world that you could go, where would it be?"

Without having to think about it, Suzanne responded "Egypt!"

"Mmmm...." Charles pondered, as if in agreement. Then tracing a finger over the lump where her nipple was protruding through the dress, he looked her in the eye and asked "Can I take this off now?"

Suzanne stood up and held her arms up so Charles could lift off the dress. Noticing that the music on the CD was still playing, Charles walked over, started it from the beginning again and turned it up loud. He removed his boxers and socks as he made his way back to the bed.

Both of them were by now bursting with passion.

That night when they made love, it was as if all the heavens, God, the angels and their ancestors were all watching and cheering them on. It felt like nothing they had ever experienced before. Suzanne cried from the bottom of her heart, and afterwards, Charles clung on to her for ages, remaining inside her long after he had ejaculated, as if not wanting to break the newly-created bond between them.

Announcement

A few days later, Charles arrived home from the office early.

"Oh! I wasn't expecting you home so soon!" Suzanne greeted him with a kiss.

"Hi Charles!" Elijah and Micah greeted him too.

"Hi boys, what are you up to?"

The boys were sitting around the dining table.

"Just homework," Elijah said.

"Okay, I'll wait 'til you've finished then."

The boys looked at each other before responding in unison "We've finished!"

"Oh no you haven't!" Suzanne interrupted.

Then turning to Charles asked "Why, what's up?"

"Oh nothing...I just have an announcement to make, but it can wait until later."

"Are you sure?"

"Of course. What's for dinner?"

"I haven't even started cooking yet! I seasoned some fish earlier, I was just going to sauté some potatoes and make a salad to go with it, is that okay?"

"Sounds good to me!"

As Suzanne headed for the kitchen, Charles followed her.

"Did you tell the boys about the Mashufaa class this Friday?" he asked her.

"Oh, I forgot! Why don't you ask them now? I'm sure they'll be up for it."

Charles returned to the living room and told the boys about the class. Of course they were eager to go; they loved doing activities with him. Returning to the kitchen, Charles asked Suzanne if she needed any help.

"No I'm fine, it won't take long...then we can hear your announcement!" she said smiling at him as she wrapped the bream.

After dinner, the boys cleared the table and loaded the dishwasher.

As they all sat around the table, Charles placed two tickets down and said "Suzanne, pack your bags, I'm taking you away!"

"Away? Where?" Suzanne asked, not quite believing what he was saying.

"To Egypt of course!"

"Egypt? But...*how*?" she asked, still in disbelief.

"What do you mean, how?" Charles questioned, amused; "You have a passport, don't you?"

"Yes...but what about the boys? And Ebony? And the business!"

"Don't worry about all that, it's all been arranged. The boys are going to stay at Janice's for the week, and I've already told Maria I'll be away for a week...I'll make it up to Ebony when we get back."

"Yes but...I don't feel comfortable about leaving them behind..."

"Mum it's okay," Elijah offered, "We'll be fine."

Charles had already discussed it with them fully before he booked the tickets. It was their idea to stay at their Auntie Janice's, so they could spend some time with their cousins. When Charles had explained to Janice why he wanted to take Suzanne on holiday, she was happy to have the boys. They were teenagers now; all they needed was feeding.

"Okay let's do it like this," Charles suggested; "We'll take this holiday together, then we'll organize another family holiday after the boys have finished their exams. How's that?"

Suzanne closed her eyes and listened to her inner voice before replying;

"Okay....But promise me you'll keep up your studies while we're gone?" she said to the boys.

"Yes mum, we will," they assured her.

When it actually sunk in, Suzanne exclaimed in delight, "Oh my god...we're actually going to *Egypt*!" flinging her arms around Charles' neck.

Ancient Kemet

Suzanne and Charles arrived in Cairo in the early hours of Monday morning after a short flight from Gatwick airport.

Arriving at the hotel around 6am, they had breakfast in the 5* hotel's restaurant, before retiring to bed for a few hours rest. They spent the rest of their first day making full use of the hotel's excellent spa facilities, swimming in the outdoor pool, relaxing in the Jacuzzi, then having a steam and sauna, before having full body massages. Charles even treated Suzanne to a seaweed facial. By the end of the day, they were totally relaxed and rejuvenated.

They undid all the pampering when they made passionate love that night.

Suzanne had put her hair in braids so she didn't have to think about what to do with it while away, as Charles had said he wanted to take her swimming in the Red Sea.

The following day, Charles arranged for them to go scuba-diving; it was like being in another world! Suzanne was amazed at the beauty of God's underwater creation; the different intricate designs he had 'painted' on all the fish… and the plants seemed to have a life of their own as they swished and swayed in the currents!

Charles was a much better swimmer than Suzanne; he offered to take her deeper underwater so she could see even more. Even though she would have probably drowned if she was on her own, she trusted him.

They picked some shells from the bottom of the ocean to bring back home. Her only regret was not having the boys with her to share

the beautiful experience, but she promised herself that she would do this trip again with them, and make it longer next time.
That evening, they got dressed up and went down to the hotel's plush restaurant for dinner.

As they searched for a free table, an older Caribbean couple beckoned them to join them at their table. It turned out they were celebrating their 28th wedding anniversary!

Mr and Mrs Jones were still happily 'in love' after being together for 30 years; their children were now grown up, and they were enjoying having 'quality time' with each other again. Suzanne wondered if they still had a sex life, but was too embarrassed to ask. They certainly *looked* as if they were still physically attracted to each other. She wondered if she would still be attracted to Charles when they were in their 60's.

Mrs Jones glanced at Suzanne's left hand and noticed she wasn't wearing a wedding ring. She blatantly asked if they were just on holiday as lovers or if they were actually in a committed relationship.

"We live together, and we're very happy with the arrangement," Suzanne informed her.

"But you look so good together, why you don' get married – wha' 'appen, you scared fe commit?" Mr Jones questioned Charles.

Charles cleared his throat;

"No, no, we're not scared, we've been thinking about it, haven't we?" he looked at Suzanne for support.

But Suzanne stood her ground.

"I don't see how getting married would help us stay together. If I'm happy in a relationship and I see it has the potential to last, I'll do my best to make it work. A wedding ring wouldn't do anything to change that," she stated.

"What, you mean you wouldn't get married?" Charles asked in a shocked tone.

"Well….*maybe.* I'm just saying, a wedding ring wouldn't make any difference to me."

Charles breathed a sigh of relief.

The Pyramids

On the Wednesday they left the hotel at 7am to join an excursion; they were going to visit the oldest and only remaining of the Seven Wonders of the Ancient World – the great pyramid of Giza. The largest of the three main colossal monuments was originally built as a burial tomb for King Khufu in the 4th Dynasty. Seeing the real thing was nothing like the pictures. But then, photographs could never capture the true magnificence of their existence. Their Egyptologist tour guide divulged much information about the pyramids, including the fact that the Great Pyramid of Giza had originally been covered in a smooth limestone casing, which had allegedly been stolen. There were a few casing stones still remaining at the base of the pyramid; one of the largest was nearly 5 feet high, weighing about 14 tons. The sheer magnitude of the Pyramid meant that a *lot* of limestone had been removed. Suzanne asked the tour guide what had been the purpose of the casing in the first place? She was informed that the casing had acted like a mirror, causing the Pyramid to reflect light.

Suzanne and Charles were both interested to learn more about the pyramids, the Sphinx and their history. They decided to do more research when they got back home.

The guided tour only left more questions in Suzanne's mind, like "*how* were they built?", "*who stole the limestone casing*?", and *"what had the stolen limestone been used for?"*

Charles had paid extra for them to enter the great pyramid, but their tour guide was not permitted to accompany them.

As they entered the tunnel, Suzanne and Charles bent down to follow the long low passage leading to the Queen's chamber. An unexplainable chill ran throughout Suzanne's body.

"Can you feel that?" she asked Charles.

"Feel what?"

"I'm not sure…I can't explain it, I just feel…*strange*."

As they entered the chamber, an overwhelming feeling came over Suzanne. She began hyperventilating.

"Are you okay?" Charles asked in a concerned tone.

"Yes…I'm not sure…"

Her inner voice advised her to go and stand in a particular spot. As soon as she did, she felt what she could only describe later as a ‘download’, and passed out.

“Are you okay?” Charles asked with concern written all over his face. By now, some of the other tourists had also gathered around her.

“Yes, I’m fine,” she responded as Charles helped her back to her feet.

“Maybe we should go,” he advised, looking around nervously.

“No it’s fine, I feel at home here.”

They continued to walk around admiring the sarcophagus, walls and ceiling carved out of thick granite stone. They both felt a residue in the air of a people who were once a great civilization.

Leaving the Pyramids, they took a short camel ride through the desert to reach the great Sphinx.

The tour guide explained that at one point it had been buried up to its neck in sand, but now, it stood 200ft long, 65 feet tall with its face measuring 13 feet wide, facing the rising sun. It had been so revered by the ancients that they had built a temple in between its massive paws. It had the body of a lion and the face of a human – but was it a male or a female, and was it the face of a Nubian or European? When Suzanne asked what had happened to the nose and lips, the tour guide informed them they had been vandalized, but they weren’t sure who by, or for what reason.

But to Suzanne and Charles, the reason was obvious.

Souvenir shopping

On the Thursday, they hired a local tour guide to take them to a traditional market where they bartered for souvenirs. Charles bought Suzanne a gold Ankh necklace to replace the Christian cross she had stopped wearing. She bought the boys a silver one each as well, and a silver bracelet for Ebony, as well as gifts for family and friends.

When they arrived back at the hotel in the late afternoon, Suzanne decided to have a nap before getting ready for dinner. Charles lay down beside her, but was too excited to sleep, so once he was sure she was out, he left the hotel room and headed down to the bar…

Surprise?

This was their last evening in Egypt. They had arranged to meet Mr and Mrs Jones for dinner again. As they left their hotel room, Charles discreetly slipped something into his trouser pocket.

Linking hands, they made their way over to table 28 where Catherine and Sydney were already waiting for them.

Charles was dressed in a pair of cream linen slacks, a white loose cotton shirt, and beige canvas shoes. Suzanne wore a knee-length cotton dress that was fitted at the bodice and waist, and white high-heeled sandals. Her skin glowed against the white material. She had styled her braids away from her face, and held it in place with a butterfly clip. Her only make-up was eye-liner, mascara and lip-gloss, giving her an au-natural look.

"You look like the perfect couple!" Catherine complimented them as they reached the table.

"Thank you!" Suzanne replied as Charles helped push her seat in, before sitting down himself.

"Today is a special day!" Charles announced loudly.

Sydney winked at him.

Just then, two brothers approached their table playing violins.

Tapping Charles frantically on the arm Suzanne whispered excitedly "Look Charles, it's *Nuttin' but Stringz*!"

"Yeah, I know." Charles replied calmly.

That's when Suzanne realized what was going on.

Turning and giving them a grateful look, Charles then smiled at Suzanne and said smugly;

"I think you'd be very happy married to me!"

'Is this his way of proposing?' She wondered, '... maybe he's using reverse psychology; maybe what he really means is he thinks *he'd* be very happy married to *me*!'

"Are you sure about this?" she questioned him cautiously. She had stopped expecting him to pop the question years ago.

Charles fumbled with his words;

"Well I wouldn't ask unless I was sure within myself. In life one can only make choices, and I choose to be happy all the time. The thought of spending the rest of my life with you makes me happy."

"So are you proposing?"

"Would you *want* to marry me?" he asked reservedly, knowing her views on marriage.

"Depends; are you proposing or not?"

He paused and took a deep breath, then slowly slid down to the floor unto one knee. Taking her by the hand, he said solemnly;

"Suzanne, it would make me very happy if you would accept my proposal to be my wife."

Suzanne decided not to give her hand away that easily, so playfully asked "Is that it? *Why* do you want me to be your wife?" Caught off guard, he shuffled unto the other knee;

"Well... I think I've met my match, I think we have something very special between us, and I think what we have can last a lifetime." He smiled up at her, pleased with his reply. He's right, it worked.

Warming to his offering, she gave him a big hug and replied "Charles, I would LOVE to be your wife!" with tears of joy in her eyes.

He reached inside his trouser pocket and took out a purple velvet box. Opening it, he took out the ring, but asked her to look at it closely before he put it on her finger.

She took it from him and examined it closely; it had a large single solitaire diamond ring in the middle in the shape of a love heart, with a small gold ankh cross flanking either side. Inside were engraved the words 'For Life'.

She exclaimed "Good heavens! Charles, it's...*beautiful*!"

She couldn't have chosen a better ring herself. She gave it back to him, and he proceeded to place the ring on her finger. As he stood up, she flung her arms around his neck, giving him a big hug and kiss.

Nuttin' but Stringz changed their violin melody to a lively upbeat tune, and everyone in the room got up and started clapping and dancing to celebrate, including Charles, Suzanne, Mr and Mrs Jones, and the staff. Afterwards, Charles asked the brothers to join them at their table for dinner, but they had to leave.

"Oh, before you leave, can we get a photo with you please?" Suzanne jumped up with her camera. She knew Micah and Elijah wouldn't believe this had happened without proof.

Mr Jones offered to take the picture.

When the two brothers had left, Suzanne exclaimed "Charles, don't tell me you flew them all the way over from America? That must have cost you a *fortune*!"

"Nah," he laughed, "I met them in the hotel lobby earlier – I recognized them from one of the boys' CD covers, got talking to them, and when I told them I was planning on proposing to you this evening, they offered to play."

They told Charles that a wealthy Arab family had commissioned them to play at their son's 21st birthday party, which is why they were there.

"Phew, that was a stroke of luck!" Suzanne sighed with relief.

"It was meant to be," said Mr Jones.

The Secret

Over dinner, Charles asked Mr and Mrs Jones "What's the secret to your long and happy marriage?"

The couple looked at each other before turning back to him and replying:

(Husband) "Always go to bed with forgiveness in your heart – never carry hurt or begrudging over to the next day."

(Wife) "Pray together. Having God in the centre of our marriage is what keeps it strong."

(Husband) "I make sure I tell her I love her every day – and I mean it!"

(Wife) "Make time for each other, even when the children start coming – do you have children?"

"Yes, three," Charles responded.

"Well it's good to see you're still taking time out to spend time together; that's important in a relationship. Ever since we got married, we've always had one weekend a month to ourselves, without the children. Either they would go to his sister's, or mine. We would 'share the care'. And we would have their children once a month so they could have *their* Time Out too – and they're still married as well!" Catherine enthused.

(Husband) "Yes, it's important to have a good support network around you, either friends who are also married, or couples like us who have been happily married for years, who can give you advice during the rough periods – because they *will* come. It's inevitable. But you've got to have *stick-ability*. Remember why you decided to get married in the first place. Remember the vows you made to each other."

Suzanne asked "Will *you* be our mentors?" and looking at Charles added "I'd love to think that *we*'ll still be in love after 30 years of marriage, like you are."

"We're not so much *in love* as in *commitment* to each other," Mrs Jones corrected.

"If you fall in love, it's just as easy to fall *out* of love again. But it's our *commitment* to each other that keeps us together, more than our love for each other."

Still, Charles joined in; "I agree, will you be our mentors?"

In unison the couple replied "Yes!"

Excitedly, they exchanged email addresses and home phone numbers so they could keep in contact.

When they arrived back in England, they couldn't wait to show the boys the photos and start doing research on the Pyramids, the Sphinx, and other places relating to Ancient Kemet – and to inform family and friends of their decision to officially 'tie the knot'.

They also organized an engagement party for family and friends to celebrate with them.

Breaking News

Charles arrived at Maria's at 6.30pm as usual.
It was a Wednesday evening. When he arrived Maria already had her coat on, and announced she was going out.

"She's had her dinner and bath, all you have to do is play with her and when she's ready to sleep, make her a cup of hot chocolate," she said as she hurried through the front door.

She was looking rather ravishing in a tight black sleeveless mini dress and high heels. 'Where's she going dressed like that?' Charles wondered as he headed for the living room. Ebony was sitting on the floor watching one of the classic Sesame Street DVD's he had bought for her.

Seeing him come through the door, she got up and ran towards him with her arms raised, crying out "Daddy, daddy!"

"Ah, come 'ere my girl!" he said, scooping her up and giving her a big hug and kiss.

He spent the next couple of hours playing with Ebony, reading to her, and singing songs with her before she finally fell asleep in his arms.

Charles looked at his watch. It was 8.30pm. He should be leaving now, but Maria wasn't back yet.

He carried his sleeping beauty upstairs and placed her gently in her bed, tucked her in, and kissed her lightly on the cheek.

Returning to the living room, he opened his briefcase and took out some papers. 'Might as well get some work done until Ria gets back'. Another hour passed with still no sign of Maria. He called her mobile...no reply. He didn't bother to leave a message, thinking she'd call him back as soon as she saw his missed call.

Another half an hour passed. Suzanne called.

"Where are you?"

"I'm still at Maria's, babe. She went out so I'm waiting for her to get back before I can leave."

A sudden feeling of panic gripped Suzanne, but she chose not to entertain the thoughts that would make her doubt Charles' integrity.

"How's Ebony?"

"She's perfect. She's fast asleep now; as soon as Maria gets back I'll be gone."

"Okay, well be home as soon as you can, I'm waiting up for you."

"As soon as she's back, I'm on my way."

"Okay babe, see you later. Love you."

"Love you too."

It had gone 10.30pm before Charles finally heard the key turn in the lock.

He had dozed off, but the sound of the door opening woke him up again. Maria entered the living room looking ravishing and slightly disheveled at the same time. She had obviously had one or two drinks; she was never a drinker.

"Hey, you still here?" she slurred.

"Where did you expect me to have gone, my daughter's here, remember?"

"It's not *me* that needs to remember, it's *you,*" Maria stated, removing her heels as she moved towards him.

Charles stood up, putting himself on guard.

"Look Ria, I'm really sorry things didn't work out between us, but you know I'm doing the best I can by you and Ebony."

"Well your best isn't good enough; I'm a woman, I'm the mother of your child, I have needs, I want more Charles...I want you back!"
He knew this was coming. He had to fight to resist the temptation.

"Now listen Maria, that's not gonna happen," he said, holding her by the arms as she tried to fling them around his neck.

"Why not? Look at me!" she backed up and began removing her clothes.

"No Maria, stop!" Charles rushed forward to stop her going any further.

"Why? Don't you still want me?" she asked seductively, stepping out of her dress. All she was wearing was the red Victoria's Secret bra and pantie set he had bought her before she had Ebony. She still looked great in it. Charles felt a stirring in his nether regions as he struggled to look away. He remembered Suzanne telling him that he was free to do as he pleased, that she had no expectations of him...but that if he cheated on her, she would know. Was it worth the risk? No, he decided. Taking his mind off her body and sex, he covered his eyes and said sternly;

"Listen Maria, I've got something I need to tell you."

Hearing the seriousness in his voice, she stopped making advances.

"What is it?"

"I'm getting married."

"What? *Married*? To who?"

"Who do you think? Suzanne of course."

"But...WHY?"

"What do you mean, *why*?"

"Why would you marry *her* when you can have *me*...and your daughter is here...we could be a *family*..."

"Stop right there Maria. We tried that, remember? It didn't work."

"Yes, but I was still getting over having our baby, I wasn't myself, you could see that..." she pleaded.

"Maria...please don't make this harder for me than it has to be. You know we were never really compatible. I'm glad we have Ebony, and you know I'll always support you both in the best way I can, but it's Suzanne I love. We're getting married Ria. I just wanted you to know."

Without another word Maria picked up her clothes from the floor, and turning away from him, headed slowly out of the room, as if in a daze.

"Ria!" Charles called after her.

Not answering, she continued heading upstairs towards her bedroom.

He gathered his things together and left quietly.

Best Man

Charles calls Dave.

"Long time no hear! How's things, bro?" Dave asked.

"Oh man, life just seems to get better and better!" Charles replied enthusiastically.

"Wow, what's that woman *doing* to you?" Dave asked in an amused tone.

Charles laughed. "I've met my match, that's all I can say. Actually, I'm calling because I want you to be Best Man at my wedding."

"You're getting *married*?"

"Yeah."

"Damn, she really has you hooked, hasn't she? What about Ria?"

"What about her?"

"How did she react when you told her you were getting married?"

"Well, she wasn't happy as you can imagine, but life goes on, you know. Besides, technically I was with Suzanne before I was with her."

"Yes but *she's* the one with your child; Suzanne already has two of her own – are you planning on having one with her too?"

"I dunno…we'll see."

Charles had never envisioned himself having children before getting married, and now the idea of having two children for two different women didn't really appeal to him, or reflect his character. But he knew he had to be true to him Self.

"Did you get your ring back from her?" Dave asked.

"Course not!"

"You mean you had to buy another ring?!"

"What, you think I'd take the ring off Ria and put it on Suzanne? You're crazy, man!"

They both laughed.

"Well I'm happy for you bro. So when's the big day?" asked Dave.

"Next July – and we're getting married abroad, so you'll have to book the week off work!"

Year Ten: A Spiritual Union

Suzanne left Charles to deal with all the legalities of getting married abroad, while she dealt with organizing the venue, booking the hotel, sending out invitations, and getting their outfits made, etc.

The last thing they wanted was to get married abroad and then find out their marriage wasn't valid in the UK, so they hired an overseas wedding planning agency to make sure everything was in order. Their plan was to keep it simple; no more than 50 guests, a small ceremony, with wedding and honeymoon in the same location – where the weather was guaranteed to be hot! However the more they planned, the more complicated it became; family members demanding free flight tickets, friends not being able to travel on the dates, other friends demanding to know why they hadn't been invited, parents complaining that the price of airfares was almost doubled because it was a school holiday, and that they would have preferred to take their children out of school... Then when Charles asked Maria if Ebony could be bridesmaid, she point blank refused, saying there was no way she was going to allow him to take her out of the country. But when he offered to pay for her flight and cover all her expenses so she could accompany Ebony, she finally agreed. Charles' mother, now in her 70's, was usually firmly against getting on a plane. But as soon as he told her he was getting married abroad she somehow overcame her fear of flying. There was no way she was going to miss her only son's wedding!

With the money they saved from having a traditional white wedding in England, they contributed towards airfares and provided accommodation for their guests.

"It's time for me to change my coil." Suzanne announced.
Charles didn't have a clue what she was talking about.

"What coil?"

"Don't you remember? I told you I'd had a coil fitted when you asked why I wasn't getting pregnant!"

"Oh! Yes...sorry, I forgot. So it's time for what?"

"To have it removed. I can either get a new one fitted, or we can try for a baby," she said sitting on his lap.

Charles rested his hand on her stomach.

"A baby sounds nice."

Build-up to the Big Day

Their wedding was scheduled for the 29th of July, a Friday. Most of their guests were due to arrive on the Thursday, but Suzanne and Charles, his Best Man Dave, Janice (bridesmaid), and the boys arrived in Cairo on the Tuesday to make sure all the preparations were going according to plan.

It was so hot that they had to spend the first day inside the air-conditioned villa acclimatizing to the heat. Suzanne had planned it so that all the men closest to Charles would stay in one villa with him the night before the wedding, and all the women closest to her would stay in another villa. Other guests would stay in a nearby hotel. They had agreed that not sharing a room the days leading up to their wedding would only add to the excitement and anticipation. They wanted their wedding night to be extra special. Both Charles and Suzanne were aware that something had happened the night they made love after returning from the African restaurant, and ever since then, their love-making had gone to another level. It was as if they could transport themselves to another dimension quite easily each time they made love, which is why they made a point of preparing themselves for each sacred sexual encounter. Charles had agreed not to eat any meat that week, and they had also agreed not to consume any dairy products or alcohol.

Suzanne had brought all the things they would need for their Sex Ritual, including incense, candles, massage oil and music.

Pre-wedding Celebrations

Charles had made sure Maria would be on the same flight as his sisters and mother so they could all travel together, and hopefully build stronger bonds. His sisters took an immediate dislike to Maria, but they loved Ebony. 'Ma Ankrah (Charles' mother) took Maria in as one of her own and by the time they arrived in Cairo, they were all like family.

The day before the wedding, Charles and Suzanne spent the afternoon and early evening entertaining their arriving guests in the hotel lounge area. They enjoyed re-uniting with old friends and family members, especially the ones they hadn't seen in years. Mr and Mrs Jones, their mentors, also came for the wedding, saying they wouldn't have missed it for the world. Charles introduced them to his and Suzanne's mothers, and the older generation formed a little clique of their own.

Dave took Maria under his wing, under Charles' request. He was attracted to her, but he could see that she still had feelings for Charles, so as it was, he just made sure she didn't feel isolated.

Micah and Elijah asked Maria if Ebony could play with them and the other children. She agreed, but under the condition that they stay away from the swimming pool. They said okay, even though they knew five-year-old Ebony was a great swimmer, since Charles had been teaching her since she was two. Suzanne decided to use this opportunity to make another effort to befriend Maria, but as she approached her, Maria got up and walked off, mumbling something about needing a cigarette. Suzanne passed a silent blessing over her and carried on mingling with the other guests.

By 6pm she was ready to head back to the women's villa for an early night. Tomorrow was going to be a long day.

Men Talk

That night, Charles and his group of men were chilling in their villa.

"I still can't believe you're getting *married!*" commented Dave, glugging from a cold can of beer.

"Why's that such a big shock to you?" Charles asked his Best Man.

"Well look how long we've known each other Charles; you've always been really picky about the women you date, and now here you are getting married to a woman with *two kids*!"

"They're not kids Dave, they're young men, and they're great, I'm proud to be part of their lives. Besides, when love strikes you're powerless to resist and the circumstances don't really matter."

"So what's so special about Suzanne?" Peter, one of their old schoolmates asked.

"Yeah, why choose her over the woman you already have a child with?" asked another.

"...And she ain't half bad looking either!" commented Dave, referring to Maria.

Charles looked around to make sure no-one else was within hearing distance.

"Promise me this won't go any further than these four walls?" he whispered.

The other brothers crossed their fingers over their chests in half-solemn oaths.

"Well it's like this...Suzanne and I...when we make love, it's like nothing I've ever experienced before...seriously...it's like we enter another world – I mean, we literally get transported into another dimension!"

The other brothers looked at each other before bursting into fits of laughter.

"That sounds like some freaky kinda sex, man!" one commented.

"So when you enter into this 'other dimension' what do you see; angels, aliens, or what?"

Charles remained silent.

"Hey, don't take it to heart, we're just messing with you bro...but were you serious about the aliens?" he asked again.

"I didn't mention aliens," Charles responded, getting up to refill his glass of water.

"How can I explain it? This woman of mine, Suzanne, she's like my soul-mate, you know? If you seriously want to know what I'm talking about, I suggest you find your own goddesses and Queens. Until you do, you won't be able to enter the gateway that leads to heaven on earth."

The Big Day

The wedding was scheduled for 11am. Suzanne had wanted it to take place early since they were both early risers, and she wanted them to be away somewhere quiet together by 6pm.

She got up at 6am and went out into the pool area to sit and meditate. An hour or so later, Janice joined her.

"Morning sis!"

"Oh, good morning Janice! Where's Keisha and Annette?"

"They're still sleeping. What are you doing up so early?"

"I *always* get up early," she informed her sister, beginning her stretches.

"Ah, it's so peaceful here!" Janice turned her face towards the sun.

"Yes, it's lovely."

"So how do you feel? Today's your big day!"

"I feel...happy and grateful. God couldn't have chosen a better husband for me."

"Yes, Charles is a nice guy – and he's got money too! I hope I find someone like him."

"Yes, well money isn't everything. Money can't buy happiness, or love...and besides, when you meet the right person, there's nothing you can't achieve together anyway."

"Is that so?"

"Of course!"

"Well you two seem to have figured it out...so how did you attract someone like Charles, anyway?" Janice asked.

Out of all the sisters, Suzanne had been considered the least attractive when they were growing up, because she was the darkest.

"Well first of all, it starts with *you*; you've got to start by loving your Self. Then whatever you desire to see in your outer world, you must first create it *within.* So if it's love you're looking for, love your Self unconditionally, from within. See what I mean?"

"Yes but I *do* love myself, and I *still* haven't attracted anyone like Charles – all the guys I seem to meet are full of themselves! Why can't *I* meet someone who's rich, handsome and spiritual?"

"Well you both have to be on the same wavelength mentally, for a start. I developed an abundance mentality, so I attracted someone on that same vibration, and we were able to achieve our goals together. I believe God was preparing us for each other long before we met."

"Really? So what about Ebony...and Maria?"

"Yes...God can have a plan for your life, and you can go off track from that path. But you can always get back on track again, it's never too late."

"So where does that leave Maria?"

"Maria will attract the right man for her, someone who's on her wavelength. The universe is abundant. She'll be fine."

Just then, Annette, Keisha and the two mothers appeared.

"Good morning! Did you have a good sleep?" Suzanne asked, hugging them all.

"Yes thanks!" they replied.

"So are you ready for your big day?" asked her mum.

"Definitely! Keisha, if I get in the shower now, will you style my hair when I come out?" she asked her sister, a hairdresser by profession.

"Of course! I brought some extra hair to make a beehive style for you…"

"No thanks, if you can just style my hair that would be great. I brought some hairpins and a tiara, that should do, shouldn't it?"

"Okay, it's *your* hair!" Keisha gave in.

"I'll do your make-up!" Janice offered.

"Fine, but not too much, Charles likes the au-natural look."

"Aren't you going to have some breakfast before you start getting ready?" asked her mum.

"I'm going to make a smoothie a bit later, nothing too heavy," Suzanne answered, pouring a glass of water for herself.

"How is that going to sustain you for the day?" her mother asked in a concerned tone.

"I'll be fine, don't worry mum. When you're ready, call the hotel and order your breakfast, they'll bring it over. I'm getting in the shower now."

Two Become One

It was an open-air wedding, held in the hotel courtyard where a large marquee had been set up. Beautiful arrangements of white and red roses decorated the walkway leading down to the altar, where the ceremony would be taking place. Two purple and gold cushions lay at the altar, along with a large white pillar candle standing upright, and two long thin candles lying on either side of it.

All the guests took their seats. Charles and Dave stood at the front in their purple suits facing the guests while they waited for Suzanne to make her entrance. She was due to enter from the back and walk down the aisle to meet her groom. Micah and Elijah sat at the front on either end of the rows of chairs, alongside Charles and Suzanne's mothers, and their mentors Mr and Mrs Jones. Soft organ music played in the background while the guests talked quietly amongst themselves, waiting for the bride to arrive.

Suddenly the music became louder, and all the guests turned around to see little Ebony walking down the aisle dropping white rose petals from the basket she was carrying. Suzanne followed about two feet behind her, with Janice close behind. Suzanne had decided to do the walk alone, since her father had passed and she didn't feel anyone could take his place. She wore a traditional white wedding dress with a long train, but had refused to wear a veil over her eyes, saying she was going into this (marriage) with her eyes wide open! She walked down the aisle slowly and gracefully at first, carrying her bouquet of red and white roses in front of her – then suddenly broke into a 'hallelujah!' dance, mixing African and contemporary dance steps together as she waved her bouquet high and low, giving God thanks that this day had finally arrived! Everyone started laughing and clapping as they cheered her on. Charles looked on in admiration, as visions of her dancing for him the night he had made the decision to marry her resurfaced. He suddenly left his position and began walking up the aisle to meet his bride, kissing his daughter on the forehead along the way. As he approached her, Suzanne realized that the dream she'd had the year they met, (of him walking towards her on their wedding day) was actually coming true! He offered her his arm, and they continued back down the aisle together, Charles with a big smile on his face. By this time everyone was standing and clapping, including Micah and Elijah. The only person who wasn't happy was Maria, who rushed out in tears. Sarah, one of Charles' sisters, followed her. Both Suzanne and Charles were so caught up in the euphoria of the moment that they were oblivious to the situation. As they reached the priest, they turned and faced each other.

After the priest had performed the traditional part of the ceremony, they incorporated their own ritual into the rest of the proceedings.

Kneeling on the purple and gold cushions, they each picked up one of the long thin candles lying at the altar. Micah and Elijah got up and lit them before returning to their seats. Holding the glowing candles, Charles and Suzanne took it in turns to make their vows to each other based on Conversations with God:

"I enter this marriage with a view towards what I can put into it, not what I can get out."

"I agree to use this union as an *opportunity* for mutual growth, full Self-expression, and for ultimate re-union with God through the joining of our two souls."

"The test of our relationship will not be how well I live up to *your* ideas about marriage, but how well I live up to *my own* ideas."

"I recognize that while we are joining as one, we each have our individual paths to follow; I will allow you the freedom to walk your own path."

"I will not impose my will upon you, or try to manipulate your mind."

"I promise to give you my love and energy without expecting the same in return."

"I will always remember that whatever I do to you, I do to my Self, and whatever I do *for* you, I do for my Self…"

As they gazed into each other's eyes while making their vows, the crowd's attention was diverted by the flicker in the candle's flames;

"...I know there will be challenges along the way, so I commit to doing whatever I can to make this relationship work, to always see the god (good) in you (even when you are showing me less), and to constantly remind you of Who You Are through my actions."

"I will remember that winning or losing is not the test, but only loving or failing to love."

"In any challenging situation, I will always ask my Self: *"What would Love do now?"*

When they had finished making their vows to each other, they simultaneously lit the large pillar candle between them, then blew out their individual candles, symbolizing the two becoming one.

Micah and Elijah then presented the rings; after Charles had taken the first ring from Elijah and placed it on Suzanne's finger, she took the second ring from Micah's cushion and placed it on Charles' finger.

The priest announced "You are now husband and wife!"

As Charles kissed his bride long and slow, their guests stood up again, giving a big round of applause.

At the reception, Charles made a moving speech telling the *'Flashback'* story of how they met, explaining the strange feeling that had come over him, as if he had known her from somewhere before – perhaps a previous lifetime? He shared how every time they split up and got back together it always felt like 'coming home', and that his inner compass had always seemed to point back to Suzanne. He told them about the night he had made the decision to marry her; the night she had danced for him. He said he was proud to have inherited two wonderful boys like Micah and Elijah, and that he would continue to do his best to be a good role model for them, then thanked Suzanne's family for adopting him into *their* family. He then addressed Maria personally, thanking her for blessing him with a beautiful daughter, and asked her to forgive him for following his heart, saying he was praying that God would provide the perfect partner for her too. Tears streamed down her face as he spoke to her from his heart; even Suzanne was finding it difficult to hold back the tears. Little Ebony left her seat and went up to her daddy who scooped her up with his left arm. Holding the mic with his right hand he continued with his speech;

"I want to thank you all for coming out here and sharing this special occasion with Suzanne and myself, and making today such a beautiful day. To all you single women, keep visualizing your Self with your perfect partner; think about what you want, not what you *don't* want in a relationship, and then ask your Self, "if that man came along, would I be the type of woman *he* would want?" Use your single time to develop your Self and prepare your Self for your mate. And men, raise your consciousness levels, there are many Queens out there waiting for their Kings. They need you, and you need them. Find each other."

With that, he sat down with Ebony on his lap, to a resounding applause.

When they had all settled down again, Suzanne stood up and walked to the centre of the floor space. She had changed into a purple and gold elaborately embroidered African-inspired dress, in a simple but elegant couture design; the material was reflected in the lapel of Charles' jacket and tie.

The backing track to her poem *'True Love'* started playing, and she recited the poem she had written based on 1 Corinthians 13:

What is the true meaning of the word 'Love'?

The thing is, 'Love' has so many meanings!
So when you say to me "I love you"
Do you mean you're in love with the way I look,
Or the way I make you feel?
Or you love the way I walk, talk, laugh, smell or appeal?
Is it my smile that captivates you?
Or the way I wear my hair?
Or is it the clothes I wear that makes you stop and stare?

Is it that you love ME because of how I treat YOU,
with Tender Loving Care?

I cook for you, I clean for you, I massage you
I dote on YOU.

Or do I love YOU because of what you can give ME
A nice home, fancy car, a lovely family
Security...
Do I love you with all sincerity
Or am I just thinking of me?

What is the true meaning of the word 'Love'?

True Love is a commitment of the HEART;
Right from the start it says
"I CHOOSE to love you,
Whether we're together or apart"

True Love says "I'm going to be patient with you;
When you try my patience, I'll <u>still</u> love you"

True Love is kind; it sows a seed
It's helpful, merciful and benevolent to those in need

True Love is never envious of what I have,
But it inspires you to reach your <u>own</u> goals,
And doesn't boast when it does.

True Love isn't proud –
Pride comes before a fall!
(giving Charles a knowing look)
But in Love you can stand tall.

True Love isn't rude or selfish
And doesn't feel the need to be loud,
Or to always have centre stage in a crowd.

True Love isn't easily angered,
It forgives and forgets
Even when it's difficult,
And it leaves no regrets.

True Love always protects
And when I'm down in the dumps
Never rejoices in my downfalls,
Only in my triumphs.
True Love always trusts, never accuses,
Always hopes, never doubts
Always perseveres, never gives up.

I love you, unreservedly
And can you say you love me, unconditionally?
LOVE NEVER FAILS.
(Track 12 on the *'Seeds of Love'* CD)

When she had finished her poem, she turned to Charles and mouthed "I LOVE YOU."

And he mouthed back "I LOVE YOU TOO".

The reception was held in an elaborately decorated hall inside the hotel.

For the opening dance, Charles chose *'Here and Now'* by Luther Vandross, while Suzanne chose *'Endless Love'* by Diana Ross and Lionel Richie. They danced as if they were the only two people in the room, reminiscent of the day they first met.

Maria left the celebrations and loitered in the hotel lobby. Dave followed her.

"Hi Maria, how are you?"

"How do you *think* I am?" she answered coldly.

"Hey listen, I'm on your side. I know this is painful for you. You're a brave woman, Maria. Not many women would have attended their ex's wedding."

"Yes, well I'm only here because of Ebony. I wish I hadn't come now...this is so unfair!" she broke down in tears. Allowing her to sob into his chest, he put a hand tentatively around her bare shoulder.

"Listen, if it's any consolation, I think Suzanne has nothing on you."

"Really?" she asked looking up at him with her big, hazel eyes.

"Nah...I mean look at you...you're beautiful, intelligent, you know how to dress, you're strong...I know who *I'd* be with if I was Charles," he said as he admired her lemon yellow mini dress against her bronze, flawless skin.

"Okay okay, I know you're just saying that to make me feel better" she responded, dabbing her face dry with a handkerchief from her yellow clutch bag.

"No, I'm serious! I tried to get him to see sense, but he wasn't having any of it. I mean, Suzanne's a nice woman, don't get me wrong, but if I had to choose, I'd choose you every time."

Maria paused, taking in the compliments before suggesting;

"I need to get out of here...d'you fancy a walk on the beach?"

The Challenge

Suzanne and Charles left the wedding reception at 5.30pm and took the short limousine ride to *Le Méridien Pyramids Hotel* on the other side of Cairo. The 5* hotel boasted a breathtaking view of the pyramids of Giza. They were due to spend two nights there, before re-joining their guests. Before she left, Suzanne had left a list of excursions that would be running each day for the guests to book if they chose to. She also left some information based on the research she and Charles had done about the pyramids and Sphinx. She wrote a short essay for their guests to give them a deeper understanding of the places they would be visiting. In it, she explained that before Egypt was raided by the Arabs and Europeans it was occupied by *Nubians*, and that it had originally been called *Ancient Kemet* which meant 'Land of the Blacks'. She informed them that ancient wisdom, knowledge and understanding had been stolen from Ancient Kemet, and that this knowledge was now being kept within the hands of a select few. She said that this small group of rich white men liked to call themselves 'the Illuminati' which meant 'enlightened ones', due to the knowledge they had acquired when they raided the tombs, pyramids and universities. They had plagiarized symbols like the Pyramid, Eye of Horus and Cross and were now using them against their original purposes. Instead of sharing the knowledge they had acquired freely, they were now using it to control the masses. Suzanne explained how these people had tried to wipe out any knowledge that Egypt had originally been occupied by Blacks, and that its ancient secrets were developed by Nubians. They had even tried to re-write history and claim Egypt wasn't in Africa, and that its history belonged to them! She gave their guests the task of looking for clues that Egypt had originally belonged to Africans during their stay. She told them the writing was on the walls. She said to look closely at the Sphinx; was that the face of a Nubian or European? Even though the nose and lips had been vandalized, it was still plainly obvious, she claimed. She invited them to spend the next two days looking for clues that Egypt was in fact, a Black land, and not to be fooled by its present occupiers.

Their guests rose to the challenge. They split into two teams and set about finding out how much of what Suzanne had claimed was true. Whichever team came back with the most information after the two days, had won.

Maria and Ebony were due to leave the day after the wedding, but Maria decided to extend their stay so Ebony could bond with her new grandmother, aunties and cousins, she said.

A Marriage of MINDS

Suzanne and Charles spent their first night together as a married couple. Their sexual union was too sacred to mention here – let's just say that for the first two nights, no-one saw or heard from them.

On the Sunday, they emerged from their hotel room looking more in love and united than ever.

They had breakfast in the hotel's courtyard where they had a breathtaking view of the pyramid Giza. 'I wonder what it would look like if it still had its original limestone casing' Suzanne thought.

"Wow, yes I can just imagine!" Charles answered, gazing up at it. That was when they both realized they could communicate telepathically! They both sat imagining the pyramid in its full original glory and splendor. They imagined it beaming angles of light so bright that they could be seen from outer space.

That afternoon they went sight-seeing on the way to re-joining their guests. As Charles stared up at a huge obelisk carved with hieroglyphs, Suzanne took a photo. When they viewed the image on her camera, it looked as if Charles was catching a sphere of light in his hand:

"Wow, how did you do that?" he asked Suzanne.

"I didn't do it, you did!"

They both looked more closely. As Charles had been paying homage to his ancestor, it was as if the soul of Imhotep had come down to greet him. It sent a chill up their spines.

It was a picture Charles would treasure for the rest of his life.

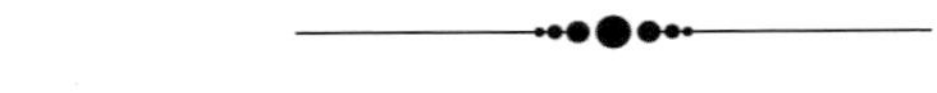

Blessings

When they arrived back that afternoon, their guests greeted them excitedly. Charles was surprised to see Maria and Ebony still there.

"Daddy, daddy!" Ebony ran up to greet him.

Charles scooped her up as they made their way into the hotel. They would be spending their last night in the Honeymoon Suite.

"Did you miss me?" Suzanne asked the boys.

"Mum look at us, we're not babies anymore," Elijah answered, giving her a hug.

They had one final get-together with their guests in the hotel's banqueting suite. Some had already left, and the rest were leaving that evening.

As they all took part in the last supper, Dave pulled Charles to one side.

"I've got something I need to tell you," he said.

"Go ahead, I'm all ears."

"Man... I don't really know how to say this," Dave stuttered.

"Hey, this is me – besides, I think I know what you're going to say anyway."

"Really? Try me!"

"You've taken a liking to Ria, haven't you?"

"How did you guess?!"

Charles laughed.

"It's kinda obvious, bro. You want to know if I approve, right?"

"You've got me all sussed, haven't you?" Dave replied coyly.

"Dave, how long have we known each other? You're practically my *brother*. Of course I could tell you like Maria!"

Dave replied in earnest; "It's just that...well, no-one's ever made me feel the way she does Charles. I couldn't help myself; I've fallen for her hook, line and sinker. I'm sorry."

"Well, you have my blessing."

"I do?!"

"Of course...what better step-father could I possibly want for my daughter than my best friend?" he answered, giving Dave a man-hug.

Year Eleven – Double Celebrations!

As Suzanne lay across her husband's lap doing her pelvic floor muscle exercises, she silently gave thanks to God for answering her prayers; she was happily married to the man of her dreams, and they had recently moved into their dream home. Together they were running a successful business, and to top it all off, they had three wonderful children between them, with another one on the way.

As they relaxed together on their large purple sofa, '*Fertile Ground*' played softly in the background; *'Let's build our home from this empty nest...'*

It reminded Suzanne of how long it had taken to build their relationship into the solid structure it was now. It had been a lot of hard work, laying the foundation, and painstakingly building upon it bit by bit. But it had been worth the effort, and now nothing could tear it down again unless they themselves chose to, and they had both worked too hard to want to destroy what they had built together. The roses on the cushions decorating their sofa made a positive affirmation of their love, stronger than thorns. One of the reasons their love was so strong was that they both spent time working on themselves; by giving each other the space they needed to grow and develop individually, they had allowed their love to blossom, like the roses on the cushions.

On a glass table beside the sofa stood a framed picture of their wedding day; Suzanne's trophy. She had also been *in*spired to collate photographs of herself with Charles in their happiest moments. Using Photoshop, she had typed each of the vows they made to each other on their wedding day unto each photo. She then printed and framed all 'Ten Commitments' and displayed them around their home, to act as a constant reminder of the promises they had made to each other.

Personally, Suzanne didn't believe in the 'institution' of marriage. She believed it was a spiritual union that only God could sanction, not a man-made ceremony. But Charles had convinced her that it made life easier if they legally married; it would provide greater stability for their children, and set a good example to the boys – not to mention the tax benefits. He had promised her there would be no messy divorce or fighting over assets. He was in this 'for life', as was inscribed on the inside of their rings. Suzanne knew Charles was committed to her wholeheartedly, and so despite her own personal viewpoints, she had happily married him. So here they were, celebrating their first year of wedded bliss. They had reason for double celebrations too, since they were also expecting the imminent birth of their first baby together!

Charles slid her top up, revealing her huge, ripe belly, tight like a drum.

"Let me see if I can hear the heartbeat," he said as he did so.

Laying his head gently on their *'Love Bump'* (as they liked to call it) he linked hands with hers as he tuned into his unborn child. They had agreed to wait until the birth to find out the sex of the baby, since they already had two boys and a girl between them. It would be a nice surprise either way, but secretly, Suzanne was hoping for a girl of her own. She already had two boys – yet on the other hand, she thought it would be nice to give Charles a son to pass his genes down to. Over the years, Charles had become a father figure to her boys. Whenever they had 'man issues' to discuss, rather than go to their dad, they would go to Charles. When they reached puberty, it was he who gave the 'pep talk'. He took them to football matches with him, and they would often go out together, just 'the men'. Suzanne didn't mind, in fact she appreciated it, as it gave her time to her Self. Now aged 16 and 18, Micah and Elijah had grown out of going to their dad's every other weekend, preferring to have their friends over instead. Their dad would take them on holiday once or twice a year, and to special family gatherings.

They had bought their 7 bedroom house in a state of disrepair at an auction a year ago, and had renovated it to their own specifications. The house was arranged over four floors; in the basement they had built a state-of-the-art cinema and a games room where they entertained friends and family. There was also a small studio in the basement for Suzanne to record her poetry. She had also planned to help other poets record their poetry too, as she felt that the wealth of literary talent within the Black community had to be recorded so it could go down in history. She would have to put that project on hold until the baby was a bit older now. Charles liked to use the basement whenever he had his friends over, as it gave them privacy. On the ground floor, they had designed a large open-plan living room with floor-to-ceiling sliding doors leading to their beautifully landscaped garden; its main feature was the water fountain. Large comfortable L-shaped leather sofas were placed near the glass doors, where the family sat together most evenings. A 52" flat-screen T.V. was built into the wall, for them to watch DVD's together. A large carved oak table with leather-padded dining chairs capable of seating up to 10 people dominated one corner of the room. Their kitchen was directly off the main living room adjacent to the dining area. Another wall was lined from floor to ceiling with their combined collection of books, but Suzanne kept her personal books in their bedroom – the ones in which she had marked all her personal notes. In one corner, a huge fish tank with all kinds of tropical fish featured. Big tropical plants were also placed strategically around the bright, airy room. Although they could afford to buy more elaborate furnishings, they were both content with the minimal look. As long as Suzanne had her fresh-cut flowers replaced weekly, she was happy. Charles' mother was getting on in age, so they had moved her in. Her living space was also on the ground floor so she didn't have to climb any stairs. She loved cooking, and had taken this on as her daily task, while Suzanne continued to make smoothies and fresh juices for the family every day. She wanted to make sure they were taking in a high content of Mother Nature's foods, which would help them to operate on a higher frequency.

The first floor was dominated by the boys; they called it the 'boyzone'; Micah and Elijah each had their own bedroom with en-suite shower rooms; they shared a 'chill-out' room where they could relax and watch DVD's or play video games together or with their friends. The entire top floor belonged to Suzanne and Charles. She had wanted to call it her Queendom (as she had always called her bedroom when she was single) but in the end, they had agreed to call it 'The Kingdom of Heaven'. You needed a key to enter, and only Suzanne and Charles held them. Entering their Haven was like entering another world – but that was their privacy. Ebony's room was also on the top floor, and they had also set up a nursery for the baby.

The road they lived on was quiet, with lots of trees and greenery. In the morning, all you could hear was the sound of birds singing. Even though there were only two other families of African descent on their road, they didn't feel out of place. Charles and Suzanne had created their own idea of 'heaven on earth'.

Suzanne had achieved her goal of being able to take her boys on holiday during school/college breaks, which was the most expensive time to travel. And even though she couldn't understand why she had to pay extra for the 'luxury' of eating food the way nature intended, she could now afford to feed her family the best foods; *organic*.
Neither did she have to worry about how she was going to manage keeping such a large house clean, since Charles had said that they could charge for a cleaner under business expenses.

She had accomplished her dream of creating an income doing what she loved; writing and performing her poetry, and was now writing her first book – a novel.

Their business became world-renowned for producing high-quality inspirational greeting cards and prints, using artwork and poetry by people of African descent. It generated a huge income from both online and high street sales. Due to the quality of their products, they were building a base of loyal repeat customers from all over the world, while constantly adding new ones. Even as she lay there pregnant, money was still going into their bank accounts. All they had to do was advertise online monthly, and place ads in various publications. Their Marketing specialist dealt with all of that. Buying in artwork and poetry helped them diversify their range, while at the same time provided a way for other 'artisans' to benefit financially from their God-given talents. What more could she ask for? They had created a way to help others while helping themselves, and were living the life of their dreams. It was almost too good to be true, she thought.

'Love is...a wonderful gift between two souls experiencing heaven on earth'.

In the Beginning...

Now in the third trimester of her pregnancy, Suzanne made sure she kept herself mentally and physically active. After her morning meditation and stretches, she would write for a couple of hours each day, as well as do research on the Internet. From the beginning of her pregnancy, she had made a conscious decision to keep her Self in a happy state, as she knew her moods would affect the baby. She also attended aqua-aerobics classes twice a week, which helped keep her flexible. Charles' mother, 'Ma Ankrah (short for 'grandma') sometimes accompanied her, as they were good for her too. Even though Suzanne had good reason to spend her days relaxing, she had a burning desire within to share the knowledge she had accumulated since asking God for 'the Truth'. What had started out as research for an article about 'Adam and Eve and the Fall of Humankind' had turned into enough material to write a whole book! She was now convinced that the bible had been written in metaphors, and wasn't meant to be taken literally. She believed the stories had a deeper esoteric meaning.

She had started a weekly blog to share bits of what she had discovered, in preparation for when her book came out.

Her first post was the one she had written about 'Adam and Eve and the Garden of Eden'. She explained how this story had been used to suppress the Feminine Energy on the planet so that the Masculine Energy could become dominant.

She also shared the connection she had made between the ancient Egyptian goddess Isis, and the book of Genesis in the bible, displaying them like this:

Genesis
Genes/Isis

She explained that the word 'Genesis' was formed from the words 'Genes' and 'Isis', hinting at the fact that Isis is the Original Mother, and that Osiris, Isis and Horus were the original Holy Trinity. While the plagiarized bible version had many similarities to the ancient Egyptian story, it made no mention of a woman 'In the Beginning'. The biblical Holy Trinity consisted of a Father, Son, and an airy-fairy 'Holy Spirit'. She wrote that when she had meditated upon this, Proverb 8 had come to mind, which revealed that Wisdom was personified as a woman, and was *with* God during the Creation process.

It was obvious to her, she asserted, that the people who constructed the bible were male chauvinist, anti-women, egotistical, and power-driven. Women had too much **inher**ent power, and the only way they could usurp that power was to degrade her.

She then decided to drop the bombshell: King James, who commissioned the King James Version of the bible, was a known homosexual who victimized women, lived apart from his wife, and openly declared his love for his male lovers. This information shouldn't come as a surprise, she said, since there was so much homosexuality in the church today, starting at the top with the Pope.

'*Can biblical history be trusted?'* she asked. The problem with 'his-story' was that it had been re-written by elitist white men. They had re-written *world* history, so why not assume they had also re-written *biblical* history? The racist Darwin Theory of Evolution was contrived, and any evidence that went against this theory was suppressed.

She went on to suggest that the 'prophecies' written in the bible could have were merely been predictions of things *they* wanted to occur in the future. She claimed that those who had constructed the bible using manuscripts stolen from ancient Egypt *knew* the creative power of thoughts. They chose to keep the masses in the dark about this, and instead, use *their minds* to achieve their goals. They knew that if they could get the masses to believe the prophecies were true, *they* would create the events at a later date, through the power of their joint-belief!

These psychopaths, she claimed, were now in control of religion, politics, education, the music and film industry, mainstream news, the pharmaceutical industry, media and sports…anything that influenced the masses. Their aim was to keep everyone dumbed down, separate from each other, and operating on a low frequency. This way, it would be easier for them to harness their thoughts and energy to achieve their own objectives, which were fear-based. They were slowly breaking down the family and community structure, so that they could take control of our children, the *future*, she wrote;

'They have already caused so much damage in the world, and need to be stopped. They are destroying the earth, right down to genetically modifying the food Mother Nature has provided for us to eat to remain healthy. Sickness is big business for them, and that's what it's all about – money and control.'

She informed her readers that religion had been created to mentally enslave her people, and politics to rule over the masses. She mentioned that her husband had suggested that everybody should stop voting and govern themselves. *'What gives them the right to rule over us anyway? Are they setting a good example themselves?'*

She declared that man-made laws only created more problems, and that God's Laws needed to be reinstated; the Laws of Nature.

Suzanne decided to write her next blog about one of the Laws; the *Law of Oneness.* She explained that everything is connected to everything else:

'We are all connected to each other and to every living thing, including 'God', the Life Force flowing in and outside of ourselves. Our thoughts are energy; when we have a thought, it doesn't just affect us, it affects everything around us as well, both now and into eternity'. She explained that the current world system was set up to keep us disconnected from each other and our Source. The same 'Divide and Conquer' tactics that had worked for them so well in the past was

being employed. Wars, racism, religions, politics, even sports, were aimed at creating divisions. The effect of this, she explained, was that on a mass-consciousness level, the human race were powerless to work together to achieve 'peace on earth'. They were too busy allowing themselves to be distracted by the news, sports, and 'programs' on the tell-lie-vision. She advised her readers to stop focusing on things that created stress, panic, sorrow, anger, fear, division and hatred. *'If we want to create a world where we can all live together in peace and harmony, we have to acknowledge the Law of Oneness'* she wrote.

We are all One

In another post, she talked about the effect subliminal programming was having on the minds of the masses. She shared some of the research she had done on the music and film industries. She encouraged her readers to notice how pop idols and film stars were influencing the masses negatively. Were these people setting a good example? Were those who emulated their idols acting more civilized or more decadent? *'Worse still, children are being targeted, to lose their innocence and become hyper-sexualized from a young age!'* She advised parents to do their own research before allowing their children to spend hours sitting watching children's 'programs', or even innocent-looking cartoons.

She wrote that people were being de-sensitized to violence, death, and all sorts of flagrant immorality through video games, music, films, porn, and the news. *'Are we losing all sense of morals and values?'* she asked. *'Instead of the recent technological advancements making us more civilized, we are becoming de-humanized'*, she warned.

'Stop allowing your mind to be programmed through the tell-lie-vision, mainstream music, films, newspapers and magazines. Educate yourselves outside of mainstream media. Remember that what you do to another, you do to your Self; if we carry on like this as a human race, we will self destruct!'

Fear Not!

Suzanne was on a mission to help her people and the whole world to heal. 'But how?' she wondered.

The answer came to her immediately: 'LOVE'.

"Love?"

'Love is the answer. Love is the complete opposite of fear, and banishes fear like a small candle lit in a dark room,' her inner voice advised.

"Yes, but how does one apply that *practically*?" she asked again.

"Fill your Self up with Love,
until there is no room left for fear"

Suzanne 'innerstood'. The more she focused on loving her Self, her people, and the whole human race, in that order, the more she would eradicate fear from her life. The biggest problem her people had was in loving themselves. They had been taught to love and put everyone else before themselves; to be good servants – obedient, humble and submissive.

Yet they weren't the only ones caught in the illusion; Caucasians had been subconsciously programmed to view themselves as *superior* to everyone else – even the least of them. Other races had their own programming. Within each race, there were further class and status hierarchies, for instance, Asians had their Caste System, which also claimed that the lighter you are, the better you are. The lower classes within each race were permitted to mix with other races, but the higher class focused on keeping their bloodlines 'pure'.

This system of class and status was based on fear, Suzanne wrote. It had been created by white 'elitists' who secretly feared the Black Man and Woman. They had created a system that put them at the top, and the Nubian race at the bottom, and had somehow managed to get all other races to see *white* as the standard of beauty and status, with black now having negative connotations attached to it. All this was based on skin colour, instead of the individual's character.

She made a conscious decision to re-mind her Self daily Who She Was:

"I am a spirit living in a body"

She had been able to create her own little ideal world with Charles, but now she imagined that if everyone on the planet did the same thing, the whole world could be ideal!

She believed that the more she embodied her true, natural virtues, the more she would attract people from *all* races who came from a place of Love instead of fear. These were the people who would join their minds with hers to create 'heaven on earth'.

When the thought came to her that '*there is nothing to fear in the future*', she made the intention that whenever she found her Self in a dark situation, she would re-mind her Self;

"I am the light!"

Breaking News

It was 9.45pm on a Friday night in June.
Suzanne lay heavily pregnant on the couch, while Micah sat on the floor in front of her as they watched a DVD together. Elijah was out with friends, 'Ma Ankrah had long gone to bed, and Charles still wasn't home yet.

There was a knock at the door.

"Who could that be at this time of the night?" Suzanne asked Micah.

"Maybe Elijah left his key at home," he speculated as he got up to answer it.

Micah returned with a concerned look on his face.

"Mum, it's the police – they want to speak to you."

Suzanne's mind immediately ran to Elijah. *'Don't tell me he's gone and gotten himself into trouble!'* she thought as she heaved herself up from the sofa. But Elijah had never been in trouble, not in school nor in college, let alone with the police. And his friends weren't the type of young men to lead him astray either. She wondered what could possibly be bringing the police to her home.
Micah supported her as she made her way to the front door.

"Mrs Ankrah?" the policeman asked.

"Yes, what is it?"

"Can we come in?"

"Is something wrong? Where's Elijah?"

"Elijah?" the policeman looked puzzled.

"Isn't that what you're here about? My son?"

"Oh! No…I think you'd better sit down Mrs Ankrah. We have some bad news for you."

"What's this all about?"
Suzanne tried not to panic as she sensed the seriousness of the reason for their visit.

"It's about your husband…Charles Ankrah?"

"Yes, what about him?"

"I'm sorry to inform you, but about an hour ago he was involved in a serious car accident. He suffered multiple broken bones and internal injuries."

Suzanne gasped.

"No…you must be mistaken…surely?"

The policeman took a set of keys out of his pocket.

"Do you recognize these?" he asked, as he held up the keys to Charles' black Mercedes with a key-ring showing a picture of Ebony on one side, and herself and the boys on the other.

"Y…yes, they're my husband's."

The policeman handed them to her.

"Is he okay? H…how did it happen?" she asked in a confused state as she took them.

"We're still investigating the cause of the crash Mrs Ankrah. But we're here to escort you to the hospital, if you like. He told us you were pregnant just before he passed out."

"*Passed out*? He *is* still alive, isn't he?"

"Yes, but they don't hold much hope for him...shall we go now?"

As Suzanne nervously gathered her things together, she asked Micah to call Dave, and to tell Elijah to meet them at the hospital.

Micah took it upon himself to also call his Aunty Janice to let her know her sister would need her.

The drive to the hospital seemed to take forever, but Suzanne remained positive within her Self that everything was going to be alright.

"When are you due?" the policewoman turned and asked.

"Any day now!" Suzanne replied, taking hold of Micah's hand.

She saw a faint look of dismay flash briefly across the policewoman's face.

Just then, she remembered that she hadn't told her mother-in-law that her son was in hospital. She called Janice and asked her to go and collect 'Ma Ankrah before meeting her at the hospital.

Arriving at the ward, Suzanne was unprepared for what she saw. Charles' broken body was barely recognizable as he lay lifeless on the bed. His head was wrapped in a large bandage, and he wore a brace to keep his broken neck in place. Tubes were attached to different parts of his body, which was connected to a life support machine.

When she caught sight of him, all the air left her lungs. Shock, horror and disbelief overwhelmed her. As her knees gave way, Micah and the policeman caught her, while the policewoman quickly pulled up a chair for her. As she sat down, a doctor came into the room.

"Doctor, please tell me…he will live, won't he?"

The doctor looked Suzanne straight in the eyes and told her gently;

"He's in a coma, Mrs Ankrah. Apart from his broken neck and internal injuries, a CT scan has revealed extensive damage to his brain. It's only the life support machine keeping him alive now."

"Oh my dear god…*CHARLES*!" Suzanne let out a blood-curdling scream as she got up, and resting her hands on his chest begged him "*PLEASE DON'T LEAVE ME!*"

Charles opened his eyes.

He appeared not to be looking *at* her, but *into* her. There was no fear in his eyes, only peace, love and contentment, as if he didn't have a care in the world. It was only for a brief second, but in that moment, Suzanne saw straight through to his soul, as if his body was just a veil, shrouding his true identity. As his real Self was revealed, his aura became visible to her. Suzanne felt as if she was being cocooned in love, light, peace, happiness and purity.

The two police made their exit.

Just then Dave, Maria and Ebony arrived. They had spoken to the doctor and were aware of the graveness of the situation. Micah spoke to them briefly in hushed tones before taking the opportunity to go and call his brother again to find out what was taking him so long. As he headed towards the Main Entrance, he saw his Aunties Janice and Keisha supporting 'Ma Ankrah in between them as they hurriedly walked towards him.

"Oh, thank goodness, there you are! Is everything okay?" asked Aunt Keisha.

"It doesn't look good," Micah replied quietly, shaking his head at the ground.

"Where are they?" 'Ma Ankrah asked anxiously.

"They're in room nine," Micah pointed the way to them.

As they entered, the silent, healing sensation of love and peace that had filled the room enveloped them as well, connecting them all. It seemed to be emanating from Charles – it was obvious that he was dying.

Suzanne, Dave, Maria and Ebony were all holding hands around his bed, as if in silent prayer. Janice and Keisha joined them.

"Oh Lord, no!" cried out 'Ma Ankrah as she caught sight of her son; "Please I beg you Lord, don' tek mi only son from me!"

She joined Suzanne in leaning over his body and praying.

Micah re-entered with Elijah. Up to that point, Elijah had been in total denial about the seriousness of the situation; the look on his face was of utter disbelief. He immediately went over to his mother and put a protective arm around her.

Suzanne was focused on willing Charles to live. She refused to believe that he was going anywhere. He was happily married. He had a beautiful daughter, two adopted sons who looked up to him, as well as the birth of his new baby to look forward to. He was the CEO of a successful business. He was rich. He had everything to live for.

But she had seen something when he opened his eyes. His soul was liberated; it no longer had any interest in the body, or its roles and responsibilities. It had let go of relationships, and detached from all the cares of this world. He had moved from *body*-consciousness to *soul*-consciousness. He was a free spirit.

She suddenly remembered two of the vows they had made to each other on their wedding day; to allow their souls to each walk their own paths, and to try not to impose their will upon each other. What was his soul trying to do? Did he want to stay, or leave?

The moment she let go of her need to keep Charles attached to this world, his spirit left his body.

Dave picked up Ebony and whispered "Say goodbye to your Daddy, princess." Ebony kissed Charles lightly on the cheek before turning away, burying her face in Dave's neck. Maria took her from him, as mother and daughter hugged each other crying. Dave tried to be strong as he put his arms around them both. Charles had been closer to him than any of his brothers.

As Charles crossed the threshold into eternal life, Suzanne began to sob uncontrollably; first quietly, then getting louder and louder as the realization of the situation sunk in.

Her and Ma's wailing brought the doctor and nurses back in, who turned off the life-support machine and began removing the tubes from his body.

The sight of the flat-line was too final; Suzanne screamed out a blood-curdling "NOOOOOOOOOO!!!"

Any moment now, she thought she *must* wake up from what had to be a horrible dream.

But somehow she knew this wasn't just a bad dream. She could feel her heart breaking all over again as she experienced an overwhelming feeling of emptiness and sorrow. Her sisters did their best to comfort her as she began to wail loudly and uncontrollably.
She began hyperventilating, holding on to her stomach.

"Doctor, I think she's in pain!" Keisha called out.

He looked over and exclaimed in his Asian accent; "Oh my gosh, I think she's going into labour! Are you feeling pain anywhere?" he asked her.
She nodded as she continued sobbing and hyperventilating.

"Where is the pain?" he asked.
Suzanne put her hand first over her heart, then on her stomach.
He instructed one of the nurses to get a wheelchair.

"We must get her to the labour ward, quick!" he ordered.

"I'm not leaving Charles!" she cried out.

"Suzanne, you're in labour – you can't give birth here!" Janice spoke firmly as she helped the nurse force her into the wheelchair.

From then on, everything became a blur to Suzanne. Not even she could tell if her loud wails were from the labour pains or her grieving. As they wheeled her up to the labour ward the nurse asked, "Did you bring your notes?"

She shook her head.

Janice told the boys to go to her car and get the baby bag, which she had seen sitting by the front door when she picked up 'Ma Ankrah, and had instinctively picked it up too.

"I'm not leaving mum." Elijah stated bluntly.

"It's okay, I'll go," Maria suggested.

"Good idea," replied Keisha. "I'll come with you."

"I'd like to stay for the birth too – if that's okay?" Maria asked "…It would be good for Ebony."

"Are you okay with that?" Janice asked Suzanne, who nodded as she grimaced in pain.

Somehow, Charles' death had created a bond between them all.

"Mummy, I want to stay with you!" Ebony pleaded.

This created a dilemma; Dave wanted to stay with Charles' body, and children weren't allowed on the labour ward.

"I'm sure if we explain the situation, they might make an exception," the nurse assured them.

For now, Dave and 'Ma Ankrah stayed with Charles' body, while Maria and Ebony left with Keisha to collect the baby bag and hospital notes from Janice's car.

By the time they returned, the nurse had explained to the midwife that Ebony's father had just passed away, and her baby brother or sister was about to be born.

"Can she stay? None of us want to miss it," Maria pleaded.

The midwife finally agreed, but insisted she would have to wait outside the labour ward until after the baby had been born. So Maria and Ebony remained in the Waiting Room.

From Suzanne's perspective, everything was one big haze; she couldn't tell if the pain she was feeling was from her broken heart, or contractions. She had no will left to push, yet nature was taking its course anyway. She could vaguely make out her sisters bending over her urging her to push, while the midwife placed a gas and air mask over her face.

As she gave birth she continued wailing and sobbing with one long groan after another asking "Why me? Why now?"

Charles had attended every pre-natal appointment, and now he wasn't even here for the birth.

Within an hour and a half, she had given birth to a beautiful, healthy baby boy. But when the midwife placed him on her chest, she turned away. Her sisters took over, helping the midwife weigh and wash the baby, and dressing him while the midwife delivered the placenta.

Suzanne continued moaning with long, painful groans even after the labour was over.

The doctor was called again.

"I think it's best if I sedate her. She's in shock – she's been through a lot this evening."

As Suzanne appeared to be delirious and sobbing hopelessly, her sisters agreed. She was in no fit state to look after the baby she had just delivered.

After the doctor gave her the injection, she slowly drifted off into sleep…

...As Suzanne entered her Alpha state, she became detached from her physical body and was immediately transported into a space of intense, bright light. Charles appeared as an ethereal form of pure love and light. As he walked towards her, he smiled with such a peaceful, happy expression. A powerful healing presence enveloped her. He didn't speak in words, but she understood everything he was communicating to her perfectly. He let her know that he was alive and well – just not in his physical body. He told her not to worry about him; he had fulfilled his soul purpose in that lifetime, and it was time for him to move on. He had been on a mission of Love, which he had completed. He reminded her that he had left a precious gift for her to cherish, and that he would always be with her in spirit.

As he drew her close to him a divine presence filled every part of her being with pure, unconditional love, until she felt part of it.
She felt warm, peaceful and happy…

…When Suzanne regained consciousness, the intensity of her grief had diminished considerably.

She had been given a glimpse through the spiritual window and had seen Charles' soul, and now *knew* that mortality is only an illusion, and death is only a separation of the true Self from the body. She felt a new sense of hope knowing that Charles could never die, and that she could never be separated from him. Death truly had no sting; it was simply a *transitioning* of the eternal spirit from the physical to the spiritual realm, back to its Source, which was Love.

She finally realized that Love isn't a *feeling*; it's a state of *being*.

In her new state of enlightenment she remembered the true and original nature of her *own* soul: She was Love. She was peace. She was joy. She was light. Seeing the real Charles had reminded her of her own immortality. She now felt as if she knew her purpose and destiny. Just as Charles' purpose had been to remind her of who *she* really was, *her* purpose was to remind others of who *they* are.

As her consciousness expanded, she remembered the lesson of loving and letting go; of being detached from outcomes and having no expectations of other souls she was in relationship with, just as God had no expectations of her.

Suzanne had loved being able to call Charles "*my* husband". But in Truth, he was not a possession for her to own or to keep, but had simply been on loan to her from the Divine, sent to help her achieve her purpose in life.

In that moment she consciously set a *new* goal for her Self; to give Love free from expectations, and to detach from everything including 'her' children – because they were not her possessions; they were sacred souls on their *own* sacred journeys, who came through her from the Divine. In Truth, nothing belonged to her; everything she owned belonged to God. When it was time for her to leave her body, she would take nothing with her.

As Maria handed her baby boy to her, the excitement of having brought forth a new life mixed with the grief of Charles' death was a bitter-sweet combination.

But it was time to let go of her negative emotions and to realize that Charles was still very much alive.

As she looked into her baby's wide, alert eyes she thought she saw something familiar; they say the eyes are the windows to a person's soul;
Could it really be…

"CHARLES?" she whispered with a trembling voice.

THE SEQUEL: YEARS 12 & 13

The sequel begins 9 months after Charles' transition…

Year Twelve: Death of a Dream

"The greatest tragedy in life is not death, it's what dies inside a person while they are still alive"
~ Norman Cousins

"Look 'Ma, he's trying to walk!"

Suzanne and 'Ma Ankrah watched as Charles jnr. took his first steps.

"Come on Charlie, you can do it!" 'Ma Ankrah coaxed him on, holding out her arms. Little Charlie focused on his goal and toddled towards his grandmother, stumbling once or twice, but immediately getting back on his feet again. When he reached her, they both gave him a big round of applause.

"Your brothers will be so proud of you!" Suzanne praised him as she walked over to where he was now sitting on his grandmother's lap. She picked him up and gave him a big hug.

Things had not always been like this; it had taken many weeks for both her and 'Ma Ankrah to get used to the idea that he had replaced his father in their home.

Memories of the first few weeks were hazy; Suzanne just about remembered her sisters and Maria coming around daily to help look after the baby, do housework, and organize Charles' cremation. He had specifically stated in his will that he didn't want to be buried in a grave, but wanted to be cremated, and his ashes taken back to his Motherland and thrown into the wind.

As if Suzanne hadn't been traumatized enough, the idea horrified her at first, but she had pledged to keep her husband's wishes, and now, his idea made sense to her.

Up to this point, Charles' ashes had been kept in an urn on a shrine she had built in his remembrance, which included his photograph and a candle which burned constantly. Every day she had sat in front of it with the baby in her arms, trying to connect with him as she had done in hospital on that fateful night. But nothing happened. Eventually she accepted that Charles had truly passed on.

Her family and friends, including Dave and Maria, had been there to support her in the early months, making sure the house and business continued to run smoothly. Suzanne had lost all interest in the business, but Elijah, now aged 19, had taken over managing the Accounts department in place of the man who had taught him so much, while continuing to study part-time.

Charles' transition had affected the staff too, who had always described him as their 'best boss ever'. Elijah saw to it that staff morale was kept high, telling them funny stories of things he and Micah had done with Charles when they were growing up. He encouraged them to make sure the business kept going to honour his memory, and sure enough, the business had continued to thrive.

While most things had remained a blur, Suzanne remembered clearly the day she had arrived home with her newborn.

Climbing the stairs to their 'haven' with the yet unnamed baby in her arms, Luther Vandross's song *'A House is Not a Home'* had come to mind, particularly the lines *'I'm not meant to live alone, turn this house into a home, when I climb the stairs and turn the key, oh please be there saying that you're still in love with me…'*

She had half expected Charles to be waiting on the other side of the door when she opened it, which only caused further heartache when she realized she wasn't going to wake up from this terrible nightmare.

Even though she had previously promised her Self that she wasn't going to listen to any more of those doomy-gloomy love songs, she downloaded the track and played it over and over again, spending night after night crying into her pillow until it was too wet to be slept on anymore.

She breast-fed the baby, but felt no attachment to it. Most nights she would just lie there in the carved wooden bed they'd had custom made, while Charles jnr. suckled at her breast, as she stared at Charles' painting *'Trust',* which hung on the wall opposite.

'Trust' by Cezanne (2009)

Charles jnr. would stare up at her with his big, brown eyes while feeding, trying to connect with his creatress.

It seemed ironic, that the painting Charles had done to honour their relationship now mocked her from the wall. *Trust?* She had trusted him not to leave her to raise another child on her own.

Upon waking from the dream (or was it a vision?) in which she had seen Charles as his ethereal body, she had looked into her baby's eyes for the first time and could have sworn she saw Charles' soul, as if he had straight away re-incarnated into his son's body. But now, she couldn't be sure. Maybe it was just the effect of the drugs she had been given? For days, she had searched her baby's eyes, looking closely for any sign of Charles. When she couldn't find any she had stopped trying, and detached. So weeks had gone by where she had refused to connect with her baby's soul.

Even though the experience of seeing Charles out of his body had helped her cope to some degree, his death had still caused a lot of grief.

But time is the greatest healer, and sure enough, over the months, Suzanne had begun to heal from the trauma of her bereavement, and to be restored from Post Natal Depression.

In the depth of her despair, the Affirmations which she had repeated so often to her Self in the past re-surfaced:

"Who Am I, and Who do I want to be, in relationship to this?"

In time, she innerstood that from the seeds of calamity – and all experiences – comes the growth of Self.

'Ma Ankrah on the other hand, hadn't taken the death of her only son very well; she hadn't had the experience of seeing Charles transfigured. "No one should have to bury their child", she had kept repeating, rocking back and forth on the bed in her room. She didn't cook for weeks (which she loved), or engage with the rest of the family, thinking she may now be put into a home. Despite her own state, Suzanne had done her best to make 'Ma Ankrah feel as if she was still part of the family, and had promised her that she would always have a place in their home.

After her first few weeks of mourning, 'Ma Ankrah had suddenly become very attached to the baby as a coping mechanism; she wanted to do everything for him, which suited Suzanne fine.

Suzanne couldn't believe that fate could be so cruel as to leave her a single mother to 3 sons – that had been her *worst fear*. But here she was, widowed at 39 with two teenagers, and a toddler to raise.

Elijah and Micah had done their best to support their mum emotionally, even though they were going through their own grief. Because there had been no funeral, they were spared from having to carry the coffin and dig the grave which had helped them to cope, but still, they had both suffered silently.

Leaving a Legacy

Charles had seen to it in his Will that his best friend Dave was well rewarded financially for taking on the responsibility of Ebony, almost as if he had known he would soon be departing his physical body.

Dave and Maria were now engaged to be married, but had decided to defer their wedding until things settled down. They had both been very active in helping care for the baby, wanting Ebony to develop a close bond with her brother. Charlie and Ebony could easily pass for brother and sister; Charles' genes were strong. Maria had been at the house almost every day along with Ebony, helping to care for the newborn, especially when Suzanne was at the height of her depression. Once Suzanne had breastfed, Maria would take over. As 'Charlie' grew, she encouraged Suzanne to put him on the bottle so she could take him home for longer periods of time at the weekends. Maria calling the baby 'Charlie' had soon rubbed off on Suzanne, 'Ma Ankrah, and everyone else.

Charles' death had brought Suzanne and Maria closer together; they were now like sisters. Suzanne was grateful for Maria's support, and was happy for her to take the baby at weekends, especially as he got older. Now, Suzanne hardly ever had Charlie – or Ebony at weekends.

9 months had passed since Charles' fatality, and life was beginning to take on some kind of normality again.

Suzanne was getting ready to hold a big Memorial for him, before making the 'Sankofa' to her Motherland to fulfill the wish he had expressed in his Will.

This would be her first trip to Ghana, which is where Charles wanted his ashes be thrown into the wind. They had planned to go there on a family holiday when the baby was a year old, but now, she would be going alone.

When Suzanne had asked 'Ma Ankrah if she wanted to accompany her she had flatly refused, saying "I just about made it on the plane for your wedding…I want my last memory of getting on a plane to be a happy one – this is *your* journey, you go."

Maria offered to look after Charlie for the two weeks Suzanne planned to be away, and had suggested she go during the school holidays, as Ebony would also be at home. That only left Micah and Elijah to decide; Elijah said he would continue managing the business and watch over 'Ma Ankrah while his mother was away, and Micah had been offered a trip to Spain with his university; he chose the uni trip. It seemed destined for Suzanne to make this trip alone, which is what she secretly wanted.

She planned the Memorial service to be held a week before she was due to leave, which would be exactly a year to the day of Charles' transition, and also little Charlie's first birthday. She had already booked the venue, and began collating pictures, videos, and a speech to share on the day.

Suzanne hadn't checked her email in months. Now that she was starting to feel in control of her mind and emotions again, she felt ready to get back on top of things. She logged into her account. Scrolling down, she felt overwhelmed at the hundreds of emails waiting for her attention, but one stood out; the subject line read 'Be Careful…'

She opened it.

'Greetings sis, I just wanted to warn you to be careful about what you post on your blog. I became a Targeted Individual for a lot less. Stay safe.

Brother Ishmael'.

"What's a *Targeted Individual*?" she wondered out loud. She Googled it:

'...With media support, criminal leaders are waging a global counterinsurgency war against empowered people with enough integrity and charisma to impact others. The ruling cabal has deemed these human obstacles to their crimes "potential enemies", enlisting congressional acts permitting 'surveillance' technology to root them out, and stalk them ***to death****. Despite growing awareness that stalking is a public health issue, available information about its toll inflicted on victims is scarce...'*

Suzanne quickly replied to brother Ishmael's email;

'Hi brother Ishmael,

Sorry for the delay replying, I suffered a bereavement.

Thank you for your information about Targeted Individuals, I'm beginning to wonder if *we* were targeted – my husband is dead!'

Suzanne could hardly wait for his response. She paced the floor while flashbacks of the night Charles died flooded her mind. She remembered the slight smirk on the policeman's face as he handed her the keys to Charles' crushed car. Working herself up into a near frenzy, Suzanne searched the internet for more information on TI's, while constantly checking to see if brother Ishmael had responded to her reply yet.

He felt like her lifeline; the only person she could talk to about this. It seemed like forever while she waited for his response.

Finally, an email came through;

"My deepest condolences, sorry to hear that – I wish I'd gotten to you sooner; when I didn't hear back from you and saw you'd stopped posting on your blog I thought something might be up. Are you okay?"

"As best as I can be under the circumstances," she typed back.

Now that he was online, she was able to have a conversation with him in real time. He asked;

"Tell me, what happened? (if you don't mind me asking)"

"No I don't mind; he died in a car crash. The police report said he lost control driving through a tunnel."

"The classic blinding tactic!"

"What do you mean?"

There was a long pause before his next reply:

"Are you on Skype by any chance? I'd like to talk to you properly, if you don't mind."

"I haven't used it in months, but I'll see if I can log in…"

It took three attempts before Suzanne finally remembered the password to her account.

"I'm in!" she typed. "Here's my Skype name, add me…"

A few long minutes passed before her Skype started ringing.

"Hi brother Ishmael, thank you for reaching out to me, I really appreciate the information you sent."

"That's okay…and please, call me Ishmael."

"Okay – Ishmael…so what are you saying about Targeted Individuals? D'you think they killed my husband?"

"I can't say for sure as I wasn't there," he replied in his strong African-American accent, "…but that's a tactic they use when they wanna take people out real quick; shine a blinding light straight into the driver's face, they lose control – and crash. I think they did the same thing with your Princess Di's driver."

"Yes I always suspected *she* was killed off…but my own husband…WHY? He was a perfect citizen, the perfect husband and father…why would they *do* that?" she broke down in tears.

"I'm sorry…I didn't mean to upset you."

"It's not your fault – I'm still healing."

"Are you sure you wanna talk about this?"

"Yes, I need to get to the bottom of it."

Taking a deep breath he continued; "Okay, well they may have killed *him* to traumatize YOU. It's something they've done since the enslavement of our ancestors."

Suzanne remembered what she had learned about enslavers torturing and killing the strongest enslaved African men in front of their women in order to send the women into an emotional state of shock and break them down psychologically.

"So they killed my husband to traumatize me? Over a *blog*? There's got to be more to it than that!"

"Well, you were also an affluent Nubian couple doing something positive for your community. If you'd just been making money for yourselves with no regard for anyone else you probably *wouldn't* have been targeted. But you were helping your community to better themselves."

Suzanne sat in shock. To think she could be targeted by the 'powers that be' for doing something *good* for others didn't make any sense. It occurred to her that their tactic had worked; she hadn't posted another blog since that fateful night. In that moment she made a decision:

"I know what I must do; I have to start writing my blogs again."

"But that's what got you targeted in the first place!"

"Yes, but if I stop, Charles' death would have been in vain. I'm *not* gonna let them win!" she spoke in a forceful, angry tone.

"Kudos to you sis, but think before making any brash decisions – there's still *your* life at stake, you know."

"I'm not afraid to die. Charles' death taught me that lesson – that you never die, your spirit is eternal…I saw him!" she blurted out.

"What do you mean, you saw him?"

"I *saw* him – out of his body! It was the most beautiful, out-of-this-world experience…" her voice trailed off.

"The tougher the lesson, the greater your blessing, use your pain to push you forward and *grow*," brother Ishmael advised her.

Suzanne took a deep breath and exhaled deeply:

"Yes, I've grown a *lot*. … Charles fulfilled his purpose in this lifetime, and also left a legacy for people to remember him by. That's what life's all about, not how long you live. I know that now."

"Are you okay financially and everything?"

"Yes, luckily, Charles being an Accountant, had everything in order; a Will, a Trust Fund for all the children, a Funeral Plan, he even had a Lasting Power of Attorney in place, which meant our assets were secure, and couldn't be taken by the government. I don't know what I would have done if he hadn't taken out that Funeral Plan, but everything was taken care of and paid for by the company. It's almost as if he knew he was going to die."

"Nah, he was just a smart dude by the sound of it; so many of our people don't put these things in place, and our children are left with nothing. White folks put those things in place from their children's birth, but we leave them to fend for themselves. That's not how it's supposed to be. We *should* leave a legacy for them, pass something of worth down to them, and give them a head start in life."

"Well he did just that, and I feel it's my duty to honour him *and* my ancestors through my work…I owe it to them to continue waking my people up. That's what he would have wanted."

"You're right. Well I'll support you in any way I can, you can count on that, okay?"

"Thank you."

Guard Your Mind!

During the early months, Suzanne's mind had been in a void for a lot of the time; a state of no-thinking. That was the only way she could cope with the trauma. But in that space, her mind had expanded. She realized that the process of life was actually a journey back to her Self, her original state. Charles had simply returned to his original form after death. She remembered how all she could feel in his presence was Pure Love & Light. There was no fear, no anxiety, no negative emotions.

Over the months, Suzanne had chosen to view her Self as a spirit living in a body, and to know that the body could die at any time, but her spirit would always live on. As a result, she had become fearless.

Her daily mantra had been;

"I am my soul, not my body. I AM Love, Love that needs no protection, Love that cannot be lost. I am fearless."

She knew that the opposite of Love was fear, so reminded her Self daily that to be Pure Love, she had to be fearless.

After her initial conversation with brother Ishmael, she immediately began writing articles for her blog again. She didn't care if they would make her a 'TI', since they had already killed her husband, and she wasn't afraid to die. For her to be targeted in the first place, meant she was doing something right, she reasoned.

While doing research on 'TI's, she uncovered lots of information about the level of Mind Control taking place on the planet. The governments by now, had it down to a fine art. You couldn't watch 'tell-lie-vision', listen to mainstream music, or even walk down the street without being influenced on a subliminal level. Suzanne started writing articles to help people become more aware of the importance of 'guarding your mind'.

She also wrote blogs about the Divine Feminine, warning that there was far too much Masculine Energy dominating the planet, due to the fact that women had been subjugated, especially through man-made religions. She explained that the masculine and feminine energies are different, but are meant to *complement* each other, and work together. Men are ego-driven, and are supposed to listen to the woman's counsel, as she is the intuitive one. However, at some point back in time, she explained, men decided they wanted more power and control, so they devised ways to suppress the Feminine Energy and Wisdom, which was mainly done through the religions they created. They claimed God was a (white) man, and that the first woman came from a man's rib; she was further degraded when blamed for the downfall of the whole human race. Suzanne claimed that the world is in the state it's in today because it lacks Feminine Energy, and because men refuse to listen to the woman's wise counsel.

She wrote that his-story was also re-written, to suppress the fact that the world was originally ruled by *Nubians* and was *Matriarchal*.

With the Feminine Energy suppressed, the Masculine Energy was able to dominate the home, religion, politics, education, business, agriculture, and every area of Western 'civilization'. She explained that because of the huge imbalance in Masculine and Feminine Energies, Mother Nature was *naturally* bringing things back into balance; the Feminine Energy was rising in order to create equilibrium (an equal balance of Masculine and Feminine Energies). She wrote that those in power were aware of this, and were trying to harness the Feminine Energy by turning *women* more *masculine*, and *men* more *feminine*, through social engineering.

She claimed that the only women they put in any form of power are the ones operating in their masculine energy.

She advised her readers to stop watching mainstream 'tell-lie-vision', reading mainstream newspapers and magazines, and listening to mainstream radio which were all controlled by the ruling cabal who used these tools to influence people on a mass-conscious level. She suggested spending that time alternatively 'going within', since that was the only way to connect with their Source. She listed a number of books and audios that they could read and listen to instead, and also suggested spending a lot more time outdoors in nature, as that would help them connect with their Source. She gave advance notice that there would be lots of *distractions*, so turning off anything that would interrupt this time was imperative.

Suzanne realized that this was her calling; to help others break free from mental slavery, and re-connect with their Source. She spent time sitting in the Silence and prayed for guidance on how best to do this.

Sometimes, when women suffer a trauma they cut off their hair. Suzanne didn't; she grew locs.

Maybe now that Charles wasn't there to comment, she felt liberated to give it a try. Even more so, it was something that occurred naturally as she lay curled up in her bed twisting her hair between her fingers, day after day in the early months. The day before the tragedy happened, she had washed it and combed it into four sections, ready to get it put in braids the following day, but she had missed her appointment. Her locs were now starting to drop; she liked the way they moved when she shook her head. Somehow, this felt more natural than straightening the hair to get movement out of it. She was almost ready to begin experimenting with different hairstyles.

"The cost of not following your heart,
is spending the rest of your life
wishing you had." ~ J. Paulsen

Follow Your Heart!

Suzanne and brother Ishmael began communicating frequently via Skype. He was easy to talk to, was on the same wavelength as her mentally, and was knowledgeable, just like Charles had been. They were developing a close friendship.

"…What Star Sign are you?" she asked him.

"Aries, you?"

"Scorpio."

"Oh, no wonder! Scorpio rules *transformation*, *death* and *rebirth*. You've certainly lived up to it, haven't you?"

"I never thought of it like that…but I suppose, yes I have…at the expense of my husband."

"Don't look at it like that sis, you're fulfilling your life's purpose, just as he fulfilled his. Death leads to rebirth, the Phoenix rising from the ashes – you're being reborn, sis. Something new will come out of this experience for you; I see a great reservoir of strength and courage within you. Call upon your ancestors and guides to help you heal to your highest perfection."

"Wow, that's deep…I never thought I'd find someone to talk to on this level again."

"Well it's like they say, like attracts like."

"Me and Charles…we had such a deep, spiritual connection, right from day one."

"Sounds like he was your twin soul."

"We were definitely soul mates; what's the difference between a twin soul and a soul mate?"

"Well, twin souls are basically the same soul split into two; sometimes, if a soul is 'too big' to fit into one body, it has to split into two in order to re-incarnate. So you'll have two parts of the same soul in two different bodies."

“Oh my god – that *would* explain the strange feeling we both had when we first met!”

“Yes, well let’s not keep dwelling on your past; let’s deal with where we are *now*.”

“What do you mean, *we*?”

“Well, um…how can I put this? (he takes a deep breath); I’ve been wanting to say this for some time now, but because of your situation I’ve been holding off…but I’ve been watching you from afar, you know, reading your blogs, listening to your poetry on your Soundcloud, having these conversations, and…I just don’t know what to do with myself anymore; I mean, there’s so many things, so many things I’d like to say to you, some things that are incomprehensible, it’s…it’s such a feeling…man, *damn*!”

“What are you trying to say?”

“Okay let me just get straight to the point…I’ve been admiring you from a distance, but I see some resistance in you and I totally innerstand, you’ve been through a lot this past year; I know you’re not ready for a relationship *right now*, but I just wanna put it out there, you know, to you, that whenever you feel ready, I hope you’ll…consider me.”

In her heart, Suzanne knew it would come to this one day – she just didn’t expect it to be so soon. Over the past few months, they had developed a close friendship bond, and it seemed only natural for it to go to the next level, but this felt premature.

“I really appreciate you being open with me Ishmael, I’ll bear that in mind for whenever I *do* feel ready, but…aren’t you already in a relationship?”

“I’m in a *situationship* but she’s not you; we don’t have this kind of connection. I love and respect her for her qualities, and I honour her for the way she’s raising our children; we keep it amicable for their sake.”

“How *amicable*?”

“I’m not gonna lie to you Suzanne, we get along really well, and every now and then, I *am* tempted into her bed, but we both know the score; we’re not an item – we think too differently. We’ve both grown a lot since we first met over 15 years ago, and now, we’re on two different paths. It's only a matter of time before one of us meets someone else."

"Oh, okay…so you're not quite ready for me either then."

"We both have time, let's put it that way."

"What about the fact that you're on the other side of the world? You live in Ferguson, and I live in London!"

"Well, Love knows no boundaries – we'll discuss that when the time comes, alright?"

The Memorial

The New Connaught Rooms main suite was packed with friends, family, employees, old school mates, ex girlfriends, ex work colleagues, and acquaintances. Because there had been no funeral, everyone wanted to take this opportunity to say their last goodbyes.

It was also little Charlie's first birthday, so this was a double celebration; they were not here to mourn, but to celebrate all that Charles had achieved in his relatively short life.

The room was decorated with balloons and flowers; Suzanne had transferred the shrine she had kept in vigil at their home to the front of the room.

As everyone took their seats, background music played Suzanne and Charles' favourite songs.

"We are gathered here today to *celebrate*, not to mourn, the life of my late husband Charles, and to celebrate his son's first birthday. The day he left his body and our son came into this world changed my life forever. With everything turned upside-down, I began to see things from a different perspective. I no longer fear death. I now know that the only thing that dies is the *body*, and that the *spirit* is eternal. Charles taught me so much about life, he helped me find my Self, and because of him I'm the person I am today. We had met before in previous lifetimes, and I'm sure we will meet again. We are twin souls, we can never be separated..."

(She took a deep breath before continuing);

"…I'm going to start by sharing his 'his-story'; I'd just like to thank 'Ma Ankrah (she indicated to where 'Ma Ankrah was sitting on the front row, who raised her hand), for helping me with my research:

Born on the 13th March 1966 at 7.32am, he was given the names Charles Quaashie Gyasi Osei Mawuli Ankrah. Quaashi, means 'born on Sunday'. Apart from his English name, the rest of his names were handed down to him ancestrally; Gyasi was his father's name which means 'one who is wonderful'. His name Osei was passed down from his grandfather, which means 'nobel' and he took the name Mawuli from his great grandfather which means 'God creates'.

This is what I learned about the family name Ankrah which I will *keep* to honour Charles and my ancestors;

'You are not a builder but a planner, and you want others to carry out your plans. You have the power and ability to choose your own destiny and achieve anything you want in life. You can expand in any direction according to your will and set of values. You have passion for justice and belong in a position of authority. You have an inherent courage and endurance to accomplish *"The Impossible Dream"*. With that power comes responsibility. You hold keys to the material world, but with this gift comes high spiritual responsibility to be fair and true to others. You are philosophical and mature, determined and intense with a desire to endure, often religious. People with the name Ankrah have a deep inner desire for love and companionship, and want to work with others to achieve peace and harmony. They are competent, practical, and can obtain great power and wealth. They tend to be successful in business and commercial affairs, and are able to achieve great material dreams.'

Looking up from her paper she asked the audience;

"Does this sound like Charles to you?"

The crowd responded in unison; "Yes!"

Suzanne continued with her speech;

"I'm *honoured* to have received Ankrah as a surname by marriage to Charles; my two older suns Micah and Elijah have also changed their surnames by Deed Poll, so that they don't pass our inherited slave master's name down to the next generation. Before I married Charles, I'd been planning on changing my surname to an African name to reclaim my spiritual roots, and to honour my ancestors. The anagram of Ankrah is *Ankh-Ra*, which means 'life' and 'Ra' is the Sun-God. As melanated people, we *need* the sun, it gives us life – I couldn't have chosen a better name myself!"

(The audience clap and cheer).

"I think it's important to re-claim our original African names not just to honour our ancestors, but to re-connect us *spiritually* to our Motherland. Our enslavers knew the importance Africans put into naming their children, even holding elaborate Naming Ceremonies for them. By taking away their *names*, they cut them off from their ancestral roots, and sadly, they lost Self-identity. Is it any wonder then, that many of us today, *especially* the descendants of enslaved Africans are lost, and don't know who we are?"

There was a deafening silence as Suzanne 'preached' from her podium.

"...By giving us *their* names, our enslavers effectively connected us spiritually with *them*, not just physically, when they branded their names into our ancestor's skin with hot irons. (She takes another deep sigh). That's the power in a name. Do you think they didn't know what they were doing? And in case you haven't studied your history, Christianity was the main tool they used to pacify our captured ancestors: Turn the other cheek. Forgive those who persecute you. Bless those who curse you. Be a humble servant to your master... When I was a regular church-goer, the only identity I had was being 'the righteousness of God in Christ Jesus' – but that wasn't enough for me. I still lacked Self-identity, because I was still disconnected from my spiritual roots. I believe that as long as we keep our slave master's names, they still have a spiritual hold over us...anyway, apologies for straying from the point..."

"No, no, it's good!" the crowd encouraged her.

"Well, let me return to the reason why we are here today; Charles was an inquisitive child, much like his own son who he never got to meet, but who displays so much of his character...."

Suzanne paused for a moment while she composed herself. She re-told his 'his-story' from when he was a child, right up to his adulthood, to the day they met, and the impact he had made on her life and the life of her two 'suns', plus the impact he had made on his 'commUNITY' through their business.

"…In the one year that we were married Charles did so much for me, and he left me with two precious gifts; (she signaled to Maria to bring little Charlie up to the stage) a son to carry on his legacy, and a *name* that connects me and our two older suns to our African roots!

(the audience applaud)

As she carried her youngest 'sun' on her hip she continued; "Charles jnr, who we've affectionately taken to calling little 'Charlie', is today celebrating his first birthday…"

(they applaud again)

"Before we sing happy birthday to him, I'd like to mention that we were supposed to have a Naming Ceremony for him on the 8th day after his birth as is the tradition, but because of the situation, it didn't happen. So today, I'd like to inform you that he has inherited his father's name, his grandfathers name, his great grandfather's name, and his great *great* grandfather's name!"

(The crowd stood up and applauded).

"So let's join together and sing happy birthday to our little prince!"

After singing 'happy birthday', all those who wanted to pay tribute to Charles were allowed to make a short speech, before everyone walked in a line past the shrine, paying their last respects.

Then the party began.

Year Thirteen: Life Goes On...

As Suzanne prepared to leave for Ghana, brother Ishmael gave her the address and telephone number of an African-American community who had headquarters in the Cantonments. He informed her that he had already let them know she would be visiting, and said they would help her with anything she needed.

'Ma Ankrah also put her in touch with some of Charles' father's family who she could stay with, and who could help her carry out his wishes.

"Make sure you keep in touch with me while you're there!" Ishmael stressed.

"Of course I will…as long as I've got battery power – I've been warned about the 'lights out' situation!"

"Yeah, well we have solar power at our headquarters, so you wouldn't have to worry about that."

"I'm spending the first week with Charles' family who are going to help me perform the ceremony, then I'll head over to the Cantonments in the second week. Do they have living quarters?"

"Yes, just ask to speak to sister Rawanda, she'll be expecting to hear from you, and if you let me know where you'll be staying, I'll send a driver to pick you up and take you there."

"Okay..."

Two of Charles' relatives were at Kotoka International Airport to meet Suzanne when she arrived.

"Akwaaba!" they greeted her.

"What does that mean?"

"Welcome!"

"Oh, thank you! How do you say thank you in…?"

"Twi (pronounced tree) – your reply would be 'Medasi'."

"*Medasi*!"

The heat hit Suzanne like a force of nature. The weather was hot, yet there was a slight cool breeze which made it tolerable. On the journey back to their house, the air conditioning kept the inside of the car at around 5 degrees, which was a bit too cold for Suzanne. She *wanted* to feel the heat, but her escorts seemed to want to get away from it. During the drive from Accra to Kumasi in the Ashanti region, Suzanne struck up a conversation with Charles' cousin and his wife;

"I'm sorry to hear of your loss, I only met Charles once, when we were youth. I remember him telling me that one day, he would return with his family when he was older. I'm sorry you have to come in such circumstances."

"It's alright, I'm just grateful that I get to see where he originated from, and to experience my own Sankofa."

"Ah, you want to experience *Sankofa*? That's good! Then you must start with a new name; what day were you born?"

"I was born on a Friday."

"Ah, then you can choose from *Afua*, or *Afia*."

Suzanne thought for a minute before replying "I'll think about it; I'd love to name myself after Queen Afua, but I might just go for Afia instead."

"Who's Queen Afua?"

"She's an African-American author, master healer, and spiritual teacher. Her books really helped me on my Self-healing journey."

"Ah, okay! So when you are ready to choose, we will do a proper Naming Ceremony for you, after we perform the ceremony to return Charles back to his Motherland….do you have his remains with you?"

"Yes, they're in my hand luggage; I wouldn't risk putting them in my suitcase in case they got lost!"

"You're a wise woman; we have everything organized to perform the ceremony tomorrow. It's already long overdue, and we didn't want to delay it any longer – I hope that's okay with you?"

"That's fine, I'm just grateful to have your help with this… difficult part of the trip."

"Don't worry, everything is taken care of. But why didn't you bring his son? We would have loved to meet him as well!"

"It would have been too much for me; he's still young, and you know what toddlers are like; do you have children?"

"Yes, but they are older; ten and thirteen."

"Oh, lovely…well I'll bring him next time, along with my two older suns, I promise."

"That would be nice!"

The ceremony was an elaborate affair, with the Chief of Charles' father's village conducting the proceedings. Suzanne didn't understand what was being said, but Kwaku did his best to translate; he explained that it was difficult because some of the words and tonalities couldn't be expressed properly in English.

Charles' ashes were removed from the urn that they had inhabited for the past year, and placed in the Chief's hands. As he spoke his incantations over them, he scattered them into the wind. With tears streaming down her face, Suzanne uttered the words "Ashes to ashes, dust to dust."

There then followed singing and dancing to the beat of the djembe drums, as everyone danced on his ashes that had just been returned to the dust.

Charles' body was finally laid to rest. He was home.

After three days, Suzanne decided to check herself into a hotel. She apologized for her short stay with Charles' family, but explained that she needed time alone. She had let her family and brother Ishmael know she had arrived safely, but hadn't been in contact since, as they had 'lights out' for two days after the ceremony, and she wasn't able to charge her phone. She hadn't taken any pictures of Charles' or her ceremonies, but other family members had managed to capture photos and short videos on their 'smart' phones, which they sent to hers. She wanted to spend some time alone going through them, and sending them to the family back in England.

Kwaku and his wife Angela (she preferred to use her European name) drove Suzanne to Labadi Beach Hotel, where they said their goodbyes.

"Are you sure you'll be okay?" he asked.

"Yes I'm sure. Thank you so much for everything you've done. I'll be in touch."

The 5* hotel had all the modern amenities, and in the four days she was there, she didn't experience 'lights out' once. She especially enjoyed hearing the sound of the waves crashing on the seashore from her room, and visiting their private beach first thing in the morning to watch the sun rise, and the fishermen pulling in their catch. During the day the beach got very busy, so she avoided it during these times. Instead, she would go sight-seeing, shopping, and visiting museums and art galleries. She had brought a suitcase filled with gifts for Charles' family, and now it was empty, she intended to fill it with gifts and souvenirs to bring back home.

As soon as she switched her back phone on, messages came through from brother Ishmael, Maria, her sister Keisha, and Elijah. She called them all, and sent pictures and videos of her stay so far, to assure them that she was fine. She let brother Ishmael know that she was no longer at the address she had given him, but to send the driver to collect her from the hotel the following Monday.

The driver arrived promptly at 10am.

On the journey to the Cantonments, they were stopped twice by corrupt policemen seeking any excuse to fine the driver, in order to extort money from him. He had been given a reserve of cash to pay them off, so he could be on his way quickly.

"Sorry madam, this always happens when they see I'm carrying an oburoni."

"A what?"

"*Oh-bro-nee* (he pronounced it). That's what we call anyone who's not from here. No offense miss."

An hour later they arrived at the Cantonments and pulled into the courtyard. She was greeted by sister Rawanda, and a tall handsome brother who looked familiar.

They were both dressed in full African garms, giving them a regal look.

As she stepped out of the car, the brother offered her a hand. That's when it dawned on her who he was.

"*Ishmael?* What are *you* doing here?"

She was shocked, surprised, but happy to see him all at the same time.

"Well it was hard for me to know you're here and not come out and see you. I hope you don't mind; I just booked the ticket on the spur of the moment – and besides, there're some things I wanna discuss with you in person, not over the internet, you know what I mean?"

"Come, let me show you to your room," sister Rawanda interjected, "Have you had breakfast yet?"

"I had some water and fruit earlier; I wouldn't mind something to eat now, thank you."

As she stepped out of the car, she hugged sister Rawanda before turning to Ishmael and responding, "I'm glad you came," giving him a warm hug too. It was a nice feeling to be finally meeting the person she had built up a relationship with over the internet.

As they all walked inside, sister Rawanda led the way, with brother Ishmael gently ushering Suzanne ahead of him by placing his hand in the small of her back. Another brother unloaded her things from the car.

"I'll show you where the canteen is first, then I'll take you to your room; we can meet back in the canteen for breakfast in 20 minutes, is that alright?" sister Rawanda asked.

"That's perfectly fine, thank you."

"I'll wait for you in the canteen," brother Ishmael added, walking off.

Ten minutes later, Suzanne entered the canteen to find Ishmael sitting reasoning with some other brothers. When he saw her, he excused himself and got up to greet her.

"This seems surreal, meeting you here," she said amusingly.

"I know, right? There's so much I have to say to you, I don't even know where to begin!"

"You can start over breakfast!"

Sister Rawanda and another sister brought in trays of vegan dishes with freshly juiced pineapple and ginger mixed together. She introduced herself before disappearing back into the kitchen.

As they sat down to eat, brother Ishmael started by asking "How did the ceremony go?"

"It was wonderful, so…right. It really brought home the meaning of the term 'ashes to ashes, dust to dust'. It's even made me think; I want to be cremated too, and *my* ashes returned to my Motherland."

"I see, well hopefully that won't be happening for a while."

"I'm not planning on going anywhere *yet*, but it's always good to plan ahead. They held a Naming Ceremony for me too, by the way – I now have a new name!"

"What is it?"

"Afia. It means…"

"…Born on a Friday, yes I know. I'm really pleased for you Suzanne – Afia. I hope the whole process has helped you to bring some closure to that part of your life."

"Yes, I feel ready to move forward now – but I'm not ready for another relationship."

"Don't worry, I'm not tryin'a coerce you into anything, I just wanted to see if I still felt this way in your presence, or whether the chemistry I've been feeling between us was just me being delusional."

"And?"

He smiled before replying "It's real, but I hope it's not all one-sided…do you feel it as well?"

"Yes, but like I said…"

"That's all I needed to hear. We can take it slow, there's no rush. I'm just happy to get to see you in person, and to know you feel the same way too."

The United States of Africa

Over breakfast, brother Ishmael explained the reason they had set up Headquarters in Ghana;

"We're here to start a MOVEMENT aimed at re-uniting the descendants of enslaved Africans like us, who are now returning to our Motherland, with those who remained on the Continent. They were never enslaved, but they haven't escaped *Colonialism.* At the moment, it's almost impossible to re-integrate because of the mindset of the people here. Then there are the descendants of enslaved Africans who are still scattered around the world, especially in the Caribbean. They've never been here and are so disconnected from their spiritual roots that they have no desire to come, because of the images they've seen in the media."

"That was me! Whenever I thought of Africa I always imagined mud huts and children with protruding stomachs."

"See what I mean! There's a lot of work to do to repair the damage caused by slavery and Colonialism. We're pushing for Reparations."

"In England, they do a Reparations March every year."

"Marching don't work. It gets us nowhere. We're galvanizing our people to *take* what is owed to us, because they're not going to hand it to us on a plate. We're owed TRILLIONS in Reparations, and we're developing a Plan to make sure we *get* it, so we can re-build our community; we need *schools* for our children, because we know the present education system is designed to hold them back. We need *businesses* so we can keep our money within our community. We need to rebuild our *family structures*. We need *community centers* for our youth to keep them off the streets. We need *counseling centers* for those still suffering from Post Traumatic Slave Syndrome. We need to get our men out of *prisons*, which means paying for top *Lawyers*, and to re-habilitate those who've been affected by the drugs trade. There's a lot of work to do."

"Yes, but we can't keep dwelling on the past, and blaming the white man for our demise. We have to take some responsibility for it as well."

"True, and we recognize our part in history that led to our downfall. But that doesn't negate the fact that Europeans have raped and plundered our Motherland, and *continue* to do so. As we speak, they've set up an oil rig in Takoradi which only *they* benefit from; they made some dumb deal with the government here, that if they provide the equipment to extract the oil, they would keep *90%* and give the government *10%*. Being the corrupt sellouts that they are, the government accepted the deal. And guess what? Not even that 10% goes towards helping their people. They live in big houses with flash cars, while everyone else suffers. And worse still, every time there's 'lights out', which is happening more and more frequently, everyone has to run and buy oil for their generators, so even the little 10% goes back to the Europeans! Black businesses here are being crippled."

"I hear you, but what can you do? It sounds as if this has been going on for a long, long time."

"It has; our first Plan of Action is to claim Reparations from the US government. The German government has been paying Reparations to victims of the Nazi regime for over 60 years. Jews are receiving Reparations for their holocaust, but what about the descendants of enslaved Africans who are *still* suffering from Post Traumatic Slave Syndrome? What help are they getting to heal psychologically, emotionally *and* financially from the African holocaust?"

"But if they haven't recovered psychologically, wouldn't they just blow the money anyway? Are they mentally prepared to *receive* Reparations?"

"There will always be the critical mass who will throw away their money because of their programming, but they're not the ones we're thinking about. We wanna work with those who are conscious enough to see their money stay within their community. We're putting financial education programs in place, because you can be sure that they won't put a dollar in a Black man's hand without a plan of how to take it out again. We've helped the Asians, the Chinese and Europeans build their empires, now it's time to rebuild our own."

Suzanne took a deep sigh.

"Well it sounds ambitious enough, but do you really think they'll give it to you in the first place?"

"We're not waiting for them to *give* it to us, we're planning on *taking* it…."

Brother Ishmael shared their Plan of how they were going to break the machine of white supremacy by galvanizing their people to unify in developing love for themselves and their own, and developing a superiority complex, so that they could at least fight on equal grounds with white supremacy. Once they were unified *as one*, they could begin to boycott mainstream media, music, religion, politics, businesses, and the education system. Their long term plan was to stop funding these Mind Control tools, and unplug from Western 'civilization'. They would set up their own TV channels, newspapers, radio shows and magazines, which would be used to re-educate their people en mass.

"Reparations won't begin to pay for the damage that's been incurred against our people, but at least, it's a symbolic gesture that's more meaningful than just saying 'sorry'. With that money we can build schools out here, and help our people set up businesses back in the USA. They will then be required to contribute a minimum of 10% of their profits to our Community Rebuilding Fund, which will help us with our operations out here. We're aiming to get more and more of our brothers and sisters to repatriate back here, so we're looking to acquire a lot of land to build homes, schools, colleges, and businesses on. There'll be no need to leave the Village if they choose not to. The USA is not for our people, we belong here, in the Motherland. Our children will thrive better in our schools; one of the biggest mistakes we ever made was allowing our children to be integrated into their schooling system. Even here in Ghana, a lot of children attend church schools, so they're being indoctrinated at a young age. It's funny how they've taken God out of European schools, but the white Jesus is still prevalent everywhere here."

"Yes I noticed! I was *shocked* when I saw the white Jesus everywhere; being advertised on people's businesses, cars, outside churches…"

"It's psychological warfare, that's what it is. They know the subconscious mind works in images, so by getting Africans to see their savior as a white man…now you can see *why* the government would allow Europeans to come and build an oil rig and take 90% of the profits, instead of building it themselves!"

"Maybe they just didn't have the *money* to build it themselves."

"What do you mean? Ghana's *rich* in gold, oil, agriculture, textiles…Africa is in the state it's in because of greedy politicians who are easily bought and sold, who sell out their people for personal gain."

"But why would they *do* that?"

"Lack of Self Love. If you can get a people to believe they're inferior to you, then you can take what you want from them. As a people we need to remember who we are, and stop believing we're inferior to others. If you want to know the truth about anything, turn it upside down. These people have put themselves in a position of power and wealth, even though they had nothing to begin with. It's time to turn the tables. If we don't fight for what's ours, they'll just keep on raping and plundering our Motherland, and claiming our stolen heritage and inheritance as their own. But as long as the blood of my ancestors cries out for justice, I cannot…*will* not rest!"

It was his warrior spirit that she 'grew' in love with.

They spent the next few days together talking, sightseeing, and shopping. Brother Ishmael arranged a group tour to Cape Castle, so Suzanne could see where her ancestors had been held captive before being transported on slave ships to the Americas, Caribbean, Brazil and Europe.

They held a small ceremony in the dungeons, where they made offerings of food and water to their ancestors, sang, and prayed.

Suzanne was deeply touched by the experience, and asked if she could perform her poem *"Who Am I?"* which seemed befitting for the occasion. In closing, they all held hands in a circle, standing in the dim candlelight, and held a minute's silence.

As Suzanne lay in bed that night, she tried to reconcile what she had learned about all souls being in bodies and returning to the *same Source*, with the unjust situation of her people. *'How is it possible that we all return to the same Source, when some of us are so evil?'* She went deep within to search for the answer. As she drifted off to sleep, she kept the question in the forefront of her mind…

…The following morning as soon as she woke up, she received the answer to her question, and wrote it into her journal:

'The Source is *Heart-centred*, and we are all connected to the Source through our *hearts*. The *mind* is meant to *follow the heart*, which is the main organ, not the other way around. During 'The Rebellion', some beings disconnected from the Source, and in doing so, disconnected from the *Heart*. This disconnection totally cut them off from their heart-centre, so they now operate purely from the *mind*; they are heart-less.

These entities can inhabit human bodies, if invited in, and when they do, they take over the *mind*; the body then becomes a host for these heart-less entities. The people you call 'evil' have simply had their bodies 'snatched'. They are acting out of their *minds*, not their hearts, because their minds have been taken over. Those who allow their bodies to be taken over by these entities become under *Mind Control*. Many of them are in your governments, and are now in positions of power and control, even *above* your governments. This is why the world is in the state it's in today; they have slowly been taking over the planet, by inhabiting bodies and putting themselves in positions of power. The real battle isn't between your people and the white man, it's between these entities and the human race.

Many of what you think are human beings, are entities inhabiting human bodies. They will not return to the Source. They are evil to the core. They chose to disconnect, and cannot re-connect to the Heart.

Their plan is to get all humanity operating from your minds instead of your hearts, so that they can *control your minds*, as they are *not able to control your hearts*.'

Genie-US

Later that morning over breakfast, Suzanne relayed to brother Ishmael the insight she had received.

"Yeah, that makes sense, being the white male has the weakest gene," he responded.

"What do you mean?"

"Well you know the Black Woman has the strongest gene – the Mitochondrial DNA – she's opposite to him in the gene pool; she has the strongest gene, he has the weakest. She's first, then the Black Man, then the white woman, then the white man."

"Mmmm….I never thought of it like that. So you're saying that because he has the weakest gene, his body was the easiest to take over?"

"Exactly."

"So it's not really the white man causing all this destruction, it's the entities inhabiting their bodies?"

"It goes even deeper than that: Because we've assimilated with them so much, many of us have also become hosts to these entities, especially through the sexual act. When they were raping our women, men and children on the plantations, it wasn't just about *sex*, it was a psychological and spiritual take-over, which has been passed down from one generation to the next. And now, many of us are also possessed by these entities."

"How can you tell if somebody's hosting an entity? That's what I'd like to know!"

"I'd imagine the first sign would be that they're cold and heartless. No real emotion, no compassion for others who are suffering, no conscience when they do wrong, that sort of thing."

"That reminds me of how the slave traders were."

"That reminds me of white men in general!"

"Well we've got to look *past* the flesh; they're just pawns in the game. We're at war, and the battle isn't between us and the white man anymore, it's between humans and these entities that are trying to take over the planet!"

Unite and Fight!

Suzanne decided to update her blog while she was getting good internet service at the Cantonments.

She didn't mention that she was in Ghana, or that she had gone there to return her late husband to his Motherland. Instead, she titled it '*The Secret Deception*', and said that many people were being deceived into thinking that their *mind* is the main organ in the body, when in truth the *heart* is.

She explained that many 'New Age' meditation techniques were created to focus on the mind rather than the heart, claiming they led people to a *false light*. 'True meditation focuses on the Heart, and connects the person with their Source, which is the true purpose of meditation,' she wrote.

She said it was imperative for human beings to return to following our *hearts*, not our minds, which are under constant mind control, psychic attack, and subliminal messaging on a daily basis.

She told her own 'her story' of how learning how to meditate had helped her take control of her negative thoughts and feelings, and how Creative Visualization had helped her and her husband create the life of their dreams, but she stressed that meditation has to be connected to the *heart*, which is connected to the *Source*.

She informed her readers that any meditation and Creative Visualization technique that focused solely on *material things* are of the *false light*. This is to distract people away from the true nature of their being, and what they are really here to be and do. She advised people not to watch and read things that create feelings of fear, hate, shock, anxiety, stress, anger and confusion, as that would only help create more negativity in the world. She explained that these entities feed off negative energy, so they propagate the news, entertainment, music and social media with images that bring up these negative thoughts and feelings. She wrote that the ruling cabal own all mainstream media, so if we as the human race want to create 'heaven on earth', we must stop allowing them to influence *our minds* to create what *they want*.

She said their ultimate goal is to corrupt all of God's creation, and take over the planet. They use various Divide and Conquer techniques to keep the human race from acting in unity; men against women, whites against blacks, young against old, Muslims against Christians, and so on. By doing this, they have slowly been infiltrating the planet.

'But we've got to galvanize ourselves; we've got to UNITE. That's the only way we're going to win this war,' she wrote.

She started getting messages from concerned people all over the world who suspected that they might have been subliminally influenced to act in ways they hadn't intended to. Some realized they were religious fanatics because of their indoctrination, others realized they were racist because they were taught that skin colour determined status. Others realized they had been oppressing their women because they were led to believe women were inferior to men. Still others realized they had been led to believe they were 'war heroes' for helping corrupt governments kill millions of innocent children, women, and men.

One woman sent Suzanne a message about an initiative she was setting up called the *Line of Hope*, in which she aimed to get as many people as possible from all over the world joining together in mind *and heart* to change the energy on the planet. She believed that rather than concentrating on issues the world currently faced, it could all change in an instant, if enough people focused on their *individual* energy fields. Once they have raised their own vibration, by joining hands in spirit and virtually through the internet with others, their energy fields would unite and magnify, creating more peace, Love, joy and harmony on the planet. As Suzanne was aware of the power of joint-thinking, she agreed to get involved.

There is no COMM**UNITY** without **UNITY**

It was almost time for Suzanne to return to cold, grey England.

She had enjoyed her time in Ghana, especially the weather, which had remained consistently hot. Her skin had benefited from the heat, and was now a darker shade of brown, which glistened from the raw shea butter mixed with coconut oil she had been applying. Her skin definitely seemed to thrive in the sun; it was now fully melanated!

On her last evening, the African-American community that brother Ishmael belonged to organized an evening of entertainment. The village children from the school they supported financially came with African drummers and put on an elaborate display of drumming and dancing, followed by griot storytelling. Suzanne promised herself that she would learn how to dance like that, and would also learn a Mother Tongue.

The following morning, she went for a walk with brother Ishmael before breakfast.

"Are you looking forward to going home?"

"Yes, I've missed my suns, and I'm sure they've missed me too. I'll miss this weather, though! And I've really enjoyed spending time with you."

"Likewise, we should do this again sometime."

"Well I did promise Charles' family that I would bring his sun next time I come, so that's a possibility!"

"When are you next planning on coming?"

"Maybe next year."

"Okay, well keep me posted on that, I'll aim to sync with you. So what's been your most memorable part of this trip?"

"Oh, all of it! From the ceremony they performed for Charles, my Naming Ceremony, meeting you here, the weather, it's all been great!"

"What's made the biggest impact on you?"

"The need for us to *unite*; there's so much work to do out here, where the mentality of our people are concerned. I think you're right; Colonialism has been just as damaging to the people here as slavery was. If not, even more so."

"Now you're getting it! We're here trying to educate the people about religion being mental slavery, but they'd rather have their white Jesus than a black man as their savior. In a way, I think those who were taken away on slave ships ended up better off in the long run; those who survived the horrific conditions had to toughen up. As the descendants of enslaved Africans, we aren't the same as the descendants of those who remained on the Continent; we became stronger both *mentally* and *physically*. Some of us are still psychologically damaged due to the trauma, but overall, we're stronger."

"I see what you mean; but how can we convince our people here that the white Jesus is psychological warfare? They're so into it!"

"We have to educate them about Colonialism. The white man's long term plan was to get everyone thinking of the white male as God. They know the subconscious mind works in *images*, so when you repeat the same image enough times, eventually the subconscious mind accepts it as *fact*. Now they've achieved their objective, they don't need the religions they created anymore. Have you noticed how they're slowly removing God out of everything, starting with schools?

"Yes, I remember praying in school and singing 'Kumbaya My Lord', but they don't do that anymore. The white Jesus image still seems to be working in their favour over *here* though!"

"We're aiming to do is eradicate it, and replace it with a Nubian one; that's how it was originally."

"Well good luck with that – you've got your work cut out for you!" Suzanne chuckled.

"It won't be easy, but that's why we're setting up our own TV and radio stations. That's the main way they're being brainwashed."

"What can I do to help?"

"You're already doing it; helping others wake up. But we as a people must *unite*; that's where our weakness lies; in our lack of unity. We have to come together *AS ONE*, so we can reclaim our rightful position in this world." He asked a seemingly random question;

"Have you watched the Game of Thrones series?"

"No, I don't watch *tell-lie-vision*."

"Nah man, you need to watch this – *everyone* needs to watch this! D'you wanna know what it's all about?"

"Yes, tell me."

"It's all about protecting *land*, *inheritance*, and the *family name*. The Game of Thrones is all about *our* stolen heritage!"

"How did you work that out?"

"Well I'm watching it with my third eye wide open; I almost felt as if they were *mocking* us, that they've stolen the wealthy resources of our Motherland, our inheritance, and even taken away our names, and what are we doing about it? Nothing! At one point I had to pause the video and take a moment to think about what I'd just seen."

"What part was that?"

"Well, this white *saviouress* had just freed thousands of slaves, and when she asked the leader of them what his name was, he replied 'Grey Worm'. Even *she* seemed horrified at it, but when she told him to choose a new name for himself, he said he wanted to *keep* it, to honour *her*. I was like – WTF! They're rubbing it blatantly in our faces! The whole series really shows their narcissistic, sociopathic, psychopathic tendencies, and how they deal with their enemies. If we treated them the way they've been treating us, they'd all be extinct by now!"

"Yes, but we've been made so docile by their religions, education system, and even their policing system which doesn't allow any room for us to display our warrior spirit," Suzanne replied.

"But if we don't rise up and fight for what's rightfully ours, it won't be handed to us on a plate – that's for sure!"

"I know what you mean," Suzanne agreed, "We've been marching for Reparations, but it gets us nowhere. We need to take *action* where it will hurt them the most; in their economy."

"You're right! We're the biggest consumers, but if we stop spending our money with them and boycott their businesses, they would *have* to start listening to us."

"Yes, but we also need to take *physical* action. When we see a brother or sister being abused by racist thugs in police uniform, instead of just standing there filming, the whole commUNITY needs to get involved in making sure the brother or sister isn't killed, brutalized or mistreated in any way. How can we stand by and watch our brother or sister being killed? It's time to take *action*!"

"But what can we do? *They* are the ones in power."

"They are the few, we are the many, and when the many stop fearing the few, then we'll see what we can do."

Negroes
Sweet and docile
Meek, humble and kind:
Beware the day
They change their mind
~ Langston Hughes

Positive Violence vs Negative Violence

'Love-sponsored action always arises out of the choice to be, do and have whatever produces the highest good for our Self. The highest good for our Self becomes the highest good for another.'

At the airport, Suzanne and brother Ishmael hugged gently but not too closely, as they said their goodbyes.

"I'm so glad I followed my spirit and booked that ticket," brother Ishmael commented, as they un-embraced.

"So am I!" Suzanne replied, smiling up at him.

"We've had some great convos, I'm sure something good will come of them. You're a powerful woman Suzanne, imagine what it would be like if we joined forces," he said with an amused look on his face.

"Yes I can imagine!" she agreed.

"There's a lot of work to do within our community, and between your operations in the UK, ours in the USA and what we're planning on doing in the Motherland, I think we can make real progress in rebuilding our community. We gotta be prepared to do whatever it takes to take back what's rightfully ours."

"I agree; but we have to remember that the battle isn't so much between us and the white man, but between the human race and these unseen forces."

"True, but I still see it as a white male thing. I mean, look who's in control of our governments, large corporations, banks, the education system, entertainment, even religion. They're all dominated by *white males*. Is it any wonder that the world's in the state it's in today?"

"What about Obama?"

"Ah, he's just a hand-picked puppet, man! D'you really think they'd put a Black man in power? The man they *fear* so much? What have they done to any powerful Nubian brother who's done anything positive for our people, like Malcom X, Marcus Garvey or Kwame Nkrumah? Killed or exiled them! So why would they turn around and make a Black man President of the United States?"

"You've got a point there; he's done nothing to help the Haitians affected by the hurricane, or the genocide going on in the Congo, nor has he stopped our brothers and sisters being killed by the police – and our brothers are still disproportionately being imprisoned. We're no better off with him in 'power'."

"He *has* no power, other than what they tell him to do. The whole government system is a farce. It doesn't matter who you vote for, they're all working for the same people behind the scenes."

"Who?"

"They call themselves Jews, but they're not – but listen, we're running out of time, you're plane's leaving soon, and there's something I'd like to ask; would you be interested in coming over to the USA? I don't wanna wait another year before I see you again."

Suzanne thought briefly before saying "Sure, why not? I'd love to!"

As he waved to her through the gates, they both knew this was the start of something great.

ACKNOWLEDGEMENTS

I first thank my Source from the bottom of my heart for the inspiration to write this book, and to share my creations with the world! Thank You for investing *so many* gifts and talents in me, which I'm happy to use for Your glory. I can now see the vision You gave me over 20 years ago beginning to unfold in my life, which at the time, I didn't believe I would fulfill. Thank you for where you have brought me from, and where you are taking me to. I now see a Divine Plan unfolding, one so thrilling, so awe-inspiring, and so beautiful, that not even I could have imagined it! I know that as long as I keep taking my Steps of Faith, I will fulfill the purpose for which You created me.

I thank my mother **Melita** for allowing me to come through you at a difficult time in your life, and for providing me with the necessary tools and experiences my soul required in order for me to develop into the person I am today. I forgive you for what I perceived to be a traumatic childhood; I now know that I had to go through that, in order to be able to do what I do now. While we may never have the mother/daughter relationship I always craved, I just want you to know I forgive you, and love you from afar, for my own sake.

I thank my 'three suns' **Zaviere**, **Sanchez** and **Azagba** who have been ever so patient, loving, and supportive of me while I nurtured my inner child through her growing pains. I would especially like to thank my eldest sun Zaviere who has always 'had my back', supporting me both financially and morally when I refused to get a job because I wanted to focus on my creativity. Now it's my turn to support you; you will be the first person on my payroll, doing my Accounts!

I didn't know why at the time, why I was being led to give you all names with the letters 'A' and 'Z' in them, just as *my* spiritual name has. The significance of this that it stands for 'Alpha and Omega, the First and the Last, the beginning and the end' – know you are gods with the power to create your future with your thoughts, words and actions!

I would also like to thank their fathers **Lofton** and **Ewemade**, who have been there for them when I couldn't be.

Thanks to all my friends and family who have supported me along my Creative Writing journey, especially Author **Kwame McPherson**, who invited me as his guest to the Millionaire Authors Bootcamp in 2011, which motivated me to publish the First Edition of this book. I'd also like to acknowledge **Errol McGlashen** for helping me edit the First Edition (titled '*Single, Spiritual…AND Sexual!*'). His creative input from a male perspective was invaluable; he fully immersed himself in the task, and got so emotionally involved in the process, that he even re-wrote things I'd written; they were meant to be a joke between us, but I thought were so funny, I left them in! For instance, it was Errol who gave Malachi his yardie accent in Year Six, and he also wrote the church scene in Year One (I edited it for a change!). You have Errol to thank for the way Year 11 ended; my original intention was for Suzanne and Charles to live 'happily ever after', but he suggested killing off one of the main characters because the ending was 'too cliché'.

At first I refused vehemently, but when I really thought about it, he was right. Charles' death became symbolic of the end of my 11-year encounters with my twin soul. We had completed our purpose for re-uniting in this lifetime – this book! (You can read my blog post about the *'Twin Soul Phenomenon'* by putting 'twin soul' in the 'Search' box at **www.journeyofasister.com**). The First Edition ended at Year 11, but my original draft *began* at the beginning of Year 11, with Suzanne and Charles relaxed on the sofa looking forward to the birth of their first child together. I had intended go back and show how they had achieved this state of bliss. It was my twin soul who suggested I move the beginning to the end, so people didn't know they got married 'in the end'. At that point, not even I knew Charles would end up passing over – otherwise I probably wouldn't have listened to him!

I also want to thank my twin soul (who wishes to remain anonymous) for his contribution to the story: When I emailed him the first draft of Year One to read (the way Suzanne and Charles met is *exactly* the way we met!) he called me up early the following morning and told me *his* version of our first meeting. Up to this point, I hadn't discussed my experience at our first meeting with him, but 8 years later, I found out that he'd had a similar experience! He told me to include his one in the book as well, but *not* to put it in Year One. "Throw it in randomly somewhere," he said, and that's exactly what I did! (It's in Year 5 '*Flashback*').

The whole process of writing this book has shown me that there is a Divine Plan in motion at all times, and all I have to do is keep taking 'Steps of Faith' (the title of my forthcoming Autobiography) even though we can't see where they are leading to. This I believe is real Faith!

I would also like to thank **Siayoum Karuma** for helping me with the Sequel. As a conduit, he 'channelled' the part about the Source being heart-centred, and us needing to go back to operating from our *heart* instead of our *minds* (page 309). He also contributed heavily to '*How to Get the Ring On Your Finger*', download it FREE when you subscribe at www.journeyofasister.com. I still have lots of info that I've typed up from our conversations (which were recorded), and plan to co-author my next book with him!

A special thanks to my Facebook friend **Viv Ahmun** who gave me permission to use his photograph to illustrate Charles in Egypt in **Year Ten** (kinda looks like him too!)

I also want to thank my sister-friend **Vanessa Reign** (who I've yet to meet physically), who contacted me out of the blue and shared lots of information regarding Temple Priestesses, Targeted Individuals and such like; (she inspired the Ishmael character in the sequel, but I also got the name from the real-life brother Ishmael who is head of the Etherean Mission). Despite her own challenges as a TI, she helped me get through some real tough times, advising how to protect myself from psychic attacks etc.

Big Love to my friend **Lorna Rhodes** who took the photo of me in *her* blue dress, and did a lovely photo shoot of me and my suns for my 50th birthday. Respect also goes to **Deiche** (Pamela) who has propped me up spiritually when I was weak.

I would also like to thank all my spiritual teachers, most of whom I've never met, but whose books and audios have helped me to grow (see 'References'). I especially give honour to **Queen Afua**, whose books *'Heal Thyself'* and *'Sacred Woman'* mentioned in this story, were pivotal in my own Self-healing journey.

Last but not least, thank **YOU** for investing in your Self by purchasing this book! If you haven't got its complimentary poetry CD '***Seeds of Love***', you can order it with its Book of Lyrics from **www.journeyofasister.com/poetry**

About Cezanne

"I write Self-help books because as I heal myself I heal others, and as I help others, I help myself"

www.journeyofasister.com

Cezanne is an award-winning Visual & Spoken Word Artist, International Author, Blogger, Events Host & Workshop Facilitator. She is also an Intuitive Counselor, specializing in helping others develop Self Love, Finding Your Purpose, Nurturing Your Inner Child, and building Sustainable Relationships.

Her Books, Poetry and Art are creative expressions of her own spiritual journey and personal development, which she shares to help others on their own journey.

"As the descendant of an enslaved African, I lacked Self-identity, had low self-esteem and self-worth, and was a blocked writer and artist for over 20 years due to lack of self-belief. Through the Self-healing work I've done, I now love my Self, know my Self, and know my worth, and I'm writing and painting freely!

My passion is to help my people break free from mental slavery, nurture Self-Love, and develop sustainable relationships, in order to build strong families and raise the next generation to be mentally free.

"The journey' back to Self is the first crucial step towards the rebuilding our relationships, families, and commUNITY" ~ Cezanne.

You have taken the first step in your Self-healing journey, take the next step by joining me on the **30 Day Mind Detox**, one of my Workshops or Retreats, or book a one-to-one counseling session to discuss any of the topics raised in my Self-help books! (see next page).

I am the proud mother of 3 'suns':

In 2014 I won the title *'International Artist of the Year'* in the **Spokenword Billboard Awards (USA)** for my poetry, my poems have also featured in a number of other books including *'Loose Muse'* (anthology of women's writing), *'Unbreakable'* by William Frederick Cooper, *'7 Shades of Love'* by Daniella Blechner, and *'Priceless Roles of a Mother'* by Margaret V. Aberdeen.

To read my weekly blogs and keep up-to-date with my activities 'follow' my blog:
www.journeyofasister.com

Join my Facebook Community**: Journey of a Sister**
Connect with me on Twitter: **@JourneySister**
'Like' my Facebook Page: **Cezanne Inspires**
Instagram: **cezanne_joas**
LinkedIn: **Cezanne Taharqa**

Continue The Journey with Me!

Join me at one of my **Book Signing & Discussion Events** where we have fun discussing the topics raised in my Self-help books! **Want to detox your mind?** Join me on the **30 Day Mind Detox** (online course). **Need to release bitterness and resentment?** Attend my One Day Workshop '**Self Healing Through Forgiveness**'! **Looking for a holiday with creativity workshops thrown in?** Join us on **The Self Love Retreat** (Women Only) or **Nurture Your Inner Child** (Mixed) Retreats! (see page 328 for more details).

Help Spread the Word!

As an indie author I rely on Word of Mouth advertising, so if you have enjoyed reading this book and know others who would benefit from reading it too, share the link to the website so they can start the journey FREE too! You can also buy copies for your friends and family – they make great gifts!

Join the Movement, Become a Distributor!

This isn't just a book, it's a MOVEMENT! If you would like to help me take the messages in this book far and wide, become a Distributor and earn 50% profit on each book sold! For details email me: **cezanne@journeyofasister.com**.

Would You Like to See this Book Turned Into A Film?

My ultimate goal is to have this story turned into a movie; many of our people won't sit and read a book, but they *will* watch a film! If you would like to help me raise the funds to turn this story into a movie to reach even more people, send your contribution to:

Cezanne Inspires Ltd.
Account Number: 04844732
Sort Code: 09-01-29
(Put your name as a reference with '*JOAS FF*')

I will publicize all funds raised on my website and the contributors names (unless you wish to remain anonymous), and progress of the filming process! All contributors over £50 (or equivalent) will get a FREE copy of the DVD and an invite to premiere screenings! **No amount is too great or too small**, help turn this dream into a reality! All contributors will be acknowledged in the film credits, and on my website.

Sponsor my Book Tour!

My mission is to help others break free from mental slavery, help my sisters heal from psychological and physical trauma, and to help us rebuild our commUNITY. If you would like to help me spread the messages in this book far and wide, support my Book Tour! Your contribution will go towards printing books to be distributed FREE to libraries, women's groups, singles groups, churches, hairdressers, and the media. It will also help fund travel and accommodation, venue hire, marketing and promotions. Make a contribution quickly and easily at: **www.paypal.me/cezanneinspires** If you are a business a £60 monthly Sponsorship package will get **your business logo on my flyers** and banners, and you'll also be able to **promote your business at my monthly Book Signing & Discussion Events**! Email me at **cezanne@journeyofasister.com** for more details!

Leave a Review!

If this book has benefitted you, please leave a Review on Amazon or Lulu, or email me at **cezanne@journeyofasister.com** with your feedback, thanks! ☺

How to Get the Ring On Your Finger

Journey of a Sister's sister-book has contributions from over 30 brothers, and takes an insightful book looks into how our PAST has affected the way we relate to each other TODAY. It will help you identify any issues you may have that may be preventing you from attracting and keeping True Love, and help you best *prepare* to meet your match. It will then guide you through the whole dating process for the best chance of getting the ring on, including doing the 'DIY Arranged Marriage', which includes doing the 6 Month Test! Get the e-book FREE when you subscribe at: **www.journeyofasister.com**

The paperback is available to purchase from
www.journeyofasister.com/books

Book Cezanne!

Cezanne is available to host **Book Signing & Discussion Events** based on the topics raised in her Self-help books. If you would like her to come to your church, library, singles group, women's group, university or commUNITY event email her at **cezanne@journeyofasister.com**.

Intuitive Counseling with Cezanne
Cezanne offers intuitive counseling if you wish to discuss any of the topics raised in her Self-help books. For more information and to book your Skype call email: **cezanne@journeyofasister.com** (put 'Counseling' in the Subject Heading)

30 Day Mind Fast with Cezanne (online course)
Do you need help with 'transforming your mind?' This 30 day online course will walk you through the process of working with daily affirmations and meditations, mental and physical exercises, your food intake, as what you eat has a direct impact on your mind. By the end of the 30 days, you will look and feel great, and will be more clear and focused on your progress forward!

Workshops & Retreats with Cezanne:

Self Healing Through Forgiveness
This one day workshop will help you realize that forgiveness is never about the other person, it's always about YOU! It will help you put things in their proper perspective, and help you release your bitterness, hurt and pain, so that you can move forward with new happiness.

The Self Love Retreat (Women only)
Join me for 5 days of *inner* and *outer* Self-indulgence on the **Self Love Retreat!** (Monday to Friday) This 5* holiday is held in exotic spa locations around the world, and will re-mind you of your Self-worth; it includes 3 half day loving workshops with Cezanne, and a full day of pampering! You will return feeling relaxed, confident, and focused. Treat your Self - you're worth it!

Nurture Your Inner Child (Mixed)
Is your inner child crying out to be heard? If you've been neglecting the creative side of your Self, this 7 day holiday will help you re-

connect with your inner child; I will be taking you through the same processes I went through to unblock as an artist and writer after 20 years! I will be preparing you for this holiday of a lifetime with small tasks, so that by the time we meet, your inner child is ready to go! You will return home with something you've created, and the tools to keep your creative juices flowing! I will also be teaching the use of **Colour Therapy** as a form of Self-healing!

These are both essentially **holidays** with some Self-nurturing thrown in! They will run once or twice yearly in different exotic locations around the world. Groups are kept to a maximum of 8 people to ensure one-to-one care with my Self is offered. Payment plans are available, so treat your Self!

For more details email me at **cezanne@journeyofasister.com** stating which Workshop or Retreat you are interested in.

Forthcoming books by Cezanne:

How to Sustain Your Relationship
(with contributions from at least 10 Nubian couples)
This is the follow-on book to *'How to Get the Ring On Your Finger'*

How to Raise a Black Child

Rise of the Phoenix (second poetry collection)

Steps of Faith (Autobiography)

'Seeds of Love' CD & Book of Lyrics

***'International Artist of the Year'* Spokenword Billboard Awards**

All 13 poems on the ***'Seeds of Love'* CD** feature in *'Journey of a Sister'*. It features acoustic guitarist **Theo Calliste,** djembe drumming by **Chi (HairbyChi) Bomani** (he also sings on the track *'Trust'*), saxophone by **George Dawkins,** and vocals by **Ras Gad** who added some ooooo's and aaaaaaah's to *'The Preparation'* and *'Equilibrium'*.
My youngest son **'Azzy'** also shouted "Your Own Universe!" on my poem-song *'Conversations Within* – the scream he did at the end was totally spontaneous, so I kept it in! (He was 5 at the time!)
In 2014 I won the title *'International Artist of the Year'* in the **Spokenword Billboard Awards** for my poetry. You can listen to some of the poems and order the CD with its Book of Lyrics from **www.journeyofasister.com/poetry**

Book References:

The Bible
'*The Secret*' by Rhonda Byrne (audiobook and DVD)
'*Conversations with God Book One*' by Neale Donald Walsche
'*The Master Key System*' by Charles F Haanel
'The Science of Getting Rich' by Wallace D. Wattles
'*When We Ruled*' by Robin Walker
'Black Scientists and Inventors' by BIS Publications
'How Europe Underdeveloped Africa' by Walter Rodney
'The Mis-education of the Negro' by Carter G. Woodson
'Message to the People' Marcus Mosiah Garvey
'Heal Thyself' by Queen Afua
'Sacred Woman' by Queen Afua
'Melanin (What Makes Black People Black)' by Dr Llaila O. Afrika
'African Holistic Health' by Dr Llaila O. Afrika
'The Secret Science of Black Male and Female Sex' by T.C. Carrier
'*Feel the Fear and Do it Anyway*' by Susan Jeffers
'A Mission of Love' by Dr Roger Cole (on death and dying)

'Be transformed by the renewing of your mind,
So that you may prove what is that good and acceptable and perfect will of God'

(Romans 12:2)

To have the most beautiful freedom
Free your mind from mental limitations
You can be, do and have whatever you can IMAGINE
So focus on your heart’s desires
(not what you don’t want to happen)
And with faith believing, take positive actions.
~ Cezanne Poetess

NOTES

NOTES